Genealogies of Difference

Genealogies of Difference

NATHAN WIDDER

University of Illinois Press

URBANA AND CHICAGO

∞ This book is printed on acid-free paper.

Library of Congress Cataloging-in-Publication Data
Widder, Nathan, 1970–
Genealogies of difference / Nathan Widder.
p.   cm.
Includes bibliographical references and index.
ISBN 0-252-02707-8 (alk. paper)
1. Pluralism. 2. Difference (Philosophy) I. Title.
BD394.W53   2002
147'.4—dc21   2001003574

For my parents,
Robert and Rachel Widder,
and my new wife, Olga

Contents

Acknowledgments

THIS WORK WOULD NOT have been possible without the advice and support of many people. Very special thanks go to Prof.-Dr. Sue Golding (johnny de philo), of the University of Greenwich (London) and the Jan Van Eyck Institute (Maastricht). As a member of my supervisory board while I was developing this project as a Ph.D. thesis, she spent hours going over virtually every sentence, offering both sharp criticism and needed encouragement and always pushing me to do my best. I would also like to thank my Ph.D. supervisor, Prof. Ernesto Laclau, and the rest of my supervisory board, Prof. Simon Critchley and Dr. Aletta Norval, all of the University of Essex. Special thanks go as well to Prof. Janet Coleman, of the London School of Economics, and Prof. William Connolly, of Johns Hopkins University, for their critical comments on various chapters and their constant encouragement; thanks also to Prof. Keith Ansell Pearson, of the University of Warwick, Prof. Tracy Strong, of the University of California at San Diego, who reviewed the manuscript for the University of Illinois Press and provided critical comments, and Bruce Bethell, whose careful copyediting and thoughtful suggestions helped me refine and polish the final text. This work also benefited greatly from discussions by e-mail and in person with Ed Kazarian (Villanova), Dr. Will Large (College of St. Mark and St. John), Dr. Andy Chadwick (Royal Holloway), Prof. Patricia Cox Miller (Syracuse), and Michael Rooney. Finally, I would like to thank my wife, Olga Nakajo-Widder, for all her support and encouragement and for enduring while I droned on about the likes of Deleuze and Duns Scotus.

Genealogies of Difference

1. The Quest for Lost Time and Space

We have to *learn to think differently*—in order at last, perhaps very
late on, to attain even more: *to feel differently.*
—Friedrich Nietzsche, *Daybreak*

To reach, not the point where one no longer says I, but the point
where it is no longer of any importance whether one says I.
—Gilles Deleuze and Félix Guattari, *A Thousand Plateaus*

TODAY IT IS COMMON to hear proclamations of an "end of philosophy" or
"end of politics" that makes our age "postmetaphysical." Such pronounce-
ments have been motivated by the perceived delegitimation of old ways of
thinking built on teleological or enchanted conceptions of the natural world,
religious beliefs in divine providence and benevolence, or a faith in the powers
of human reason to disclose an underlying Truth. But what does it mean to
be postmetaphysical? Responses to this question have diverged widely.

For many, the loss of enchantment permits an empirical, scientific approach to the world, which forgoes any aspiration to find a mysterious or
divine meaning in nature and instead develops models capable of most closely calculating and measuring phenomena (a view of science most famously
challenged by Kuhn [1970]). A somewhat related approach to human affairs
holds that the lack of a foundational Truth about good and evil sets the conditions for a liberal society, wherein individuals may seek the good life for
themselves (see Berlin 1969:118–72). This view accepts that modern secularism and pluralism limit the possibilities for an inclusive community and so
proposes a minimal institutional framework to which all may rationally agree
(see, for example, Rawls 1971). Here reason in both the hard and soft sciences
assumes a reduced role consistent with an instrumental pragmatism or empiricism.[1]

Some who object to the atomism and anomie of these approaches to nature and society seek to rearticulate seemingly discredited cultural and social bonds that nevertheless remain implicated in a shared history. What was

previously taken as a moral law provided by a divine being or built into a natural order is now sanctioned as part of the contingent but nonetheless settled traditions or conventions constituting "our" identity (see, for example, Taylor 1989). In this approach, to be postmetaphysical means to historicize what has hitherto been viewed as unchanging and transcendent. Not all who make this historicizing move attempt to reestablish a stable morality. But when the attempt is made, although the goal often seems problematic, the latter remains viable in the present environment to the degree that the historical approach does not appear to reinstitute previously rejected transcendental foundations.[2] What is accepted in both historicist and empirical-scientific attitudes is that modern Western society, whether celebrated or lamented, must be acknowledged as a contingent formation whose legitimacy rests on at best strategic or pragmatic considerations.[3] Whether these considerations suffice to construct a strong community identity or produce merely a common set of basic rules remains an open question.

But such positions efface important dimensions of thought by equating antifoundationalism and "ontological minimalism." Whether one turns to empiricism, historicism, or even a form of "postmodern ironism," the aim is always to become postmetaphysical by *scaling down* speculation, so that the objects of thought are reduced to what is verifiable, what conforms to minimal standards of rationality or pragmatic or utilitarian principles, or what can be historicized. Such positions thus converge in holding that once the search for an ultimate Truth and all its accompanying transcendental or divine frameworks are rejected, thought is compatible with groundlessness to the extent that it rests on the fewest fundamental assumptions possible. In short, a theory in this intellectual climate is considered postmetaphysical to the degree it can minimize the base on which it is built while acknowledging the precariousness of its ground and exposing its opponents' unwarranted assumptions, which it can supposedly avoid. Unsurprisingly, the contemporary philosophies that take this route are usually more successful in knocking down their competitors than in defending themselves from similar attacks (on this point, see Connolly 1995: ch. 1).

Such views are easily compatible with a retention of those components of metaphysical philosophy that can survive the abolition of traditional metaphysical guarantees. Thus, despite the aspirations of their proponents, these contemporary positions become a recipe for thoughtlessness, since their minimal assumptions need be nothing more than those previously accepted postulates that appear sustainable after appeals to transcendence are forsaken. As a result distinctive possibilities are overlooked, leaving a continuation of metaphysical remnants by other means. It is in this sense that

Nietzsche writes: "God is dead; but given the way of men, there may still be caves for thousands of years in which his shadow will be shown" (1974: §108). In other words, even though our enlightened modern thought has taken on a decidedly more secular appearance by turning to the empirical, scientific, rational, pragmatic, and historical, it has failed truly to come to terms with what this move entails. *If* we moderns have really surpassed the need for the Judeo-Christian God, Nietzsche contends, we must seriously consider why we still understand evil as the opposite of good, falsity as the opposite of truth, and chaos as the opposite of order. We must also question why we hold on to the traditional alignments made among such oppositions, whereby what is ordered and stable is considered good, true, and beautiful. Finally, we must ask whether the correlate to opposition—identity, which may be recognized as essentialist or contingent—is indeed an indispensable precondition for politics, ethics, meaning, and even thought as such. What is required, Nietzsche holds, is that the entire panoply of principles and concepts surrounding both identity and opposition—which are all, at bottom, valuations—must be revalued in order to determine whether other modes of thinking, being, and feeling are possible.

As Nietzsche knew well, opposition incorporates only limited forms of difference according to two general models. The first, expressed most prominently in Platonism and Christianity, elevates one term in an opposition to a positive and pure identity and defines the other as a lack or absence, so that beauty, for example, is the beautiful in itself and can exist independent of ugliness, which is nothing but a falling away from the beautiful. The result is a crude idealism. The second model, found in Hegelian dialectics, insists that each term of a binary opposition invokes and passes into its other, creating an identity of opposites that relates and reconciles them. Nietzsche takes a different route: he declares, "The fundamental faith of the metaphysicians is *the faith in opposite values*" (1966a: §2) and declares opposing values to be "merely foreground estimates, only provisional perspectives, perhaps even from some nook, perhaps from below, frog perspectives, as it were" (ibid.). Opposition, in short, is a crude cutting tool dealing with a phenomenon—difference—that requires more subtle instruments.

To aspire to a Nietzschean revaluation of oppositional values, therefore, is not to fall into a nihilism that, in rejecting even the most minimal assumptions, leaves us with "nothingness." Nor is it to call for a return to an old metaphysics and its bulky mechanisms of unity. Rather, it is to engage in deeper ontological speculation precisely to move away from metaphysical remnants still active in our unthinking reliance on the categories of identity. And so, if antifoundationalism is to mean something other than ontological minimalism, if the "death of God" is to provide an opportunity to press forward to a new way of thinking and feeling, we must investigate differences exceeding the logic of identity and opposition, differences that are not merely different in reference to sameness. Taking seriously Nietzsche's call that "we still have to vanquish his shadow, too" (1974: §108) thus requires a reexamination of pluralism—or rather, the *inauguration* of the thought of pluralism, even though this beginning is in no way a *first time*. For as will become clear in subsequent chapters, thinking that attempts to conceive difference and plurality through the strictures of identity must invariably introduce exogenous factors that compromise the very task it has set itself. Nonetheless, this very defeat offers a glimpse of an excessive difference providing another content, meaning, and necessity.

A difference that differs from identity and difference must be strange and paradoxical, since it is incompatible with naming or locating as standardly understood. It is an otherness that cannot be identified, because its being erased or forgotten is a condition of identity as such and more important, because being named or identified is one way in which this difference is effaced, compressed into a schema by which it can be comprehended and known. We might compare this nameless something to another dimension that we do not perceive but that structures our reality, a situation similar to the one described by Hermann Minkowski when, developing the implications of Einstein's special theory of relativity, he explained that what humans experience as reality is really a three-dimensional slice of a four-dimensional space-time manifold—and we cannot rule out the possibility of dimensions beyond this (Krauss 1997:27–29). To treat this additional dimension as one of the perceptible three would undoubtedly be to misrepresent the way it both exceeds and remains implicated in our perceptions. Similarly, to locate or identify this unlocalizable difference risks distorting it onto a field of representation it surpasses. We must therefore avoid treatment of this otherness as a mere opposite to identity, calling it Jew or woman or person of color or homosexual or "not-X" in general. Once this is done, it is possible to use the negation of X to give meaning to X, and vice versa, the space that one of them occupies serving to demarcate the space of the other. In this way, however, the nameless excess is compressed onto the common denominator of space, and its import is lost, for its alterity comes not from its being in opposition to and thus definable against some X but in its being *neither* X *nor* not-X. This difference, then, is one that can never be reduced to a place within a system or whole.

Nonetheless, thought cannot proceed without naming, even if it must recognize the problematic nature of this endeavor: as Adorno writes, "We

cannot think without identifying . . . [, but] the mistake in traditional thinking is that identity is taken for the goal" (1995:149). It is within this necessity
that various names are given for this namelessness, such as "jews" or "unsayable something" or "Real" or "*différance.*" But the name that will be privileged here is *event,* which has the strategic advantage of expressing the "newness" of this excess vis-à-vis any opposition. This event is not the opposite
of the everyday or banal. It is a kind of change or irruption, but one that is
neither spectacular nor ordinary. The novelty of the event consists in the way
it is always more than a particular occurrence in a specific time and place:
an event may be dated, but its meaning and effect are never exhausted by its
date, so that it is always strangely also sometime and someplace else.[4] In this
way the event is both singular and multiple. It is singular in being absolutely
unique, never fully susceptible to classification within a greater whole and
so irreducible to any order of identity; in this way, however, it is also a difference and hence implies a multitude, although this multitude is not the
opposite of unity. The event is a "multiple singularity" (see Golding 1995)
different from traditional philosophical conceptions of the One and the
Many.

Continuing with the physics analogy, this extra dimension must be seen
as immanent in the other three, residing within them as something else. It is
another space—and, indeed, another time—although it stands at no distance
from the empty space and continuous time of representational thought but
is rather folded into them. Further, it is determined by these other dimensions insofar as its own being is conditioned by the objects that move through
three-dimensional space. Yet it also structures these three dimensions, doing so in a way that always twists and contorts their relations to one another,
so that normal mapping procedures are always inadequate, because the space
on which the mapping must take place is inevitably curved or warped. This
additional dimension is therefore not prior to the others as a first cause or
unmoved mover, and to the extent that it holds the privileged status of structuring the others, it does so in an always precarious and discontinuous way.
There is thus a relation of mutual imbrication and reciprocal determination
similar to Foucault's "rule of double conditioning" between constitutive and
ever-present but hidden micropower relations and local and unstable
macropower formations (1990a:92–102, esp. 99–100).

The event is therefore more than a meaningless remainder, an unstruc-
tured Lack never fully integrated into structures of meaning and identity.
Such a view follows from a perspective still committed to a metaphysical
understanding of structure that then pictures the event as structure's chaotic opposite. It is instead necessary to conceive of this difference as holding

together differences, synthesizing them, but through a kind of *disjoining* that *links them through their difference,* so that, although such differences may be mapped to one another through a common space and time, they are also related through another element that sustains their heterogeneity. In this sense, in relation to oppositional understandings of differences, the excess is a surface that, no matter how thin, always differs from what it both divides and holds together; it is the slash (/) that makes any binary, such as good/ evil or order/chaos, always more than a mere binary, confounding any attempt to treat it in simple, oppositional terms that could be strictly separated or harmoniously resolved.

This singular-multiple event, precisely by being unlocalizable, implies a certain movement: a flux by which it consistently surpasses itself while eluding capture by a telos, dialectic, or other representational schema; and a repetition that involves a recurrence not of "identical states" but rather of the excessive heterogeneity that destroys all models of identity. Recall Nietzsche's claim that the great error of rationalist philosophy lies in its positing the eternal, identical, or final as ruling over the world of becoming: God, telos, natural law, the thing-in-itself, the "real" world, and even the theory of events cyclically repeating, which comes close to, but never quite reaches, the thought of eternal return. In each case difference, mutation, and contingency are subordinated to some form of identity. It follows, however, that the becoming released from the control of such principles must be very different from the one that remains governed by them. It is with this idea in mind that Bergson counterpoises his concept of duration to representation's reduction of movement to symbolism. On the one hand, duration is akin to both the rolling and unrolling of a coil—an unrolling toward an indeterminate future but also a rolling up of each passing present into an ever-enlarging memory of the past. The simile of the coil is insufficient, however, insofar as it implies the homogeneity of a line or surface. On the other hand, then, duration must be compared to a tinted spectrum, with insensible gradations in shades that nonetheless remain external to one another, making it a passage from heterogeneous to heterogeneous (Bergson 1955:25–27; on the limits of Bergsonian duration for the rethinking of temporality, see Boundas 1996). Bergsonian duration, in short, is a moving synthesis of differences that, even while defining one another, nonetheless relate through disjunction. When the conditions of the event, its being or eventness, are sought without appeal to identity, they are revealed to be this very synthesis and becoming; the event, in turn, is the *being* of this becoming.

This disjoining of differences presents a distinctive kind of pluralism. Deleuze and Guattari refer to a rhizome—a subterranean plant stem that grows horizontally, sending out roots below and stems above—opposing a rhizomatic pluralism with no central point, and therefore no definable limit, to an arboreal one, in which differences are unified by a common trunk or base (see Deleuze and Guattari 1987:3–25). The ungrounded, nomadic differences expressed by the rhizome demonstrate the genuine lesson of antifoundationalism or the postmetaphysical to be not simply the affirmation of the historical, empirical, or contingent but a shattering of any identity-based model, which, by reducing differences to a unitary base, never achieves pluralism even in the last instance. Such a model is overturned by an excessive event that not only multiplies sites within common spatial and temporal dimensions but multiplies the dimensions as well.

A new subtlety must be introduced once the old differentiations of identity and opposition are rendered inadequate. Theory cannot be distinguished from practice as an abstract doctrine providing a priori rules and justifications. Political theory in particular can no longer simply explicate procedures within which disputes are conducted and policed, elaborate the conditions for a more inclusive social milieu that would resolve them, or develop a utopian model to inspire political action, for all these options in some way occlude recognition of groundless difference. As Foucault maintained, it is necessary to resist any humanist discourse giving primacy to the reconciliation—in the form of simple inclusion or exclusion—of divergent elements: submerged within any binarism is a multiplicity to be exposed. Some may hold that this is the province of neither politics nor ethics but rather art. The danger here, as Foucault notes, is that aesthetics is already designated the holding ground for what this humanist thinking otherwise rejects (see Foucault 1977).

This study aims to develop this pluralism against the ontological minimalism of other contemporary approaches. Doing so involves above all two interrelated tasks. The first is to gain some insight into the manner in which mainstream discourse omits groundless difference; the second is to plot alternative lines of thought through which it can appear. The result will be another mode of time and space in which both point and instant become plural. That all this should involve passage through key strategies of metaphysical thinking is not surprising, for it is only when the question of difference is forgotten that the postmetaphysical appears as an uncomplicated move beyond metaphysics. In fact, however, the difference at issue remains at the heart of the very philosophies that seek to ignore or evade it.

How the Forgotten Is Forgotten: History versus Time

It is clear that contemporary thought has generally ignored a difference at once singular and multiple. This neglect has been propagated by sophisticated means. Nonetheless, it is easy enough to perceive the tenuous nature of the way in which the turn to groundlessness is deployed to make the question of difference inconsequential. It rests on a particular understanding of the history of philosophy and a concomitant perception of time that reduces it to historical analysis. Whether one focuses on unmoving continuities beneath ephemeral circumstances or distributes discontinuities that separate epochs, the event is always domesticated insofar as it is serialized within a chronological time. This is the case whether the aim is to denigrate the historical in favor of a purportedly rational present or to tie the present back to its constitutive past. When this attitude is applied to the history of ideas, what Nietzsche calls the untimeliness of thought—its encounters with excess—is replaced by a smooth economy of transitions. It is certainly true, as Augustine points out, that we need memory to perceive and measure the linear passage of time (1961:11.14–31), yet Nietzsche shows how this recollection rests on an even more profound amnesia that does not forget established memories but instead constitutes the experience of memory and identity, of the unhistorical within history:

> Imagine the extremest possible example of a man who did not possess the power of forgetting at all and who was thus condemned to see everywhere a state of becoming: such a man would no longer believe in his own being, would no longer believe in himself, would see everything flowing asunder in moving points and would lose himself in this stream of becoming: like a true pupil of Heraclitus, he would in the end hardly dare to raise his finger. . . . A man who wanted to feel historically through and through would be like one forcibly deprived of sleep, or an animal that had to live only by rumination and ever repeated rumination. Thus: it is possible to live almost without memory and live happily moreover, as the animal demonstrates; but it is altogether impossible to *live* at all without forgetting. (Nietzsche 1983:62)

Without this amnesia, neither the self nor the objects around it would have sufficient unity to be grasped. They could not be identified and placed on a temporal continuum—understood, say, as having vanished from a previous existence or now developing toward a future finished form. In this way identity, knowledge, and chronological time are interdependent: "The principle of identity has behind it the 'apparent' fact of things that are the same. A world in a state of becoming could not, in a strict sense, be 'comprehended' or 'known'" (Nietzsche 1967a: §520).

When the logic of identity and negation continues in the analysis of history, it inevitably results in the same domestication of becoming through the mechanisms of forgetting that characterizes metaphysics. This effect goes unnoticed when the test for a postmetaphysical concept is mere compatibility with the rejection of foundations, which is why Foucault declares that the epistemological mutation in history will remain incomplete as long as the focus on discontinuities retains the coherence and sovereignty of the subject (1989:3–17). The narrative of history will consign the past to its "proper" place in its evaluation of the present and establish uniform linkages. Discontinuities may occur, but only *within* an already established continuum of time.

Secularized accounts that retain the chronological conception of time present a postmetaphysical version of this same error while indicating through the selectivity of their omissions the difference that exceeds them. One example, Hans Blumenberg's *Legitimacy of the Modern Age*, will suffice here. In this metanarrative of Western thought, Blumenberg holds that a path to the modern "self-assertion of reason" is made available by the successive failures of teleological and enchanted worldviews to provide the foundations necessary to secure themselves. The Greek cosmic view, which left the question of evil unanswered; the later Christian solution, which posited a God at once omnipotent and benevolent but who nonetheless allows evil to exist; and the early modern aspiration to rationally grasp the totality of human history without recourse to the divine—all collapsed by turn, leaving in their wake "the needliness [*sic*] of a consciousness that has been overextended and then disappointed in regard to the great questions and great hopes" (Blumenberg 1983:89). The result is a modern world left cold and uncaring, which in turn justifies a project of rational, scientific mastery over a nature now devoid of any innate purpose. This enterprise succeeds where its predecessors failed not by relying on the truth value of its own ontology to operate effectively but by simply presupposing it as given, "or at any rate as not open to meaningful doubt" (191). Given technology's success and the absence of any alternative that does not make a metaphysical appeal to transcendence, self-assertion wins out in a contingent historical process of elimination, a method that itself appears to hold to a minimum of ontological assumptions. In this way Blumenberg opposes both modern foundationalists, who seek an ahistorical ground for post-Enlightenment rationality, and "secularization theorems," which contend that modernity has secretly retained the Christian deity by transferring the concept of divine infinity into the universe and that of providence into secularized versions of the "end of history." According to the second group, the modern age has occluded dependence on this theological substance, thereby incurring charges of illegitimacy as it has attempted to provide itself with self-foundation. In response to this, Blumenberg argues that the modern age has legitimacy not through its capacity for self-foundation but rather from its ability to provide an alternative after the internal deconstruction of Christian ontology.[5]

Because of the priorities of this justificatory enterprise, Blumenberg must treat whatever thought he examines as a forebear of modern rationalism, a carrier of teleological thinking, or something in between. But this situation similarly confronts opposing histories of Western thought, such as the secularization theorems offering another appraisal of modernity. It is not surprising that Blumenberg addresses certain philosophies only to illustrate how they defeat the transcendental foundations of premodern ontologies, clearing a path for the self-assertion of reason. These include Gnosticism, whose dualistic solution to the problem of evil Augustine had to overcome to establish his God as both omnipotent and benevolent, and medieval nominalism, which pressed the issue of divine omnipotence to the point where transcendental certainties were dissolved. Any creative alternatives advanced by these doctrines are left unexamined. Even more suspect, however, is Blumenberg's treatment of philosophers who openly attack any demand for existential guarantees, whether by the appeal to a heavenly world or the promise of continual rational development and mastery on earth. Such thinking is clearly anathema to Blumenberg's analysis, yet since it appears in the history he recounts, he must address it, even though his own terms of engagement limit his options.

The most prominently addressed figures in this regard are Epicurus and Nietzsche—the first, because he offers the most obvious alternative to the Augustinian response to the crisis of Gnosticism in the ancient world by developing a lifestyle and ethic of joy from the rejection of purpose in the cosmos; the second, because he critiques modern science and reason as a continuation of the Christian will to truth. In each case Blumenberg's dismissal follows a one-dimensional reading. With Epicurus Blumenberg notes a continuing reliance on providential elements despite the general rejection of teleology. Specifically, "the nature that was not created out of divine providence for man necessarily continues to owe man a great deal" (Blumenberg 1983:165) in the form of providing minimal human needs. "*Necessary* wants can be satisfied without great exertion and expense, and the satisfaction of *natural* wants does not leave much to be wished for because nature itself holds ready at hand the wealth with which they can be satisfied; only *empty* wants find neither measure nor satisfaction in nature" (ibid.). Epicureanism is accordingly rendered defunct in a postnominalist era, when this last vestige of providence is extinguished. Its lack of a "technical implication" is its fatal flaw, although this is a product of its historical position: "The ultimate epochal difference is that Epicurus does not recognize the postulate of domination of nature as the consequence of his consideration of man's situation in the world. . . . what he wants is to be able to put the phenomena at a distance, not to be able to produce them. . . . But precisely this ancient way out . . . was closed during the decline of the Middle Ages" (182).

Nietzsche's fate is similarly decided by his historical location, which Blumenberg says prevents him from recognizing science's ability to break free from its initial reliance on the theoretical truth of its method. The success of technology, despite its ultimate lack of foundation, thereby makes his criticism obsolete. Nietzsche could not see this because the idea "that technique also could surpass the character of pure self-assertion, that it could not only disguise the element of need but even eliminate it in the immanence of becoming an end in itself, that it could break out of competition with nature's accomplishments and present itself as authentic reality, was still beyond the horizon of experience at the time" (Blumenberg 1983:142). For Blumenberg, then, Nietzsche becomes a footnote to modernity, useful for highlighting a dead end it must avoid. In his critique of science, "the inner logic of the connection between self-assertion and the 'disappearance of order' becomes clear with a unique sharpness" (140), and so "we are concerned here only with this effect of making visible, not the dogmatics employed in achieving it—that is, with the optics, not the analysis" (142). Blumenberg thus treats Nietzsche's alternatives to both history and science—presented through the language of art, will to power, and eternal return—as thought experiments invoking a minimalist conception of nature. Because these alternatives share the idea that humanity's "right should consist in imputing the least possible binding force to reality, so as to make room for [its] own works" (141–42), they are really no different from the historicism and technological self-assertion they seek to condemn. Nietzsche's philosophy is thereby left "among the approaches to a kind of thinking that removes problems by specifying the conditions under which they no longer arise" (143); for that same reason, however, it "has only illuminated better what it was meant to destroy" (ibid.).

Within these readings numerous connections between Epicurus and Nietzsche are severed, including a common location of ressentiment in the demand for existential guarantees, transcendental or otherwise, and the cultivation of strategies to orient the self properly to death. Most significantly, however, Nietzsche and Epicurus converge in a concern to articulate ontologies of unlocalizable and unrepresentable discontinuities relating to space and time. Both, in short, present groundless differences exceeding the logic of identity and difference. As will be seen in chapter 3, Epicurus, followed by Lucretius, expresses this through the *clinamen* as a random atomic swerve occurring in a time and place smaller than the minimum thinkable continuity. In Nietzsche it underlies a genealogical investigation into the nature of lost origins and an eternal return as a movement of perpetual novelty irreducible to a cyclical identity of events, both of which are examined in chapter 2.

Precisely because of the way they call into question the traditional orderings of events in time and space, serialization and contextualization are inappropriate to Nietzsche's and Epicurus's thought. Thus we cannot alleviate the problems they pose by more widely incorporating their ideas into the narrative of Western thought. It is not simply that they present alternatives to premodern telos and modern mastery. Rather, they expose how such a historical approach, despite its antifoundationalist pretensions, smuggles aboard the metaphysical spirit it purports to reject via the continuities of time and space it invokes. This will be the case regardless of whether this history is used for the justification or criticism of modern rationalism. The modern rejection of God, insisting on both an ontological minimum—which may be welcomed or lamented—and consciousness of the contingency of the present, thus signals a maximum retention of the beneficent certainties of metaphysics.

Alternative Routes

If in the aspiration to being postmetaphysical one must not conflate antifoundationalism and ontological minimalism, and if continuity and linearity are as much at issue as foundation and identity in the task of thinking the event, then a genealogical rather than historical analysis is required. Genealogy does not do away with standard historical analysis but nonetheless refuses to be reduced to it. It would be absurd to deny that recognizable sequential connections lead from past to present, but such connections, no matter the degree of their detail and complexity, are always insufficient to the task of thinking the event. Conversely, however, it would be thoughtless to fall back on the contingency of all history, for this would similarly fail to grasp those differences that go unnoticed when the eventness of thought is forgotten. Genealogy articulates not only the character of the event but also the ways in which it appears within and mutates traditional categories and concepts of political and philosophical thought, disrupting the attempt to trace these through an ordered narrative. Genealogy thereby expresses what Nietzsche calls "historical sense," which is not just an awareness of past events, even in their contingency, but also a refusal to interpret the past according to familiar representations.[6] Most important, genealogy teaches that although there is no transcendent "higher world," this world is not what it is usually thought to be. The lesson of genealogy is that we cannot transcend temporality, but temporality is something more than linear, chronological time.

This study's genealogical endeavor begins in chapter 2 with the development of an ontology of the singular-multiple event, rendered through an engagement with Hegelian dialectics, followed by the examination of a number of contemporary exponents of nondialectical difference. Chapters 3, 4, and 5 further flesh out the qualities of this difference through analyses of ancient and medieval philosophers, from Aristotle to William of Ockham, some of whom posit identity and continuity only to give way to a difference exceeding these terms, whereas others build on this surplus and develop its implications. The philosophers chosen are situated at key moments of transition in the history of Western metaphysics: the articulation of the fundamental categories of teleological thought in the final moments of the life of the Greek polis, the emergence of a theology of transcendence at the late stages of the Roman empire, and the attempt to synthesize these past moments at the close of the Middle Ages. The point of these forays into ancient, early Christian, and medieval thought is not historical but rather genealogical, for they are designed to locate alternative routes that can be glimpsed at these historical junctures. Deleuze and Guattari speak of a becoming-minor from which all genuine creativity emerges. This minor is not the minority that is the simple, quantitative opposite of the majority, nor is it the periphery opposed to the center (Deleuze and Guattari 1987:105–6). It is rather that which puts the oppositions of center/margin and majority/minority into question by bringing forward the strange newness of the event. Nevertheless, it is not surprising, even if it is not strictly speaking necessary, that the minor is also marginalized. Put in these terms, the later chapters of this study especially comprise a series of explorations into both "minor philosophies" (which have often also been minority philosophies) and the becoming-minor of "major philosophies"—in both cases showing how thought can pass from the logic of identity, continuity, and chronology to that of excess and disjunction.

It is precisely the rethinking of time that connects these various components: if past, present, and future are in something more than a linear relation, then the ancient and medieval cannot be reduced to precursors of the modern or postmodern, treated as either a defunct metaphysical monolith or an underappreciated source of inspiration for contemporary thought. Likewise, the present cannot be understood in terms of the simple choice of being a radical break from its past or a continuation of it. An ontology that appreciates the shortcomings of this chronological conception of time both compels a reexamination of these discourses and provides another mode through which to analyze them; put simply, postmodernity itself demands a reengagement with the very past it has infamously criticized. The later chapters, which pursue this reengagement, do not read a contemporary concept into premodern discourses, even if some of them—particularly Epicureanism and Gnosticism—are being raised to the eventness that marks the "postmodern condition" (see Lyotard 1984:71–82). Rather, the chapters attempt a double move, trying not only to read these thinkers on their own terms (ultimately an impossibility, given the problems of context and perspective) but also to locate the points where on their own terms their theories break down or yield something new—but a newness that is always *untimely*. One could obviously write a history of Western thought linking these theorists together, or a history of a concept or set of concepts they all address. That is not attempted here. Instead, these thinkers are examined in their different engagements with excess in order to think through what is required for a philosophy of difference. Aristotle, for example, presents a logic that stresses both a teleological concept of movement and the linear continuity of time and space as preconditions for truth and understanding; Epicurus and Lucretius invert such thinking to develop a philosophy privileging discontinuity and contingency. Augustine articulates a conception of hierarchical order grounded in a transcendent source; the Gnostics, in rejecting this, advance a notion of order that remains decentered and rhizomatic. Aquinas, Duns Scotus, and Ockham endeavor to understand the relation between an infinite deity and a finite world heterogeneous to him but in doing so are unable to sustain a coherent synthesis of reason and faith while opening the space for another ontology of the heterogeneous and different as such. Together, these excursions provide a blueprint for a political theory and philosophy of the event.

Historical analysis holds the ambiguous position already discussed—seeming to reject metaphysics while nonetheless continuing it—precisely because the reduction of time to history marks the final attempt to escape appeals to transcendence that the logic of identity musters. Since genealogy must distance itself from this method of inquiry, it is appropriate to begin by examining the dialectical thought of Hegel, who makes clear how identity must rest on a mediating synthesis actualized only in history and whose sophisticated pluralist philosophy is today both appealing and inadequate. If, from the perspective of a history of Western thought, Hegel appears as the culmination of the metaphysical tradition, it is no small irony that he also points the way toward the demolition of the ideas of linear time and space.

Hegel presents a fundamentally relational conception of identity. There can be no identity in itself prior to its relations to others, he says, for in that case no determination could be given for this identity, and no law could be provided for its being. Any identity must instead be always already mediated and thus a product of its relations, which are both negative and oppositional. The identity of any X is determined only by its not being not-X, and this negative relation to not-X both separates it from the identity of X and, by virtue of constituting that identity, holds both together. The dual nature of this relationship means that identity and difference are intimately bound together, with the consequence that a totality of an identity and its constitutive differences can be thought. It is therefore possible to glean the nature of absolute knowledge as the identity of identity and difference.

The argument at this early point in Hegel's *Phenomenology,* however, provides only the conditions for truth understood in terms of identity. The unity of the rational and real requires that these conditions be actualized. Hegel thus proposes to show the incarnation of the identity of identity and difference in human history, since only here is an ordered mediation of differences possible. This is the task of the historical chapters of the *Phenomenology,* which culminate in the mutual recognition of one self-consciousness by and through another, in an ethical community bringing the divine to earth. But this history is fraught with contingencies, depending at each stage on recognitions that the agents of the history need not make. Hegel is aware that he cannot overcome this difficulty by positing an external telos to guide this movement. Thus, as is well known, it is necessary that the end of history already be reached, so that the historical dialectic merely retraces a development that has already transpired. Demonstrating this end is the task of the largely ahistorical dialectic of the modern state in the *Philosophy of Right.* The appeal to world history in its closing pages signals its failure, however, since it is precisely history that needs redemption.

As a result, history becomes that which both is invoked by and exceeds dialectical movement, presenting its point of nonclosure. The dialectical understanding of time—which, as Kojève puts it, is the negation of the immediately given, or "space," into a mediated unity (1969: chs. 5–6)—shows itself to be insufficient, a result that opens the possibility for another difference relating to both space and time. The remainder of chapter 2 explores the mechanisms of this difference through engagement with a series of problematics: Lyotard's conception of "the jews" as a nondialectical excess to dialectical thought, Nietzsche's will to power and eternal return, Deleuze's understanding of the virtual and Foucault's theory of micropowers, and Blanchot's unavowable community. What aligns these diverse approaches in their antagonism to dialectics is the thought of a difference that escapes the dialectical mediation of opposites while invoking another form of synthesis that relates differences through their difference. This disjunctive synthesis and its implications for meaning, truth, ethics, and politics constitute the central themes of this half of the second chapter.

Chapter 3 examines issues of totality, infinity, continuity, and discontinuity in Aristotle and Epicureanism. Heidegger maintains that Aristotle provides the first rigorous delineation of fundamental metaphysical categories, one grounded in a metaphysical understanding of the origin that combines notions of genesis and domination (Heidegger 1976). But this rigor also indicates the path toward an antimetaphysical thought, insofar as it is directed at and so draws attention toward a chaotic difference that dissolves any foundation for determination and knowledge. Aristotle displays the fundamental priorities of his thought when he asserts the rights of pluralism against the Eleatic One and the Platonic Forms but also attempts to wrap this plurality into a totality. The fulcrum of this strategy is the primacy given to telos, which is secured through a metaphysics of potency and act: the priority of the actual over the potential grounds that of the whole over its parts and over the movement by which a thing progresses toward its end. Nevertheless, this same reasoning, which elevates the determinate limit of telos over the indeterminate and unlimited, also requires the reduction of the unlimited or infinite to an always potential being, leaving it an unexplained exception to the rule that whatever exists potentially must be capable of becoming actual. Meanwhile, the theory of an always only potential infinite grounds the Aristotelian understanding of continuity, so that this proposed settlement for the indeterminate violates its own rules in a manner that points toward a discontinuity within any continuum and a becoming that escapes determinate principles. Epicurus and Lucretius build their ontology around such discontinuities and a concomitant rethinking of the limit that the actuality of the infinite demands. They view the limit no longer as a simple determination of a thing but as a paradoxical site in which a heterogeneous beyond disrupts any claim to continuity and wholeness. Consequently, beneath the world of becoming lies the discontinuous realm of the atom, which persists through all change, and within the movements of the atom "as swift as thought" lies an erratic swerve so slight and quick that it cannot be conceived as occurring within a continuous space and time. This primordial indeterminacy gives rise to an always open pluralism, which translates into an ethical critique of metaphysical thought, since the metaphysical demand for order now appears grounded in a fear of death. This anxiety is not overcome by the development of virtue, for virtue itself presupposes the very notion of order in dispute; nor, however, does it entail the hedonism for which Epicureanism is historically ridiculed. Rather, it entails a "care of the self"[7] whereby the violences spawned from the demand for unity are tempered.

Chapter 4 focuses on positivity, negativity, hierarchy, and transcendence through Augustine and the Gnostic tractates of the *Nag Hammadi Library*. Augustine recognizes a difference that does not participate in the hierarchy of the One and the Many, but he can admit it only as an evil impersonating the good, to be overcome by a God who is omnipotent and benevolent yet not responsible for sin. Establishing the coherence of this arrangement constitutes a central task for Augustine, yet each of his several accounts entails unacceptable concessions. He presents evil at one moment as merely illusory but at another as necessary for a greater good; he holds it to have no cause yet blames the free choice of angels and humans for its existence; and when divine power or goodness appears compromised by the persistence of this evil, he leaves its existence as a mystery of faith. Ultimately Augustine cannot rationally keep the hierarchy of the good separate from that difference that neither participates in it nor disappears. This failure, however, comes as no surprise from a Gnostic viewpoint, which inverts the principles governing orthodox Christian thought. In Gnostic ontology and theology, evil is not a pale image of a divine hierarchy grounded in a transcendent One; rather, it is the One together with its hierarchy that falls away from—and so is a pale reflection of—a multiple, decentered, rhizomatic plurality. Indeed, a belief in the One characterizes the very ignorance that gnosis is meant to overcome. Gnosis not only indicates the incomplete nature of metaphysical thought, which fails to find its genuine origin in difference, but provides the basis for a positive ethic built around the location and cultivation of the energies of multiplicity within the self.

Chapter 5 investigates the way being relates to primary diversity, an ontological question central to the thought of Aquinas, Duns Scotus, and Ockham. In medieval philosophy generally, the issue appears along three main axes: the relation among the categories; the divergence of individuals, which prevents their being fully subsumed by the common identity of their species; and the relation between the created world and an infinite God transcending it. The predicament was made salient by the Latin world's rediscovery of Aristotelian texts, a development that gave philosophy an apparently new independence from theology and compelled the search for a new synthesis between reason and faith but also provided answers to the problem of the categories, which could be extended to the other two realms. Aquinas extracts from Aristotle an analogical relation among the categories that he adapts to theorize a proportional relation between the finite and infinite, building from this a ladder of being that allows reason to approach the divine but that reserves a place for grace to complete the journey. This solution, however, must restrict God's omnipotence for the benefit of his goodness. Duns Scotus, attacking the coherence of an asserted analogy with a deity who remains mysterious, draws from Aristotle a univocal conception of being. While a hierarchy with and among creatures remains, it is now grounded in a common notion of being that remains indifferent to the differences between beings, so that the hierarchy must instead be developed through an essential order of causes. Yet this answer requires both denying any rational demonstration of divine omnipotence and presuming it in rational arguments for the existence of such a being. Ockham finds in both these philosophies unnecessary and illegitimate excesses regarding the powers of reason. After using Aristotle to support his assault on the reality of universals, the distinction between essence and existence, and the hierarchical notion of essential order, only a minimal proof for God's existence can remain. Ockham thus expands the place of faith even while he leaves it without any rational support. This development marks the close of Christian Scholasticism but does not end its relevance. The question of individuation remains, and Scotus addresses it with the idea of haecceity, an excess within all concrete beings that is irreducible to formal categories but that provides the ultimate actuality of form. Once this excess and the univocal conception of being are freed from the restrictions placed on them by the Christian demand for an omnipotent and benevolent God buttressed by a unity of reason and faith, a philosophy of difference can be born.

A philosophy of the event is a philosophy of chaos, but chaos is not mere indetermination or accident. It embodies contingency, but unlike so many contemporary formulations, contingency is maintained in its heterogeneous meanings, which include both chance (A is a contingent or random event) and relations of dependence (A is contingent on B). In one way or another, metaphysical thought—and much that claims to be postmetaphysical—has subordinated the first meaning through emphasis on the second while ascribing to its opponents a simple reversal of this ordering. This is the move by which skepticism, Epicureanism, Gnosticism, and postmodernism have often been conflated.[8] Conversely, a philosophy of genuine pluralism that neither denies the difference exceeding identity nor laments it as a fault or loss, thereby stretching beyond good and evil, maintains this manifold of determinations in its irreducibility. Identity and opposition are consequently displaced by a groundless ground by which differences are related through dispersion. This is an ontology far more appropriate than the minimalism that characterizes contemporary secularism, which Nietzsche scorns for retaining a metaphysical faith and piety (1974: §344). To vanquish the shadow of the God of identity is to show that it is precisely that: a penumbra of a more primordial multiplicity that can be reached neither historically nor empirically but only genealogically.

2. Force, Synthesis, and Event

> But to make a real escape from Hegel presupposes an exact
> appreciation of what it costs to detach ourselves from him. It
> presupposes a knowledge of how close Hegel has come to us,
> perhaps insidiously. It presupposes a knowledge of what is still
> Hegelian in that which allows us to think against Hegel; and an
> ability to gauge how much our resources against him are perhaps
> still a ruse which he is using against us, and at the end of which he
> is waiting for us, immobile and elsewhere.
>
> —Michel Foucault, "The Order of Discourse"

WHAT WOULD IT MEAN to "escape" or "forget" Hegel? The crux of Hegelian philosophy is the totalizing movement of the dialectic. Examining the
derivation, character, and utilization of this movement is therefore crucial
to determine the path that a post- or anti-Hegelian thinking might take.

Other philosophies, Hegel maintains, remain trapped by abstraction by
insisting on a foundation that exists positively as an identity in itself, whether
this be a transcendent Form or an empirical fact. Such a view of identity must
always remain one-sided insofar as it suppresses the differences that define
and give meaning to any being. Hegelian abstraction thus differs from, for
example, the Aristotelian view of a universal category expressing the commonality of particulars within it. Indeed, Hegel views such a general concept
as more concrete insofar as it mediates immediate particulars so that they
can be known. What is concrete on these terms is what is relational and
mediated, so that what is ultimately real in Hegel's thought is the Notion, or
Concept, that synthesizes all differences, leaving nothing outside it in the form
of a thing-in-itself that would condition or limit it. The concrete Notion thus
unifies but also separates and defines the opposites of universal and particular, being and nonbeing, identity and nonidentity, and so on. The dialectic
is both the mechanism by which thought traces the way each opposite gives
itself over to its other in mediation and the process by which reality itself
unfolds as a mediated unity in history. The culmination of the dialectic is the

concrete unity of thought and being, the rational and the real, in the identity of identity and difference.

As will become clear, however, Hegelian dialectics remains abstract on its own terms, the Notion amounting only to a postulate of thought that gives meaning to reality but remains mysterious, mystical, and unreal itself. This failure does not necessitate a return to some pre-Hegelian conception of an identity in itself but instead compels another form of synthesis. Put simply, the source of Hegelian abstraction is to be found in the oppositional understanding of difference that Hegel's dialectic synthesizes; in pressing beyond opposition, however, a space opens for another synthesis that does not link differences through the identity of identity and opposition but instead relates them through a disjoining that characterizes the event.

Hegel and the Circle of Dialectics

The first chapter of the *Science of Logic* presents the dialectical synthesis of being and nothing. As the highest category, being is indeterminate and undifferentiated, having no other category to delineate it. Being is thus identical to emptiness and nothingness. Yet being and nothing are also opposites and must be recognized as such. How can this identity of opposites be grasped? It can be understood, Hegel insists, only as a *movement* of opposites into sameness and back into opposition. This movement is becoming.

> *Pure being* and *pure nothing* are, therefore, the same. What is the truth is neither being nor nothing, but that being—does not pass over but has passed over—into nothing, and nothing into being. But it is equally true that they are not undistinguished from each other, that, on the contrary, they are not the same, that they are absolutely distinct, and yet that they are unseparated and inseparable and that each immediately *vanishes in its opposite.* Their truth is, therefore, this movement of the immediate vanishing of the one in the other: *becoming,* a movement in which both are distinguished, but by a difference which has equally immediately resolved itself. (Hegel 1969:82–83)

Becoming is not a midpoint between the infinitely distant extremes of being and nothing. Nor is there simply no interval or spacing between being and nothing, even though the slightest departure from one instantly and completely invokes the other. Finally, becoming is not merely a trait of a thing that moves from X to Y or between states of being and nonbeing that are indifferent to it. In all these cases being is understood independently of both change and nothing. But being necessarily *becomes* nothing, and nothing *becomes* being, and in this movement each has always already become its opposite. The immediacy of this transition in fact introduces a mediation, but one in which the spacing between differences is not an indifferent element. Becoming is therefore a middle term encompassing and sustaining its extremes within it. Both being and nothing presuppose becoming as their common ground, but it is an immanent ground consisting of nothing other than the necessary, internal movement of each into the other. Conversely, becoming is the whole that divides itself into being, nothing, and their mutual passing. As Hegel says of any oppositional pair: "They are just as much in a unity, as this unity, which appears as the middle term over against the independent extremes, is a perpetual diremption of itself into just these extremes which exist only through this process" (Hegel 1977: §136). The resulting foundation is neither a transcendent One nor a simple totality but a perpetual self-transformation, whole and complete because nothing lies beyond it. The being of becoming is the virtual movement—what Hegel calls "pure change" (§160)—that sustains the identity of identity and difference, totalizes its moments such that they cannot escape it, and raises the Absolute from Substance to Subject (§§17–18; see also Taylor 1975: ch. 1). Becoming is also the first determination of being and so is the internal transformation of pure, indeterminate being into determinate being. Following this originary movement of becoming, the dialectic can continue as the derivation and envelopment of the moments of determinate being, eventually reaching the doctrine of essence and finally the doctrine of the Notion as knowledge of the Absolute.

The dialectical synthesis is also a movement of negation. Only negation is capable of totalization by virtue of its dual function: it at once marks a distinction from an "other" (X is not Y) and the supersession of this difference (X negates or annihilates Y), a moment of independence and one of relatedness. Thus, "in the negative judgement the 'is' (copula) holds together as well as separates the terms" (Hegel 1977: §578). Negation is poorly understood when considered to be simple nothingness or denial—the mode of the skeptic—for this forecloses the possibility of development (§79). Similarly, difference is misconstrued if one seeks to avoid or displace the negative. "Positive difference," Hegel maintains, is actually a condition of indifference: a thing in a positive relation relates in the first instance to itself, making all other relations secondary and unessential. Such a thing is an abstraction, a being-in-itself that is merely the initial moment of the dialectical passage to being-for-another and back to concrete being-for-self (§19).

Without negation, a thing must be understood through external predicates, so that "one never learns what the thing itself is, nor what the one or the other is" (§50). Moreover, as the opening pages of the *Logic* demonstrate, being as a positive source, refusing to recognize its dialectical relation to nothingness, collapses into its other (on this point, see also Hardt 1993:2–4, 13–19). Thus, inverting the ancient doctrine that negation refers to a prior positivity from which it is merely a lack, Hegel maintains that positive essence can exist only as the product of a more encompassing negative movement.

Through these principles, Hegel insists, one can understand reality as a rational totality. The movement of negation means that no difference or otherness can remain "outside" as an opaque essence or "thing-in-itself" conditioning appearances. The perpetual return to relatedness likewise reveals the idea of infinity as endless extension, a "progress to infinity," to be spurious. Such an infinite remains indeterminate and ethereal: "This spurious infinity is in itself the same thing as the perennial ought; it is the negation of the finite it is true, but it cannot in truth free itself therefrom. The finite reappears *in the infinite itself* as its other, because it is only in its *connection* with its other, the finite, that the infinite is. The progress to infinity is, consequently, only the perpetual repetition of one and the same content, one and the same tedious *alternation* of this finite and infinite" (Hegel 1969:142). Genuinely infinite freedom reconciles liberty and determination in the form of concrete autonomy or self-determination (Hegel 1967:5–7). Similarly, genuinely infinite knowledge grasps even infinitely distant contradictory differences. The Notion is therefore greater than a genus, which organizes contrary entities into a common identity, but at the same time capable of more precise determination than a species, which fails to reach the level of individual variety, in both ways fulfilling the strict demands of science by providing universality without abstraction (Hyppolite 1974:134–35). Holding all differences within it, the only positivity is the self-moving and therefore autonomous totality itself, as nothing remains beyond it—or rather, what remains beyond is merely a nothingness that, as the negation of being, is already accounted for within its schema. Dialectical movement thus reduces any apparent outside to nullity, so that "in pressing forward to its true existence, consciousness will arrive at a point at which it gets rid of its semblance of being burdened with something alien, with what is only for it, and some sort of 'other,' at a point where appearance becomes identical with essence, so that its exposition will coincide at just this point with the authentic Science of Spirit. And finally, when consciousness itself grasps this its own essence, it will signify the nature of absolute knowledge itself" (Hegel 1977: §89).

But if this absolute knowledge—and the unity of subject and object it entails—were merely posited above ordinary knowledge as the ideal form of science, it would remain nothing more than a postulate concerning reality based on faith and would invoke an insurmountable separation of being and thought that is at best externally mediated by an instrument or test for knowledge (Hegel 1977: §§73–89). Moreover, if it remained only abstractly related to the reality it purports to explain, it would not truly account for anything. It is therefore necessary to show how this totality is derived from the experience it is to measure and then how, from this abstract totality, thought can move through a series of internal transitions toward a derivation of the concrete reality of the modern condition. Hegel sketches the first task, in which the Absolute is conceived as a rational whole, in the first three chapters of the *Phenomenology of Spirit,* where he traces the development of consciousness from sense certainty through perception and into understanding.

The truth and meaning of a thing may seem most certain in its immediate presentation, but this is not the case. For if one writes down what one experiences here and now—for example, that it is now night—the statement becomes, after a short time, false.[1] The being of night is thus not immediate but conditioned by circumstance. Further, if its certainty does not lie in the particular object, it is no more to be found in the specific subject witnessing it: night exists whether or not an individual beholds it. What remains unconditioned is not the presentation of a particular object to a particular subject but the categories of here and now, as well as subject and object, which are all constant and indifferent to their particular contents. The truth of an immediate presentation thus lies in the universal categories by which it is perceived—or, put differently, what immediately appears is only a part of the truth and merely an abstraction if taken to be truth in its entirety. In this way, sense certainty negates itself and passes to perception.

The truth of a sensed thing is found in its status as an object, but the question then becomes how the object's meaning is determined. The object is a collection of universal properties, at once independent and indifferent to one another but also joined in unity. It thus appears paradoxically as both one and many. One might think that the subject/object distinction accounts for this opposition: the thing may be considered objectively one but subjectively many, or vice versa. The unity of a thing is tied to its determinateness, however, and it is determined by its multiple properties, so neither aspect can be dismissed as subjective caprice: "Things are therefore in and for themselves determinate; they have properties by which they distinguish themselves from others" (Hegel 1977: §120). Further, since the properties of an object relate it to other objects that either share these properties or give the properties their own meaning through contrast, the unified object cannot be separated from its relations with others. The ensuing paradox is that insofar as it relates to itself, the object must negate otherness, but it thus relates to this otherness and so cannot exclude it: "The Thing is posited as being *for itself,* or as the absolute negation of all otherness, therefore as purely *self*-related negation; but the negation that is self-related is the suspension of *itself;* in other words, the Thing has its essential being in another Thing" (§126). This contradiction within the perceived object amounts to its self-annulment. It is now a movement between the opposing moments of being-in-itself and being-for-another, of existing as an isolated object and dissolving in its relations. No object of perception fails to pass over into this movement as the condition of its truth and meaning. Hegel calls this form of being "force."

It is through the concept of force, introduced in the stage of understanding, that Hegel overcomes the distinctions between essence and appearance and subject and object.[2] What is presented is a plurality of forces, each expressing itself as multiple (thereby relating to others) in one moment and withdrawing into unity (relating to itself) in the next. The second aspect becomes a moment of the first, however, since one force is determined only in and through another. The result is a reciprocal determination: one force determines another, but it does so only insofar as it is itself a force, and so is determined as such by another—or, in Hegel's terminology of "soliciting" and "solicited" forces:

> The soliciting Force, e.g., is posited as a universal medium, and the one solicited, on the other hand, as Force driven back into itself; but the former is a universal medium only through the other being Force that is driven back into itself; or, it is really the latter that is the soliciting Force for the other and is what makes it a medium. The first Force has its determinateness only through the other, and solicits only in so far as the other solicits it to be a soliciting Force; and, just as directly, it loses the determinateness given to it, for this passes over—or rather has already passed over—to the other. (1977: §139)

Primacy is thereby given to the relations between forces, not the forces in themselves: "They do not exist as extremes which retain for themselves something fixed and substantial, transmitting to one another in their middle term and in their contact a merely external property; on the contrary, what they are, they are, only in this middle term and in this contact. In this, there is immediately present both the repression within itself of Force, or its *being-for-self,* as well as its expression" (§141). Force therefore differs from the object of perception, in which the atomistic thing is defined by external predicates. Difference and relationality gain priority. Further, because each force is both determining and determined, the distinctions between them in both form and content vanish (§140; see also Heidegger 1988:119–20), and "in this way there vanishes completely all distinction of *separate,* mutually contrasted *Forces* which were supposed to be present in this movement, for they rested solely on those distinctions; and the distinction between the Forces, along with both those distinctions, likewise collapses into only one" (Hegel 1977: §148). The relationship between forces thereby draws them into a moment of unity as well, but a moment in which "the Forces seem to make an *independent* appearance" (§139).

One may try to reduce this play of forces to a phenomenal appearance for consciousness covering a true essence. It would thus be a totality, but "a *totality* of show" (Hegel 1977: §143) reflecting a deeper noumenal realm. Hegel brilliantly debunks this appeal to a heterogeneous, suprasensible world. To speak of a static thing-in-itself governing the movement of appearances is to relate the two by law. But what form does this law take? We may say first that the law is a simple universal into which differences are resolved—in other words, that different apparitions are governed by the same law. Then, however, the differences among appearances are not fully accounted for within the law but instead are conditioned by circumstance, the result being that the thing-in-itself does not truly govern them. Conversely, if each appearance is given a different law, there is no universality. Clearly law must account for both these moments, and so it must be a movement of each into the other. If so, then the Notion of law, as the relation between the thing-in-itself and appearances, is identical to the play of forces. The thing-in-itself is therefore no different from the moment of force driven into itself, which immediately gives itself to another. As a result, there is no truth buried behind appearances, and so no appearance arising from a hidden essence (§143–55). Nothing can remain outside the play of forces—that is, the movement by which the totality divides and returns to itself—which means that there can be nothing that is by its nature alien or unknowable. Hegel thus proclaims: "Appearance is its essence and, in fact, its filling. The supersensible is the sensuous and the perceived posited as it is *in truth;* but the *truth* of the sensuous and the perceived is to be *appearance*. The supersensible is therefore *appearance qua appearance*" (§147). Put differently, the realm of appearance—the play of forces—is no longer simply a medium between the conscious observer and the impenetrable suprasensible but rather the totality in which subject and object are vanishing moments. With this, the Notion of absolute knowledge in its skeletal form is reached. Consciousness discovers its truth in self-consciousness: as its dialectical development has led it to a point where no object can appear to it as simply alien, it finds itself in its object. Anything posited outside the totality of relations would be related to it and so accounted for within its schema. And so no difference escapes the movement of negation; there is literally nowhere else to go.[3]

This is the most abstract presentation of the Absolute: a movement of force relations providing the condition of possibility for the truth of any sensuous experience, which is the only way that such experience can literally "make sense." This account presupposes the possibility of truth—that is, the identity of thought and thing—but since Hegel views the skeptical denial of truth to be self-defeating, he maintains that this is the only possible route that thought can take. However, the attainment of absolute knowledge does not mean that everything can be known. This is not surprising, since absolute knowledge must include its own negation within itself, as being must include nothingness. For this reason, when the level of the concrete is finally attained, it is only in the realm of collective human self-consciousness or spirit that the Notion becomes actual, for only here does the middle term encompass its extremes: both individual self-consciousness and Absolute Spirit are actualized only in and through community. In nature the middle term of the organic syllogism (genus-species-individual) does not contain its extremes, for although the genus is actualized in its species, the individual is not; instead the species is actualized in the individual.[4] There is thus no true mediation here, so that nature has no history or determinate development and can be only described, not known. Conversely, only Spirit is real, not because nature does not exist, but because only in the former are mediation and totalization fulfilled.[5] Nature does not, however, escape the Notion. It is rather the latter's failed actualization, the first blind steps of a barely conscious Spirit coming into being. It is therefore of no concern, Hegel claims, that nature is ambiguous; it is sufficient that nature embodies the Notion, albeit in an imperfectly sketched rather than fully presented manner, so that a philosophy of nature is still possible (Hyppolite 1974:232–58). This claim remains mere faith, however, inasmuch as no rationality can be drawn from the movements of nature. Further, since a dialectical relation requires that all possible relationships of difference be accounted for as moments, the mediation of absolute knowledge and its opposite requires Hegel to show that, in the realm of Spirit, self-knowledge is indeed achieved. In short, the claim that dialectical mediation permits the negation of knowledge to appear freely implies that self-conscious certainty displays a moment of independence too, so that the lack of certainty in the realm of nature in no way undermines the self-certainty of Spirit.

The bulk of the *Phenomenology* details the actualization of the Notion in collective human spirit. Through its dialectical transitions, human consciousness learns that the Absolute—manifest in social institutions—is not alien to it, while the Absolute or World Spirit gains self-consciousness only through its embodiment in human communities. Each element alone shows itself to be a self-negating abstraction, so that only within a mediated whole does it attain concreteness. The mediating term is the state: the modern nation-state resolves the conflict between individual and universal by governing each individual's being-for-self in his being-for-another and in others' being-for-him. The state thereby embodies the movement of the Notion, making it whole unto itself. The four levels on which this path to harmony is traced— self-consciousness, reason, spirit, and religion—are each connected logically. The completion of the still abstract dialectic of self-consciousness, for example, allows the same development to be retraced in a more concrete fashion as the unfolding of reason, and so on.[6] This process culminates in absolute knowledge, the totality of moments that together produce and redeem the modern condition by accounting for the meaning and place of nature, history, God, and humanity.

The previously traced dialectic of consciousness seeks the meaning of an object presented to consciousness and ends with consciousness and its object being absorbed and reconciled in a higher unity. Here consciousness discovers that its object is not truly alien to it and passes into self-consciousness. The concept of self-consciousness, Hegel says, presents a more concrete depiction of reality than that of a merely abstract consciousness examining an external world. To seek the truth of self-consciousness, in turn, will similarly lead toward a mediating synthesis. Thus, moving from the master/slave dialectic through the transitions of stoicism, skepticism, and unhappy consciousness, it becomes clear that self-consciousness finds self-certainly only when the individual is united and so reconciled with the universal. Only in this way can self-consciousness surpass the many one-sided forms of freedom embodied in the master, who is free but lacks self-reflection; the self-reflective slave, who remains unfree; the stoic, who attains freedom by retreating to an inner citadel, negating all surrounding standards; the skeptic, who, in taking such negation to its conclusion, destroys any basis for its freedom and action; and the unhappy consciousness, which seeks to give itself over to a universal standard that it posits in a transcendent realm beyond its reach. Hegel calls the unity of individual and universal "reason," which again is more concrete than an isolated and thus incomplete self-consciousness. The "idea of *Reason*" is "the certainty that, in its particular individuality, it has being absolutely *in itself*, or is all reality" (Hegel 1977: §230). Christianity announces the form of this reconciliation, although it cannot actualize it.

The dialectic of reason demonstrates that the mediation of individual and universal can take place only in the realm of community self-consciousness or spirit. Its subdialectic of "Observing Reason" shows that the observation of nature and even of humanity—through the sciences of psychology, physiognomy, and phrenology—yields descriptions that cannot attain the status of truth. When consciousness turns to itself, however, declaring itself to be a thing, it exceeds its own thinghood and particularity, passing over into universality. This is "the *infinite judgement* that the self is a Thing, a judgement that suspends itself. Through this result, then, the category is further determined as being this self-superseding antithesis" (Hegel 1977: §344). But attempts by individual consciousness to generate a universal on its own are futile, as is shown by the persistent failure of subjective standards such as pleasure, the "law of the heart," and virtue to sustain a consistent moral law; conversely, a static, objective moral code cannot realize itself unless it already embodies a dynamic that ties it directly to individual subjects and circumstances. Only when individuals unconditionally affirm the law can the opposition between them be overcome: "If they are supposed to be validated by *my* insight, then I have already denied their unshakeable, intrinsic being. . . . Ethical disposition consists just in sticking steadfastly to what is right, and abstaining from all attempts to move or shake it, or derive it" (§437). This attitude, which absorbs and reconciles the opposition of subjective and objective, particular and universal, defines "the spiritual being" (§435) and thus the spirit of a community.

The dialectic of spirit recounts the history of lived communities culminating in the real reconciliation of individual and collective freedom and self-knowledge. It begins in ancient Greece, where the willing of the universal, precisely because it is immediate and unreflective, retains a mysterious and transcendent element, dividing into a knowable human and an unknowable divine law and making conflict inevitable. Oedipus thus breaches family law in fulfilling human duty, whereas Antigone transgresses human law in observing divine command. From Roman legal citizenship to feudal courtiership, the dialectic of culture presents a series of ultimately one-sided attempts to surpass this dualism. Finally, with the Terror that follows from the Enlightenment's turn to rationality against faith, consciousness surrenders itself to a universal—albeit a purely destructive one—that comes from nothing other than itself. The dialectic of morality then details the negation and sublation of this negative universal into a positive reconciliation, culminating in the confession and forgiveness of acting and judging consciousness that establishes the reciprocal recognition of individuals as autonomous moral agents. To be self-conscious is to recognize others and to be recognized as a universal individual—a self-reflective being who attains being-for-self through action that is both for itself and for another. And this is achieved with the passage into a society of true reciprocal recognition that appears, Hegel maintains, in the modern state. The dialectic of spirit thus concludes with the passage from consciousness given over to its absolute to self-consciousness, which actualizes the Absolute, to which it is identical. The collective self-consciousness of the modern state is thus "God manifested in the midst of those who know themselves in the form of pure knowledge" (Hegel 1977: §671).

The dialectic of religion retraces the same history from the perspective of the universal that is progressively more embodied in spiritual communities (Hegel 1977: §672). From primitive religions, which posit the divine in nature, to religions of emanation, which see the divine as the Light from which all beings receive sustenance, to pantheisms, which locate it within plant and animal life, Spirit exists as an unreflective source. Religion advances with the conception of Spirit as an artificer and later as the spirit of a particular nation. Nevertheless, the gods remain separate from their worshipers in all the various manifestations of this religion. Christianity and the incarnation of the divine in Christ overcome this separation. The Christian's God presents the movement of the Notion: the universal becomes particular and through the negation of death returns to the universal. Yet even here the divine is only an image, an object of worship for believers.

All that is needed is to realize that the content of religion comes not from a foreign source but from the religious community itself. But this is exactly what the previous history of spirit has demonstrated. The Absolute thereby becomes self-conscious in its identity with the self-conscious community, and consciousness passes from religion to science, in a dialectic of absolute knowledge that traces the most recent developments bringing the dialectical unfolding to its conclusion in the modern state. Whole and complete, the state, as the divine become real on earth, represents the end of history, leaving only the occasional recollection of the history that has culminated in it.

> The *goal*, Absolute Knowing, or Spirit that knows itself as Spirit, has for its path the recollection of the Spirits as they are in themselves and as they accomplish the organization of their realm. Their preservation, regarded from the side of their free existence appearing in the form of contingency, is History; but regarded from the side of their [philosophically] comprehended organization, it is the Science of Knowing in the sphere of appearance: the two together, comprehended History, form alike the inwardizing and the Calvary of ab-

solute Spirit, the actuality, truth and certainty of his throne, without which he would be lifeless and alone. (Hegel 1977: §808)

All this, at least, is what the *Phenomenology* purports to fulfill. But while the dialectic does culminate in the reconciliation of universal and particular, it is less certain that it is an *internal* and *necessary* movement. Rather, each transitional point for consciousness appears marked with contingency. From the initial surrender of one consciousness to another that commences the dialectic of lordship and bondage to the confession and forgiveness of acting and judging consciousnesses that establish universal self-consciousness, nothing within these situations compels their sublations. All depend on a series of realizations that consciousness need not make. Hegel does elaborate the logical contradictions within the circumstances consciousness faces in its attempts to reconcile itself with the universal. But the existence of a logical contradiction does not oblige its resolution. Here the dialectic fails to account for the motor force it demands, so that mediation remains incomplete insofar as the Notion does not account for its own becoming.[7] These difficulties appear even more markedly in the later *Lectures on the Philosophy of World Spirit*, where Hegel asserts the order of human communities that instantiate World Spirit to be determined by geographical conditions and natural circumstances, so that history transpires in the Old World and not the New because the former comprises three continents but the latter comprises only two, and the path of development moves from the Orient and travels westward, leaving Africa with no place in world history at all (Hegel 1975:152–96).

Kojève, while dealing specifically with the history of the *Phenomenology*, recognizes this deficiency and holds that "desire" accounts for dialectical advancement. This claim seems to satisfy the requirement of internality while making the progression of consciousness a determinate movement, but it fails because it invokes the Notion it is supposed to actualize. Desire is inadequate to explain history if it is simply the desire to have (that is, to negate the independence of) an object, for that is a quality of all life. Desire becomes human only when it seeks something beyond the objects of life and becomes the desire for desire—that is, the desire to be the desire of another, to be held as an object of value, rather than simply to value an object (see Kojève 1969: chs. 1–2). The desire that drives history is thus self-consciousness's desire to be recognized by another self-consciousness—but this is then a desire for the final form of human life, in which the Notion is actualized. None of this is surprising, given that the crucial passages that begin the chapter on self-consciousness forgo any dialectical derivation of desire but rather assert a definition from the perspective of the phenomenologist standing at the end of the dialectical unfolding (Hegel 1977: §168).[8] Therefore, if desire is indeed Hegel's motor force, as Kojève argues, it is nothing less than the desire for the Notion to be realized.

Now if the purpose of the historical dialectic is to locate the causal chain through which human development produces the Notion, it cannot introduce the desire for this end to account for this evolution, for then it becomes a simple tautology: consciousness advances toward the Notion because it desires the actualization of the Notion. As Hegel himself points out, such a teleological account explains nothing.

> The necessity, just because it cannot be grasped as an inner necessity of the creature, ceases to have a sensuous existence, and can no longer be observed in the world of reality, but has withdrawn from it. Finding thus no place in the actual creature, it is what is called a teleological relation, a relation which is *external* to the related terms, and therefore really the antithesis of a law. It is a conception completely freed from the necessity of Nature, a conception which leaves that necessity behind and operates spontaneously above it. (1977: §255)

Given this, the only way to redeem the historical dialectic is to excuse it from having to provide a causal chain wherein the Notion becomes actual in human history by demonstrating this realization to be an already established fact. In other words, history must already have terminated, so that the historical dialectic simply recounts its fulfillment, bypassing the need to explain it. As Hegel declares: "We must first of all know what the ultimate design of the world really is, and secondly, we must see that this design has been realised and that evil has not been able to maintain a position of equality beside it" (1975:43).

The onus therefore falls on Hegel's account of the modern state in the *Philosophy of Right,* and it should not be surprising that Hegel explicitly rejects any historical analysis of modern law and institutions.

> By dint of obscuring the difference between the historical and the philosophical study of law, it becomes possible to shift the point of view and slip over from the problem of the true justification of a thing to a justification by appeal to circumstances, to deductions from presupposed conditions which in themselves may have no higher validity, and so forth. To generalize, by this means the relative is put in place of the absolute and the external appearance in

place of the true nature of the thing. When those who try to justify things on historical grounds confound an origin in external circumstances with one in the concept, they unconsciously achieve the very opposite of what they intend. Once the origination of an institution has been shown to be wholly to the purpose and necessary in the circumstances of the time, the demands of history have been fulfilled. But if this is supposed to pass for a general justification of the thing itself, it turns out to be the opposite, because, since those circumstances are no longer present, the institution so far from being justified has by their disappearance lost its meaning and its right. (1967: §3)

Precisely because the modern state must rescue its historical origins from mere contingency, the *Philosophy of Right*—although presenting the state in a developmental and dialectical character—is largely ahistorical. In addition, it is paramount for Hegel to demonstrate that modern life achieves the reciprocal recognition required for true self-consciousness—or at least that it contains concretely within it the institutional and social mechanisms to achieve this recognition—not only for the sake of his account of history but also to avoid reducing the Notion to an ideal and self-consciousness to a utopian faith that he vehemently opposes.

Since philosophy is the exploration of the rational, it is for that very reason the apprehension of the present and the actual, not the erection of a beyond, supposed to exist, God knows where, or rather which exists, and we can perfectly well say where, namely in the error of a one-sided, empty, ratiocination. . . . It is just as absurd to fancy that a philosophy can transcend its contemporary world as it is to fancy that an individual can overleap his own age, jump over Rhodes. If his theory really goes beyond the world as it is and builds an ideal one as it ought to be, that world exists indeed, but only in his opinions, an unsubstantial element where anything you please may, in fancy, be built. (1967:10–11)

Nevertheless, Hegel fails both to show that modern life achieves reciprocal recognition and to avoid the use of historical argument. We need not recount the text's entire logic, for it suffices to recall that in the closing pages of the *Philosophy of Right*, Hegel is compelled to turn to World Spirit's historical development when justifying the state's need to employ the chaos of international relations and war in securing its internal unity. This unity appears to be threatened by such internal forces as the necessary creation of pauperism in free-market economies (see Hegel 1967: §§236–45); the recalcitrant sub-jectivism within state institutions designed to act objectively (§320); and the uncertain stability of the family (§§158–81), the institution that underpins the ethical life of the state. Hegel suggests that the threat of war can suppress these divisive elements, aligning otherwise self-interested individuals with the uni-versal good (§323), so that a society of reciprocal recognition can be achieved. But he then must maintain that the destruction inherent within this condi-tion is wrapped up in historical progression (§§341–60). World history thus justifies its violence by the creation of the nations that, at each stage in histo-ry, embody more fully the Notion, moving from the Oriental, Greek, and Roman eras to Hegel's Germany. With this final appeal to history, however, the dialectic simply falls apart: the final condition of the state appears to be marked with the contingencies of war unless the latter can be seen as part of a necessary historical development, but the historical account itself devolves into a mere interpretation of contingent events unless it can be shown that the modern state realizes the end of history.[9]

Exactly as the young Marx claims, the unity of Hegel's state is nothing more than that of an abstract and mystified Spirit hovering above an actuality rec-ognized as lacking the means to overcome its obvious antagonistic divisions (see Marx 1970; Marx 1964:170–93). This is fatal to the entire Hegelian dia-lectic. If the Notion is no more than an unactualized thought, a hoped for mediation posited above a reality that remains divided, then Hegel will have shown only that every being, insofar as it relates oppositionally to other be-ings, presupposes a movement of totalization. Nonetheless, although this claim is certainly effective in dismissing simple skepticisms or empiricisms, it is far from invulnerable. Because it remains abstract, it fails to foreclose the possibility that every being might also paradoxically presuppose that which deconstructs or decomposes the totality and a movement that escapes the power of the whole. In other words, the failure to redeem the modern con-dition presents a possible route to "escape" or "forget" Hegel.

"Beyond" the Identity of Identity and Difference: The Singular-Multiple Event

The possibility of a new ontology follows directly from the previous exam-ination of the dialectic.[10] Hegel draws the necessity of negation from the in-ability of being as a simple positivity to distinguish itself from nothingness. This creates a movement purporting to be autonomous. Given Hegel's in-ability to show the Notion's actualization in history, however, it becomes clear that the dialectic itself rests on a final cause that remains external to it. Only if history had indeed been completed could Hegel dispense with the need to assert a desire for actualization to make the various developments compulsory for consciousness and with a World Spirit to inspire unity in a world that is actually divided. As Hegel himself maintained (1974: §255), however, an external cause in such a teleological form can have only an accidental relation to its effects. The dialectical synthesis of opposites thus remains only an abstract unity unable to grasp the conditions of modernity that are meant to incarnate it. The inability to illustrate the embodiment of the Notion in the mediating institutions of the modern state does not signal a definitive failure of dialectics, but it does enable a rethinking of the being of becoming not as the identity of identity and difference but rather as a relation of what Foucault termed originary dispersion. The paradoxical thought of this difference must now be engaged.

Lyotard provides a point of entry with his conception of "the jews" as a nondialectical excess that cannot be brought into any representational schema except through violence but that remains implicated in dialectical and representational thought as such. This singular-multiple difference demands an alternative synthesis of differences that links them not through identity but rather through a sameness of that which differs. Heidegger suggests such a sameness as the genuine principle of identity misunderstood by metaphysics, but it is the Nietzschean conceptualization of forces and the movement of becoming as eternal return that presents its power of linkage and production. Deleuze's understanding of the virtual event organizing actual relations of difference and Foucault's conception of micropowers underlying disciplinary systems show how the synthesis of forces yields structure and meaning. Nietzsche's rethinking of the friend/enemy opposition, Foucault's engagement with politics as ethics, and Blanchot's theorization of the unavowable community together illustrate the ways in which the affirmation of this groundless difference demands a rethinking of key terms of political discourse.

In Excess of Dialectics

The logic of dialectics rests on the claim that positivity is an abstraction, for it is only a moment in a more encompassing negativity that accounts for both inclusion and exclusion. In this way, one speaks of Hegel's having accounted for all forms of difference, for he shows its various appearances—independence, interdependence, and identity—to be vanishing moments. This thinking rests on a prior understanding of difference as spacing: between the oppositional terms to be synthesized, there must be a distance or space that separates them but which cannot be consistently included or excluded from the identity of either, just as the distance separating two cities is a gap at once external to each and a necessary element in their definitions (see Rorty 1967). Any thing thus invokes a topography of relations through which it gains specificity. If this yet to be thought difference is to escape this rationality, it must not fall into a formulation of spacing that allows for dialectical mediation or into a movement that can be recuperated by that of contradiction.

Lyotard approaches this issue through Freud in *Heidegger and "the jews,"* speaking of a disturbance unable to be registered by psychic mechanisms. An event occurs, he says, that cannot be depicted as inside or outside, located on a linear continuum of time, or even known as an "absence": "This excitation need not be 'forgotten,' repressed according to representational procedures, nor through *acting out.* Its 'excess' (of quantity, of intensity) exceeds the excess that gives rise (presence, place, and time) to the unconscious and the preconscious. It is 'in excess' like air and earth are in excess for the life of a fish. . . . We are confronted with a silence that does not make itself heard as silence" (Lyotard 1990:12). This "first blow," which is "like a whistle that is inaudible to humans but not to dogs, or like infrared or ultraviolet light" (15), is an "unsayable something" that may be traumatic or merely banal.[11] It must not, however, be subsumed under forms of secondary repression, understood as excluded according to the various figures of representation. For this reason, Lyotard insists on distinguishing anti-Semitism from xenophobia. The latter seeks to place otherness "outside," an exclusion that can be sufficiently answered as a dialectical impossibility. The former, however, "is one of the means of the apparatus of its culture to bind and represent as much as possible—to protect against—the originary terror, actively to forget it" (23). It attempts to signify "the jews," the nomadic, unrepresentable difference—the differend— in the name of control over the time and space constituting the possibility of representation and then to forget the cruelty it concomitantly performs. This is the maneuver that makes dialectics possible.

This event is thus neither "inside" nor "outside," surpassing space and time without being marked within them as their beyond. It remains an unrecuperable excess, a surplus that cannot be reduced to an opposition to what it surpasses. Hence it is an otherness, but precisely because it problematizes the relation of self and other, identity and difference. Its "identity" can be only as that which differs from itself. It may be called a "singular" difference escaping the logic of universal and particular, and thus quite different from the Hegelian singular;[12] an "absolute" or "multiple" negation (see Golding 1997) that pluralizes by negating the positive/negative dichotomy itself; or a "virtual" difference that is unidentifiable yet real. Such an event is forgotten not by being lost in time but by being "lost time," strangely "in between" past, present, and future. It is forgotten by virtue of being "left out" but never simply excluded or left behind. As a difference, it must display notions of spacing, movement, and temporality—or rather, as a rethinking of difference, it must revise these terms as well. It will be not a dialectical difference but something nomadic and noncategorizable that through its operations levels hierarchies, deconstructs totalities, and decomposes identity.

To pull this event into a symbolic logic would do violence to its nature, for if the first blow comes too early for a system that cannot catalog it, the second blow comes too late, and the psychic reaction and representation miss their mark. To ignore the event is as great a misdeed as to represent it, however, for it is then reduced to a mere absence.

It follows that psychoanalysis, the search for lost time, can only be interminable, like literature and like true history (i.e., the one that is not historicism but anamnesis): the kind of history that does not forget that forgetting is not a breakdown of memory but the immemorial always "present" but never here-now, always torn apart in the time of consciousness, of chronology, between a too early and a too late—the too early of a first blow dealt to the apparatus that it does not feel, and the too late of a second blow where something intolerable is felt. A soul struck without striking a blow. (Lyotard 1990:20)

This double refusal of incorporation or dismissal is political by definition: "The differend, transcribed as 'tendency,' as 'faction,' gives rise to negotiations, lies, maneuvers, concessions, denunciations. . . . If this is horrifying, then one 'cannot engage in politics.' One has others do it" (57). Politics in this sense is the always strategic engagement with a difference that cannot be grasped by normal mechanisms of procedural justice and representation.

Lyotard's ontological thought here converges with his concerns regarding the Holocaust. His imperative for silence regarding Auschwitz is neither the erection of a moral taboo nor a call for resignation and dismissal. It denies authorship to speak, but only to expose the paradox of the double bind: on the one hand, those who would have authority are already dead; on the other, the Holocaust, which must receive the greatest moral condemnation, nonetheless reveals the limit at which moral discourse, positing a subject with moral claims and responsibilities, subverts itself (see Readings 1991:121–25). The point is that attempts to represent the extermination, through the exactitude and detail they employ to guarantee the horror will not be forgotten, invariably domesticate the event. They recite the dehumanization of the victims, their treatment as animals, and yet "it is not as men, women, and

children that they are exterminated but as the name of what is evil—'jews'—
that the Occident has given to the unconscious anxiety" (Lyotard 1990:27).
Similar difficulties arise when examining the Nazi actions themselves. It is
not simply that there is no reason to see "the jews" as enemies, and hence
the insanity of the massacre. They are not treated as enemies in the first place:
"They have not been declared the enemy. They have no claim to the spot-
light of confrontation on stage" (28–29). Hence the extermination takes place
offstage, managed so as to leave no trace (25–29). The subsequent political
reassertion of human rights and toleration, while certainly laudable, presents
only a ruse of respect for the alterity of this otherness. Even a revolutionary
politics shares complicity, since the call for the new "is the slogan of the general economy that governs hell by imposing the rule of forgetting and turning the spirit exclusively, foreclosingly, toward the future" (47). In each form
of protest, the silent voice of the event is lost. "It can be surmised what advantages a well-led indignation can derive from the word of reality. And what
is spawned by this indignation is the embryo of the justice-maker. It is indignation, however, with its claim to realism, which insults the name of
Auschwitz, for this indignation is itself the only result it derives from that collective murder. It does not even *doubt* that there is a result (namely itself)"
(Lyotard 1994:153).

One must therefore remember the Holocaust indirectly, through strategies that betray their own attempts to represent. Certain forms of literature
provide one method, and aesthetics another, for art can bear witness to the
always returning aporia of the sublime. It must be sufficient "that one remembers that one must remember, that one should; and it must be sufficient
that one remembers that one does not remind oneself of it anymore; it must
be sufficient to save the interminable and the waiting. Ordinary memory
accomplishes forgetting, covers up the promise. But the promise is not gone,
it is always there" (Lyotard 1990:37–38). After Auschwitz, then, "it is necessary, according to Eli Wiesel, to add yet another verse to the story of the forgetting of the recollection beside the fire in the forest" (47). But this attitude
does not remain fixated on the past. It invokes a newness—"One must con-
cede to art and writing that they cannot escape this requirement of being new,
of 'bringing on' something new" (48)—but that of "the impossible newness
of the more ancient, always new because always forgotten" (ibid.).

The New Synthesis of Forces

In "The Principle of Identity" Heidegger addresses Parmenides' statement,
"For the same perceiving (thinking) as well as being." Heidegger maintains

that this sameness between thought and being cannot be that of the metaphysical understanding of identity subsumed within being. It rather points to a nonmetaphysical "belonging together."

> If we think of belonging *together* in the customary way, the meaning of belonging is determined by the word together, that is, by its unity. In that case, "to belong" means as much as: to be assigned and placed into the order of a "together," established in the unity of a manifold, combined into the unity of a system, mediated by the unifying center of an authoritative synthesis. . . . However, belonging together can also be thought of as *belonging* together. This means: the "together" is now determined by the belonging. Of course, we must still ask here what "belong" means in that case, and how its peculiar "together" is determined only in its terms. . . . Enough for now that this reference makes us note the possibility of no longer representing belonging in terms of the unity of the together, but rather of experiencing this together in terms of belonging. (Heidegger 1969:29)[13]

The equation A = A must be distinguished from the principle that "A is the same [as A]." The former necessarily implies two distinct entities: "An equation requires at least two elements. One A is equal to another. . . . For something to be the same, one is always enough" (23–24). Metaphysics here fails in the very task it gives itself, never saying what a thing is but asserting only that to which it is equal or identical. If sameness rather than equality is the principle of identity, however, and if it invokes a "belonging together," then identity can be neither a being-in-itself nor a being-for-itself. Identity must invoke a synthesis, but one that is prior to any dialectical formulation of unity.

Nietzsche indicates the form that such a synthesis must take when he tackles the consequences of the "death of God" for the central question of philosophy: how can a thing come from its opposite? Whereas metaphysical thought has maintained the separation of one term from the other by "assuming for the more highly valued thing a miraculous source in the very kernel and being of the 'thing in itself,'" historical philosophy "has discovered in individual cases (and this will probably be the result in every case) that there are no opposites, except in the customary exaggeration of popular or metaphysical interpretations, and that a mistake in reasoning lies at the bottom of this antithesis" (Nietzsche 1986: §1; see also Nietzsche 1966a: §2). Nietzsche in this way rejects the route from Hegel taken by Marx, who, remaining committed to a dialectical understanding of the real as the movement of contradiction and reconciliation, holds that Hegel's fault stems from his remaining in the realm of idealism and abstract consciousness, failing to realize the primary role of labor and the fact that it is being that determines consciousness, not the reverse (see Marx 1964:170–93). Against this, Nietzsche locates the source of Hegelian abstraction in the oppositional understanding of relations. Where opposites are strictly separated, any constitutive relationality is denied, resulting in a crude idealism; alternatively, where such opposites are dialectically mediated, Nietzsche objects that this signals an abstraction by establishing an equivalence among differences. This does not mean that everything falls into an abyss of indifferent nothingness. Rather, with no God to hold opposites apart, to reduce evil to a lack of good, or madness to a lack of reason, "a *chemistry* of the moral, religious and aesthetic conceptions and sensations" is required (Nietzsche 1986: §1). Historical philosophy, later renamed "genealogy," aims to fulfill this role while accounting for the appearance of oppositional logic. In doing so, it provides a glimpse of this nondialectical difference.

The death of God razes the distinction of essence and appearance: "The sore spot of Kant's critical philosophy has gradually become visible even to dull eyes" (Nietzsche 1967a: §553). Hegel himself shows that the thing-in-itself and the logic of causality are incompatible and that no thing can be distinguished from its relations to others. Without these others, the thing could not exist. As Nietzsche says:

> The properties of a thing are effects on other "things":
> if one removes other "things," then a thing has no properties,
> i.e., there is no thing without other things,
> i.e., there is no "thing-in-itself." (§557)

There is no thing-in-itself, no physical atom, except perhaps as the secondary effect of relations among forces or as an interpretation of phenomena that is itself a product of forces (§§624–25). These forces in turn give any thing its meaning and sense: as Deleuze says in his famous analysis of Nietzsche, "We will never find the sense of something (of a human, a biological or even a physical phenomenon) if we do not know the force which appropriates the thing, which exploits it, which takes possession of it or is expressed in it" (1983:3). As Deleuze argues, however, Nietzsche's concept of force must be rigorously distinguished from Hegel's.[14] For Nietzsche, relations among forces cannot be reduced to equality, nor can their differences be measured by a fixed scale, for both these maneuvers presuppose a Sameness, identity, or ground. This indicates that force necessarily engenders resistance, even in scenarios where forces can be said to "cooperate." The movement of forces therefore cannot be one of a totality dividing and returning to itself, a becoming other followed by a becoming same, and no line of equivalences can be drawn between the individual, its constitutive relations, and the universe that the latter forms, for the equivalence by which such a dialectic functions is the expression of abstraction. Instead, encounters among forces are contingent, irreducible to any order that would determine them. The "death of God" thus demands a fundamental antagonism and disequilibrium installed within force relations and a movement that results from and continues this asymmetry.

All this necessitates rethinking quantity and quality to free them from the hierarchy and abstraction of quality-quantity-measure found in Hegel's *Logic*, whereby all qualities, through dialectical synthesis, can be quantified and therefore measured (see Hegel 1969: bk. 1). As Deleuze explains, Nietzsche views differences in force relations that cannot be gauged on a fixed scale as quantitative differences because, understood strictly from the viewpoint of quantity, there is nothing to reduce them to sameness. One can speak only of an equality (e-quality) of quantities, invoking quality as a separate measuring rod. To reject such a metaphysical remnant means that there is no quantity in itself, that quantity is always a difference in quantity, just as the essence of a force is always its difference from related forces, making it appropriate to call differences between forces quantitative differences. But to say that force is a quantitative difference is to assert both its relationality and its heterogeneity with respect to the forces related to it. This heterogeneity is more than a difference in type that can be subsumed into a higher category, as red and green are brought under the realm of color, for such an understanding of difference would reinstate the very abstraction being contested. Nor is it a relation of contradiction resolvable through a negative synthesis. A Nietzschean force is therefore neither a thing-in-itself nor part of a dialectical synthesis establishing an identity of identity and difference but rather a component of a *disjunctive synthesis* that relates forces *through their difference*. It is a disjoining that, precisely because it cannot be dialectically mediated, cannot be understood as a separation or spacing. It is a synthesis *through* difference that invokes an "excess of the in-between" in the form of an unlocalizable warping that underpins the meaning and sense of any thing. And it follows from the elimination of any equality among forces that would signal an abstraction. An unnameable excess thereby accompanies any thing within the irreducible, paradoxical concatenation of forces that embodies the latter's synthetic being: an ineliminable discontinuity that remains unrepresentable while structuring representation and meaning.

Qualities, however, are by definition irreducible to one another, or at best reduced only through abstraction. Understood in this way, quantity, as inseparable from difference in quantity, *is* quality (see Deleuze 1983:43–44), but of a peculiar sort. As Deleuze continues to explain through Nietzsche, in differential relations, one force necessarily dominates the other. Through this difference in status, the quantitative difference of related forces gives rise to a qualitative difference—the will to power of each force as active or reactive. The quality of force is expressive and judgmental: a force is constituted so as to express a judgment concerning Being, thereby introducing value and evaluation into philosophy.[15] Given this, the genealogical task is a simple matter of asking what relations would constitute a will that, rather than acknowledging inequality and heterogeneity, insists instead upon an equality that is by definition an abstraction—or what sort of will would establish oppositions between goodness seen as pure, unadulterated, and unrelational and evil seen as the former's lack or absence. The answer is that such a will must be that of a being unable to affirm relationality or *unable to affirm itself in its relations*—in other words, a being that can be described only as weak, dominated, and slavish. The obviously limited perspective from which such demands are expressed, however, indicates another mode of valuation from beings who act and dominate. Here, then, are the wills to power that express noble and slave moralities.

"Active" characterizes a will to power able to express itself immediately; "reactive" designates a will that must defer action and so judges in the first instance rather than acts. The first, noble mode of being goes to the limits of what it can do and transcends them; the second, slavish form separates force from what it can do in order to hold it accountable for what it does. Noble morality is characterized by its nonoppositional character. The master affirms himself as good, but in doing so he affirms not a self-identity but rather an agonism by which he transcends his limits and overcomes himself. He therefore requires another noble as a worthy opponent: "How much reverence has a noble man for his enemies!—and such reverence is a bridge to love.—For he desires his enemy for himself, as his mark of distinction; he can endure no other enemy than one in whom there is nothing to despise and *very much* to honor! In contrast to this, picture 'the enemy' as the man of *ressentiment* conceives him" (Nietzsche 1967b:1.10). The nobles' valuations come from their high station—"It was out of this *pathos of distance* that they first seized the right to create values and to coin names for values: what had they to do with utility!" (1.2)—but crucially, their affirmations do not emerge from

comparisons with what they stand above. Rather, strife and conflict themselves are affirmed, whereas the weak, base, and therefore unworthy are labeled "bad." Nonetheless, even though good and bad are defined relational-
ly, they are not established through an opposition that sets the boundaries
of the one against the other. The name "good" *identifies* the noble but does
not establish his *identity,* and in this way it expresses not a mediation between
self and other but an overcoming that dissolves this binary relation. Noble
affirmation thereby pays homage to excess.

In this way active wills *affirm their difference,* which is to say, they affirm a
groundless difference. It is the slaves who, too weak to affirm themselves in
conflict, call themselves good only by first defining evil as its polar opposite.
Demanding a justification for their suffering and their being reduced to reaction, and driven by a paranoia that those who harm them do so intentionally, they will an equalization of forces or a ground to measure differences,
allowing them to label aristocratic actions as unjust. The slaves secure their
own identity through a distortion of noble identification that pins it within
boundaries parallel to those the slaves seek for themselves. Nietzsche's
"jews,"[16] then, like Lyotard's anti-Semites, witness an affirmation so far exceeding their capacities that it is ultimately distorted and reduced into an
oppositional schema of good and evil: they are evil, and hence I am good;
they are stronger, but I am superior. The slaves' logic here shows itself to be
abstract and one-sided.

> That lambs dislike great birds of prey does not seem strange: only
> it gives no ground for reproaching these birds of prey for bearing
> off little lambs. And if the lambs say among themselves: "these birds
> of prey are evil; and whoever is least like a bird of prey, but rather
> its opposite, a lamb—would he not be good?" there is no reason to
> find fault with this institution of an ideal, except perhaps that the
> birds of prey might view it a little ironically and say: "*we* don't dis-
> like them at all, these good little lambs; we even love them: nothing
> is more tasty than a tender lamb." (Nietzsche 1967b:1.13)

If this distortion is not appreciated, then Nietzsche's calls for an aristocratic
society are apt to severe misunderstanding.[17]

It is also incorrect to understand noble affirmation as a *causa sui.* That the
masters define themselves as good prior to judging the slaves implies not that
their wills are not the product of relational forces but rather that they affirm
difference in the form of *amor fati*—the contingent clash of forces and the
necessity that follows from the dice roll (see Deleuze 1983:25–27). Converse-

ly, that the slaves affirm themselves as good only by first labeling the masters evil indicates a will that misunderstands the ontology of forces. What Nietzsche admires in noble morality, despite its obvious brutishness and stupidity, is an affirmation of difference beyond any negative moment, for to affirm this groundless difference is precisely to value as good that which dissolves the oppositional relation between identity and difference. This is the ethical judgment that does not bow to ressentiment in the encounter with the unsayable difference. It is an innocent affirmation, in the sense not of being pure and unadulterated but rather of not being implicated in a Law establishing innocence and guilt (22–25). What is both acted and affirmed, then, is not a ground but a mutation that dissolves the self as an identity, though it does not dissolve it into nothingness. Put differently, the power and domination this will exercises operate by linking beings in a disjunctive synthesis, producing dispersion. Noble affirmation may resemble a *causa sui* in its immediacy, but what is immediate is not self-identity but a self-overcoming singularity, a repetition of difference that Nietzsche labels the "eternal return."[18]

Nietzsche's presentation of the eternal return is clearly incomplete and ambiguous, being largely underthematized in relation to that of the overman. The internal coherence of both doctrines and their compatibility with each other are uncertain. Few commentators who accept either one hold that they can be reconciled,[19] and many of those who do resort to dismissing certain aspects of one or the other.[20] Nevertheless, if the unlocalizable excess of the event and the nondialectical disjoining of the disjunctive synthesis are kept in mind, it is possible to see the eternal return as the very decentering affirmed in overcoming and overcoming as an affirmation that involves a circular remarking of the past.

It is first necessary to distinguish an eternal return that does not overcome but instead embodies nihilism: the recurrence of identical events.

> Let us think this thought in its most terrible form: existence as it is, without meaning or aim, yet recurring inevitably without any finale of nothingness: "*The eternal recurrence*."
> This is the most extreme form of nihilism: the nothing (the "meaningless"), eternally! (Nietzsche 1967a: §55)

This eternal return is the product of science, "the most *scientific* of all possible hypotheses" (ibid.). Given a definite quantity of force and a finite number of centers of force (both following the law of conservation of energy), in an infinite period of time the contingent combinations of forces will repeat themselves eternally. Although based on the same principles as mechanism—

including its spatialized, chronological conception of time extending infinitely forward and backward[21]—this doctrine nonetheless goes beyond it, for
mechanism invokes a final entropic state that should, given an infinite time,
have already been reached.

> If the world could in any way become rigid, dry, dead, *nothing,* or if
> it could reach a state of equilibrium, or if it had any kind of goal that
> involved duration, immutability, the once-and-for-all (in short,
> speaking metaphysically: if becoming *could* resolve itself into being
> or into nothingness), then this state must have been reached. . . .
> *Because* the world has not reached this [final state], mechanistic
> theory must be considered an imperfect and merely provisional
> hypothesis. (§1066)

However, by reinvoking a ground in the form of the self-identity of a circular series, this eternal return exposes the will to nothingness of science itself.[22]
Such a movement not only implies Zarathustra's nightmare that the small
man will return but also lacks the ability to act as "a *selective* principle, in the
service of strength (and barbarism!!)" (§1058).[23]

Moving beyond this nihilism does not mean positing eternal novelty
against eternal repetition. The suggestion that "the world intentionally avoids
a goal and even knows artifices for keeping itself from entering into a circular course" is a theological remnant, which arises from the error of imputing to "a finite, definite, unchangeable force of constant size, such as the world
is, the miraculous power of infinite novelty in its forms and states" (1967a:
§1062). Employing Boscovitch against Spinoza (see Whitlock 1996), Nietzsche argues that if force cannot have infinitely great magnitude, then the
power of infinite novelty is chimerical. But what Nietzsche rejects here is
infinite novelty *posited as the opposite of finitude.* The error, in short, comes
from insisting that the universe fit into one or the other term of a binary that
is nothing more than a human, all too human construction: the universe,
Nietzsche maintains, is neither purposeful nor accidental, neither an organism nor a machine, and death is not the opposite of life (Nietzsche 1974: §109).
It is therefore hasty to conclude that in rejecting infinite novelty Nietzsche
is falling back to its opposite, a return of the finite and the identical.

We will return to this issue in detail in chapter 3, but here it suffices to say
that there is another understanding of infinity that can be incorporated into
the eternal return. This is neither the infinite extension of time that follows
from the rejection of a point at which a created universe began; the infinite
magnitude of force of theological doctrines; nor the potential infinity of

divisibility, accepted by Boscovitch (see Whitlock 1996:211–13), that defines spatio-temporal continuity. It is rather the infinite as an excess that, by virtue of being unlocalizable in space or time, goes *beyond the limit* of spatio-temporal continuity. As an excess that remains immanent to what it exceeds, it does not oppose infinite to finite. While it introduces novelty, it does not do so as a creativity ex nihilo.

A close reading of "On the Vision and the Riddle" is requisite here. Zarathustra confronts the dwarf with the image of a gateway, inscribed as "Moment," from which two infinite pathways extend to the future and the past. They "offend each other face to face." But their contradiction is not eternal.

> "Behold," I continued, "this moment! From this gateway, Moment, a long eternal lane leads *backward:* behind us lies an eternity. Must not whatever *can* walk have walked on this lane before? Must not whatever *can* happen have happened, have been done, have passed by before? And if everything has been there before—what do you think, dwarf, of this moment? Must not this gateway too have been there before? And are not all things knotted together so firmly that this moment draws after it *all* that is to come? Therefore—itself too? For whatever *can* walk—in this long lane out *there* too, it *must* walk once more.
>
> "And this slow spider, which crawls in the moonlight, and this moonlight itself, and I and you in the gateway, whispering together, whispering of eternal things—must not all of us have been there before? And return and walk in that other lane, out there, before us, in this long dreadful lane—must we not eternally return?" (Nietzsche 1966b:3.2.2)

This description initially appears to affirm a return of identical states, but Zarathustra has already scolded the dwarf for suggesting that time is a circle: "'You spirit of gravity,' I said angrily, 'do not make things too easy for yourself!'" (ibid.).[24] What complicates the situation is that the gateway also resides in both past and future—not the state of being grasped by the moment but the moment itself. To say that the present moment is also past and future is to say that it is no longer a mere marker on a temporal continuum but becomes instead an "untimely" event. The moment, in short, stitches together all time only at the cost of cracking it, of moving it "out of joint."[25]

What returns then, is the fissure of lost time, invoking the impossible newness of the always forgotten, returning eternally because it can never be forgotten "in time." It is an eternal recurrence of the same, but a sameness that differs from the identical or the similar and that invokes a nondialectical synthesis of disjoining. As a result both time and space are cracked. The untimeliness of the moment means that time cannot be reduced to a continuum measuring movement in space. And the imbalance of the rift puts space itself in motion: "That a state of equilibrium is never reached proves that it is not possible. But in an indefinite space it would have to have been reached. Likewise in a spherical space. The *shape* of space must be the cause of eternal movement, and ultimately of all 'imperfection'" (Nietzsche 1967a: §1064). The notion of empty space is an "erroneous conception" (§520), necessary for human life but of no higher value: "Between ourselves: since no one would maintain that there is any necessity for men to exist, reason, as well as Euclidean space, is a mere idiosyncrasy of a certain species of animal, and one among many" (§515).

To affirm this eternal return is to affirm a temporality that is more than chronological time, one that ties together events not only in contingency and strife but also in such a way that they always exceed their linear date and place, thus "returning" in strange and subtle ways. This in turn has distinctive consequences for an overcoming that stretches beyond identity and opposition, beyond good and evil. Overcoming is not an escape from the world but rather a renewed immersion in it, so that it is not an ideal of infinite and unconditioned creativity but a "newness" implicated in the way all moments are conditioned and tied together. Moreover, the figure of overcoming, the overman, is not a radical break from humanity.[26] Overcoming arises as much from behind as from ahead, from a "prehistory" that "is in any case present in all ages or may always reappear" (Nietzsche 1967b:2.9), as well as from a present in which God has been murdered, yet the murderers themselves do not yet recognize this (Nietzsche 1974: §125), and a future of an overman who "must come one day" (Nietzsche 1967b:2.24). In other words, overcoming occurs at every moment (see Ansell Pearson 1997:15, 78n), because the untimeliness of the moment transverses all time without being localized within it.

Given all this, it is not surprising that overcoming takes the form of a willing of all time to repeat itself eternally. The moralist error, Nietzsche says, is to insist that one change oneself without regard to how the self is woven intrinsically into all temporality: "The individual is, in his future and in his past, a piece of fate, one law more, one necessity more for everything that is and everything that will be. To say to him 'change yourself' means to demand that everything should change, even in the past" (Nietzsche 1990:56). In contrast, to affirm the moment means affirming all time in its relations of dependency, uncertainty, and strife, and even the "small man" implicated in it, because all is at play within this moment: "If we affirm one single moment, we thus affirm not only ourselves but all existence. For nothing is self-sufficient, neither in us ourselves nor in things; and if our soul has trembled with happiness and sounded like a harp string just once, all eternity was needed to produce this one event—and in this single moment of affirmation all eternity was called good, redeemed, justified, and affirmed" (Nietzsche 1967a: §1032). Seen on a linear model, overcoming re-marks the past, redeeming it by transforming every "it was" into "Thus I willed it!" and, even more, into "I will its eternal return." The novelty that follows from the return of the fissure is thus accompanied by an apparently more conventional circular return—a point that further illustrates how "any attempt to locate the overhuman outside the human, including outside of history, and to give the overhuman different origins, is fundamentally misguided" (Ansell Pearson 1997:15). But the conventional return neither asserts nor depends on the reality of the repetition of identical events. It instead follows from affirming in the strongest possible way a world of disjunction and nonlinearity. Through rewilling, the self is dissolved as an identity, opening it to another becoming. In so doing, however, it becomes impossible for this untimeliness not to have already appeared innumerable times before, although it must necessarily have been forgotten precisely because its effect is to throw the self outside itself, so that the present revelation must be forgotten too (see Klossowski 1997:56–60). A circle is the form in which overcoming is actualized, but this is also only a superficial image of a more complex and vicious dynamic.

Through the ontology of forces, then, Nietzsche explains how the death of God implies a movement of decentering that compels a rethinking of both time and space and furthermore accounts for both a will that acts this movement and another that denies it, the latter remaining wrapped up in the search for foundations, an original fullness, and a justification of contingent suffering, losing sight of its "true" genesis in differential force relations. The human and natural sciences and philosophy all stand convicted of lacking historical spirit or sense, which is not just a recognition of the contingency of past events but also a refusal to reduce the past to familiar representations (see Nietzsche 1967b:1.2; 1974: §§83, 337). They suffer from a misrecognition of force that treats it only in terms of reaction: "Physiologists should think before putting down the instinct of self-preservation as the cardinal instinct of an organic being. A living thing seeks above all to *discharge* its strength— life itself is *will to power;* self-preservation is only one of the indirect and most frequent *results*" (Nietzsche 1966a: §13). As a result, they conflate a thing's origin and its use: "But purposes and utilities are only *signs* that a will to power has become master of something less powerful and imposed upon it the character of a function; and the entire history of a 'thing,' an organ, a custom can in this way be a continuous sign-chain of ever new interpreta-tions and adaptations whose causes do not even have to be related to one another but, on the contrary, in some cases succeed and alternate with one another in a purely chance fashion" (Nietzsche 1967b:2.12). Genealogy traces the discontinuous history of objects to show how their meanings and iden-tities relate to the forces that seize them. In doing so, however, it recovers a more than historical becoming that always returns to dissolve identity and a corresponding ethic that overcomes the nihilistic implications of the death of God, stretching "beyond" good and evil.

The Power and Meaning of Virtual Folds

The first three chapters of Hegel's *Phenomenology* make clear that the mean-ing of a thing cannot be found in its immediate presentation. It is instead always already mediated, first through various universal categories and then, more profoundly, by a relational movement of forces constituting a totality that includes within it even infinitely distant contradictories. This is an im-manent movement that enables real experience to have meaning by provid-ing a link among differences that would otherwise remain buried within the immediacy of their actual, sensuous presentation. Given a singularity exceed-ing this framework, however, this representational understanding of mean-ing cannot be sustained. It is thus appropriate to ask how the belonging to-gether of differences provides their contouring and specification.

Deleuze, in both his solo works and collaborations with Félix Guattari, presents the structuring operation of dispersion in terms of a passage from a virtual field of forces into actual relations of difference. The schema of vir-tual and actual is not unlike the Hegelian system already examined. The lat-ter presents two levels, of actual experience on the one hand and a movement of forces that gives it meaning on the other. This second level remains con-stitutive but hidden—microscopic, as it were, in the Foucauldian sense—but is nevertheless fully real: it is not a possibility that may or may not exist but instead a condition necessary for experience to "make sense." Similarly, Deleuze distinguishes his coupling of virtual and actual from that of possi-ble and real: "The possible is opposed to the real; the process undergone by the possible is therefore a 'realisation.' By contrast, the virtual is not opposed to the real; it possesses a full reality by itself. The process it undergoes is that of actualisation" (1994:211). The possible, Deleuze maintains, is nothing more than an abstraction of the real, a concept made indeterminate by extrapo-lating existence from it, so that it remains well within the realm of represen-tation. The realization of the possible thereby functions in terms of a fundamental sameness conditioning difference: realization is a coming into existence, and existence resembles the possible that it realizes.

> To the extent that the possible is open to "realisation," it is understood as an image of the real, while the real is supposed to resemble the possible. That is why it is difficult to understand what existence adds to the concept when all it does is double like with like. . . . The actualisation of the virtual, on the contrary, always takes place by difference, divergence or differenciation. Actualisation breaks with resemblance as a process no less than it does with identity as a principle. Actual terms never resemble the singularities they incarnate. In this sense, actualisation or differenciation is always a genuine creation. (212)

Deleuze breaks with Hegel here. The specter of the possible still plagues the latter's thought because Hegel insists on the unity of rational and real. Hegel's Notion thus unfolds so that each more concrete formulation is identical to those from which it is derived. This requires a symmetry by which one can move from the actuality of phenomenological experience to its virtual preconditions and back to the actual structure of nature, spirit, and logic, so that one may begin at any point within the system and derive the rest. Without this symmetry, Hegel maintains, the Notion would remain merely a postulate of thought that, like Kant's transcendental categories, is purely formal.

Deleuze reproaches Kant for providing the conditions of only possible rather than real experience (see, e.g., Deleuze 1991:23; Deleuze 1994:154), and this criticism can be leveled against Hegel as well. That the identity of identity and difference applies only to possible experience is indicated by the way its actualization remains abstract on Hegel's own terms—that is to say, improperly synthesized and so one-sided. It is therefore necessary to press toward another form of difference beyond any oppositional synthesis. Such a synthesis is inadequate, Deleuze says, because it presupposes a space of representation on which mediation takes place—a space that is no more than a slice of a more multidimensional terrain.

> As for opposition . . . [,] it is as though things were spread out upon a flat surface, polarised in a single plane, and the synthesis itself took place only in a false depth—that is, in a fictitious third dimension added to the others which does no more than double the plane. In any case, what is missing is the original, intensive depth which is the matrix of the entire space and the first affirmation of difference: here, that which only afterwards appears as linear limitation and flat opposition lives and simmers in the form of free differences. Every-

where, couples and polarities presuppose bundles and networks, organised oppositions presuppose radiations in all directions. (1994:50–51)

Thus, in the Deleuzean passage from actual experience to its virtual preconditions, what is obtained is not a mediation of opposites but a more originary disjunction that relates irreducibly heterogeneous differences *through their difference*—in other words, what provides the conditions of real experience is the singular-multiple event. This event is not the particular being-in-itself that Hegel himself shows to be an empiricist abstraction (see Baugh 1992:140) but is rather what follows when the remaining abstractions of dialectics are razed. Deleuze holds this event to be a univocal sense or voice speaking through all beings (1994:35–41, 303–4).

The event as a disjoining of differences should be enough to refute interpretations of univocity as a kind of unity or Oneness grounding Deleuzean multiplicity. The most notable of these is Alain Badiou's argument that Deleuze's philosophy is a "Platonism of the virtual" that affirms an actual but unreal and simulacral multiplicity grounded in a still transcendent virtual One and that domesticates the contingency of actual events by submitting them to a virtual Event (Badiou 2000:46, 27).[27] The conflation of the univocity of being and the Oneness of being on which this criticism rests cannot stand up to an examination of the medieval background from which Deleuze draws the concept, a point that will be demonstrated in chapter 5.[28] But even leaving this aside, Badiou struggles to make his reading stick, never using Deleuze's words to substantiate the claim that Deleuze holds actual multiplicities to be unreal and being hard-pressed to sustain the characterization of the virtual as a realm of Oneness against Deleuze's explicit analyses of multiplicities that are constitutive and so not *merely* simulacral in the sense Badiou uses.[29] Unsurprisingly, Badiou is left vacillating between a conception of this virtual One as a "single voice" and as a self-differentiating whole, and in the latter case between the whole's differentiation as the production of simulcra by the One and as a "real" plurality of the One that actual multiplicities simulate.[30]

Rather than affirm a One beyond representation that produces an unreal simulacrum, Deleuze insists on the reality and primordiality of simulacra by virtue of an unrepresentable difference. It is now identity that is a mere simulation, lacking reality: "We should say of this identity and this resemblance that they are 'simulated': they are products of systems which relate different to different by means of difference (which is why such systems are themselves simulacra)" (Deleuze 1994:126). The virtual is thus a field combining the maximum of "differentiation"—that is, the power of dispersion—with the inability to be "differenciated"—the capacity to be grouped into genera, species, and parts. In contrast, the actualization of this virtual plurality permits categorization by the terms of identity, but these terms always remain inadequate because of the virtual differentiation and becoming inhering within the actual (see 187, 207), so that dialectical negativity and mediation never genuinely appear in either realm except when the dispersion of the virtual is abstracted away (207). For Deleuze the simulacral nature of the virtual comes from its being structured through a difference that, instead of being located in a common space of differentiation, folds this space, disjoining the differences that relate through it. The fold is therefore something different from a dimensionless point that could be treated as a minimum of differentiation or even a kind of indifference. The point is only a marker on a continuum, whereas the fold carries out a synthesis of spatial dimensions, but at the cost of destroying spatial smoothness, just as, in the formulation of the eternal return, the moment can stitch together the dimensions of time only by moving them out of joint. Any continuity is thereby littered with immanent warps: "The irrational number implies the descent of a circular arc on the straight line of rational points, and expresses the latter as a false infinity, a simple undefinite that includes an infinity of lacunae; that is why the continuous is a labyrinth that cannot be represented by a straight line. The straight line always has to be intermingled with curved lines" (Deleuze 1993:17). In this way, the fold implies a dispersion that does not *extend* anywhere and so a novelty that remains immanent to the conditions that create it and that it distorts. It is "a leap which would not amount to throwing oneself *elsewhere* (as if another world would open up) but rather leaping in place. Folding, leaping in place, and thus distorting or displacing the ground (the foundation, or its un-founding)" (Nancy 1996:109).

This dispersion is the vehicle through which the virtual carries a sense that is also "nonsense," circulating within the folding interstices of the series it brings together, without being definable by either of them (Deleuze 1990:81). Deleuze presents this paradoxical sense through an analysis of the relation between words and things (12–22). In a representational understanding of meaning, he says, a proposition is considered grounded if it denotes a state of affairs, manifests the intentions of a speaker, or signifies universal concepts. But each of these possibilities subverts the other two. It seems that the manifestation of a founding cogito must be primary to ground the signification of concepts and designate states of affairs. Nevertheless, words must signify concepts before they can be used to manifest or designate anything. Yet if a proposition signifying concepts is supposed to refer to a state of affairs, it must presuppose that this state of affairs determines the truth of the proposition independent of the logical coherence of its significations, so that designation

turns out to be original. A fourth dimension of the proposition remains un-
deniable—namely, its meaning or sense, which is presupposed by manifestation, denotation, and signification but which exceeds both states of affairs
and propositions. The sense of the proposition, "The tree is green," for example, is given in the verb "to green" or "to become green." As an infinitive,
it remains indifferent both to the tree's being green or not being green and
to the active and passive modes of becoming green (214–15; on this point see
also Boundas 1994:105). The sense carried by the infinitive thus exhibits a paradoxical becoming that cannot be subsumed by a telos or form, a becoming
in two directions at once that forever eludes the present. This virtual sense
cannot be judged true or false on the basis of formal logic ("How are we to
reconcile the logical principle, according to which a false proposition has
sense . . . [,] and the no less certain transcendental principle according to
which a proposition always has the truth, the part and the kind of truth which
it merits, and which belongs to it, according to its sense?" [Deleuze 1990:96])
or empirical verification ("'God is' and 'God is not' must have the same sense,
by virtue of the autonomy of sense in relation to the denotatum" [33]). It does
not represent an actual state of affairs but rather is *applied* to this state of affairs while nonetheless residing only in the proposition. It links together word
and thing in a way that denies any correspondence between them.

It remains to be seen how the virtual is actualized—how, in short, folds
"unfold." Here we must recognize that the passages between virtual and actual do not operate according to a correspondence or identity: one can move
from virtual forces to actual states of affairs, but "if we go back up in the
opposite direction, from states of affairs to the virtual, the line is not the same
because it is not the same virtual" (Deleuze and Guattari 1994:156). At times
Deleuze speaks of actualization as a dramatization (Deleuze 1994:216–21)
where the actual is itself a simulation—a "copy" without original, or a coming into being whose (non-)origin is constituted as an effect of its movement.
Actualization is also presented in terms of problem and solution: the virtual
is an open, problematic structure of singularities that sets the transcendental horizon of its actualizations or solutions. Solutions, in turn, never do away
with the problematic that gives them meaning, and the latter inheres within
them as what generates and subverts them (see ch. 4; Deleuze 1990:52–57;
Deleuze and Guattari 1994). But the key to actualization is the disjunctive
synthesis itself: the unfolding of folds is itself a macrofold. If a "thing," understood as a formed unity, is constituted through the interrelation of heterogeneous forces, then the organization of things is exactly that which relates this plurality through an irreducible difference—the virtual—that
muddles any understanding of actuality based on correspondence, identity,
or representation. This movement of actualization forms not a precarious

identity but rather *a dispersion of which any formulation in terms of identity is always incomplete and uncertain.* Actualization, then, is a "contraction" of microscopic, virtual singularities that is not continuous with the virtual. And the virtual inheres within this actual dispersion as that which both constitutes it and into which it dissolves.[31]

Clear parallels can be drawn between this actualization of the virtual and Foucault's understanding of micropowers as a "moving substrate of force relations which, by virtue of their inequality, constantly engender states of power, but the latter are always local and unstable," and which constitute the repetitive mechanisms of repressive power as "the over-all effect that emerges from all these mobilities, the concatenation that rests on each of them and seeks in turn to arrest their movement" (Foucault 1990a:93). Power relations are immanent in all things—power is everywhere, although importantly it is *not* everything—but they have inscribed within them a plurality of sites of resistance as part of their relational nature. Power is therefore never in simple opposition to freedom (Foucault 1988a:12), and large-scale forms of power are neither the sum of these relations nor simply other to them: "There is no discontinuity between them, as if one were dealing with two different levels (one microscopic and the other macroscopic); but neither is there homogeneity (as if one were only the enlarged projection or miniaturization of the other); rather, one must conceive of the double conditioning of a strategy by the specificity of possible tactics, and of tactics by the strategic envelope that makes them work" (Foucault 1990a:99–100). It is through a composition of microforces that is not a mere aggregate or totality that "far reaching, but never completely stable, effects of domination are produced" (102).

Foucault opposes this analytic to juridico-discursive theories that reduce power to restriction, including psychoanalytic models in which the law constitutes the very desire it prohibits. These models, he insists, treat power as "poor in resources, sparing of its methods, monotonous in the tactics it utilizes, incapable of invention, and seemingly doomed always to repeat itself" (Foucault 1990a:85). They are inadequate not simply because resistance is internal to power but because they theorize only a limited set of (negative) relations, restricted to prohibition and transgression, thereby misunderstanding the complexities of power that follow from its dispersive dynamic. Hence they conceive of the fracturing of actuality in terms of a failure of power relations to engender a closed system rather than as a condition that follows from the disjunctive synthesis that both links together microscopic force relations and governs their actualizations. The result is the irrelevance of these juridico-discursive models to a society "that has been more imaginative, probably, than any other in creating devious and supple mechanisms of power" and that "has gradually been penetrated by quite new mechanisms of power that are probably irreducible to the representation of law" (86, 89). In short, the model of law—even in the inverted form presented by psychoanalysis—retains a metaphysical understanding of synthesis at the expense of other, more relevant possibilities.

This force of fracturing and dispersion highlights the great irony in the workings of disciplinary society. We live in a society, Foucault says, that is driven to name, observe, locate, measure, and know. More specifically, it is compelled to identify deviations from a norm that, strangely, does not exist in the first place[32] and then to police and correct these deviations to promote conformity with this fictitious standard. But all this identifying and policing yields the opposite effect: it multiplies differences, producing dispersion and disjunction rather than gathering difference under an umbrella of normality. Meanwhile, the modern will to truth, vigorously seeking to secure stability and identity by locating, mapping, and comprehending every anomaly as a form of deviance, presses for such normality more stringently, thereby stretching into new areas of life. The greater the applied power, however, the greater the resistance in the form of dispersion that follows. It is therefore not surprising, Foucault says, that today's prisons look like factories, which look like hospitals, which look like schools. Nor is it surprising that when one examines the personal histories of the various "deviants" that modern society seeks to contain, they have all already passed through a myriad of institutions purportedly designed to normalize them. And the entire system of disciplinary power seems trapped within its own logic, unable on its own terms to do anything more than increase its policing.

The operative rule of this analysis is that of noncoincidence within relations of complete intimacy and imbrication, for again, the linking of differences does not invoke a separation within a homogeneous space. On the relation of knowledge and power, for example, Foucault states, "Between techniques of knowledge and strategies of power, there is no exteriority, even if they have specific roles and are linked together on the basis of their difference" (1990a:98). As Deleuze notes, Foucault's entire corpus identifies a noncorrespondence between objects and discourses of knowledge and the sites of their production: the hospital as an institution to deal with insanity has its origins not in medicine but in law enforcement, and the discourse on madness is located not in the hospital but in the courts; the delinquent, as an object of penal law, is produced within the walls of prisons, whereas prisoners themselves are created by the mechanisms of the judiciary (see Deleuze 1988: esp. pt. 2). Actualization is the specification of singularities by a synthesis that links them through their difference. As such, it establishes meaning, but not through an appeal to the identity of identity and difference. This allows us to plot a route away from Hegel in which differences presuppose not a totalizing ground but rather the "groundless ground" of a decentered and unlocalized virtuality.

The Friend, the Enemy, and the Community of Those with Nothing in Common

What would a multiple affirmation of difference or, perhaps better, an affirmation of difference as multiplicity mean? Certainly it does not entail a blanket sanctioning of all differences, an interpretation behind the relativist charge that such thought would have to accept fascism, racism, sexism, and so on. Nor does it imply what Deleuze calls a "beautiful soul" who "sees differences everywhere and appeals to them only as respectable, reconcilable or federative differences, while history continues to be made through bloody contradictions" (Deleuze 1994:52). Rather, it is affirmation of a groundless difference that muddles all relations that might otherwise be seen in simple, oppositional terms. It affirms a virtual excess that relates beings through their difference, establishing a dynamism among them and a folding within each. In the light of this theorization, the binarisms on which politics and ethics often rest show themselves to be lacking.

Nietzsche registers a concomitant sensibility in his rethinking of the friend/enemy relation. The friend is one who intervenes between "I" and "me" to prevent the fall into the abyss of self-identity, of the nothingness that would be an I = I relation: "I and me are always too deep in conversation: how could one stand that if there were no friend? For the hermit the friend is always the third person: the third is the cork that prevents the conversation of the two from sinking into the depths" (Nietzsche 1966b:1.14). The friend resides within the fissure as the excess driving one to overcome oneself, opening the self to multiplicity. But then the friend must also be an enemy: "In a friend one should have one's best enemy" (ibid.). The friend is no longer the one who is closest, while the enemy is the furthest and most alien. Against the Christian exhortation to love thy neighbors, Nietzsche proclaims: "It is those farther away who must pay for your love of your neighbor; and even if five of you are together, there is always a sixth who must die. . . . My brothers, love of the neighbor I do not recommend to you: I recommend to you love of the farthest" (1.16). Against the Church's desire to destroy its enemies, he calls for the "spiritualization of *enmity.* It consists in profoundly grasping the value of having enemies: in brief, in acting and thinking in the reverse of the way in which one formerly acted and thought" (Nietzsche 1990:53). The strife and conflict with the "enemy" (and the "friend") remains, but no longer in the brute form of opposition.

In this way one endeavors to move beyond good and evil or, in Foucault's terms, struggles against the fascism both around us and inside us (see Foucault's preface to Deleuze and Guattari 1983). The danger presents itself whenever the possibility of serious discussion or cooperation is foreclosed by a political practice caught up in a "model of war," in which success and failure become a zero-sum game.

> Furthermore: might not this "struggle" that one tries to wage against the "enemy" only be a way of making a petty dispute without much importance seem more serious than it really is? I mean, don't certain intellectuals hope to lend themselves greater political weight with their "ideological struggle" than they really have? . . . And then I'll tell you: I find this "model of war" not only a bit ridiculous but also rather dangerous. Because by virtue of saying or thinking "I'm fighting against the enemy," if one day you found yourself in a position of strength, and in a situation of real war, in front of this blasted "enemy," wouldn't you actually treat him as one? Taking that route leads directly to oppression, no matter who takes it: that's the real danger. (Foucault 1991:180–81)

This reason underlies Foucault's refusal to engage in ideological forms of politics that, by virtue of being totalizing, "are always, in fact, very limited" (Foucault 1984c:375). Instead, he seeks to raise political problems not determined by established political outlooks. This is a task of thought, governed by a certain ethical sense, that flows into politics: "Thinking and acting are connected in an ethical sense, but one which has results that have to be called political" (377).[33]

> Let's take an example that touches us all, that of Poland. If we raise the question of Poland in strictly political terms, it's clear that we quickly reach the point of saying that there's nothing we can do. We can't dispatch a team of paratroopers, and we can't send armored cars to liberate Warsaw. I think that, politically, we have to recognize this, but I think we also agree that, for ethical reasons, we have to raise the problem of Poland in the form of a nonacceptance of what is happening there, and a nonacceptance of the passivity of our own governments. I think this attitude is an ethical one, but it is also political; it does not consist in saying merely, "I protest," but in making of that attitude a political phenomenon that is as substantial as possible, and one which those who govern, here or there, will sooner or later be obliged to take into account. (Ibid.)

It is further necessary to raise the problems ignored by the normal mechanisms and institutions of politics, such as those in the asylum, prison, and clinic. These are specific fields, but they nonetheless illuminate the most general problems of modern Western society: power relations and the disciplinary strategies that organize them.

The ethical rejection of the friend/enemy binarism, then, signals neither the "death of politics" nor a withdrawal into apathy. It rather invokes an ethical sensibility with political effects, one drawn from an ontology of belonging together and a decentered pluralism that Deleuze and Guattari label "rhizomatic" and oppose to "arboreal." The latter form demands that differences converge like branches and roots on a central trunk, whereas the former releases them into a multiplicity that escapes the dialectic of One and Many (see Deleuze and Guattari 1987:3–25). Blanchot calls this the "unavowable community," which shows itself in the defection or betrayal of community itself. It is again the denial of transcendence that leads to this paradoxical thought.

The modern turn from God, Blanchot holds, undermines community in two senses. First, the "exigency of an absolute immanence implies the dissolution of everything that would prevent man (given that he is his own equality and determination) from positing himself as pure individual reality, a reality all the more closed as it is open to all" (Blanchot 1988:2). This further demands an opacity among individuals, who cannot be related through a common ground: "If the relation of man with man ceases to be that of the Same with the Same, but rather introduces the Other as irreducible and— given the equality between them—always in a situation of dissymmetry in relation to the one looking at the Other, then a completely different relationship imposes itself and imposes another form of society which one would hardly dare call a 'community'" (3). But the lack of foundation also repudiates this apparently pure individualism by denying any self-identical being-in-itself. In short, "There exists a principle of insufficiency at the root of each being" (Bataille, quoted in ibid.:5), even though "it follows that this lack on principle does not go hand in hand with a necessity for completion. A being, insufficient as it is, does not attempt to associate itself with another being to make up a substance of integrity" (Blanchot 1988:5). For this reason beings must relate, but the resulting "society" would be subject to the same objection as the individual if its assemblage simply gave rise to a "supra-individuality" (7).

Community can therefore link beings only through a self-renunciation more penetrating than any self-criticism, which is "clearly only the refusal of criticism by the other, a way to be self-sufficient while reserving for oneself the right to insufficiency, a self-abasement that is a self-heightening"

(Blanchot 1988:8). Blanchot gives two names to this self-abdication: death and love. He calls it death because it exceeds any representational category, remaining an untimely event already inscribed within any finite being that never occurs in the present: one *is* dead only *after* the moment of death. Consequently, it can never be retained as "my death," and the significant death can be only that of the other.

> What, then, calls me into question most radically? Not my relation to myself as finite or as the consciousness of being before death or for death, but my presence for another who absents himself by dying. To remain present in the proximity of another who by dying removes himself definitively, to take upon myself another's death as the only death that concerns me, this is what puts me beside myself, this is the only separation that can open me, in its very impossibility, to the Openness of a community. (9)

Similarly, love presents an obligation to the other that follows the abandonment of self to singularity. It connects one to an opaque other, but for that very reason it inscribes within itself indifference, lack of recognition, and apathy (see pt. 2). In both cases the impossibility of belonging is inscribed in its very operation: "for the 'I' and the 'other' do not live in the same time, are never together (synchronously), can therefore not be contemporary, but separated (even when united) by a 'not yet' which goes hand in hand with an 'already no longer'" (42). It is a community that can be no more than a representation to itself of its own failure—a community, in short, of those with nothing "in common."

The injunction of this community does not follow from its possibility of becoming present. At best, it appears only in the most fleeting moments, when it does not even seem to have taken place.[34] For this reason, however, it is also a false marker that, if treated as anything more than an ephemeral strategy of engagement, hardens into being no more than an inverse of the Hegelian ethical community. To maintain its efficacy, it must not actively forget the always-forgotten nonorigin that gives it authority: the silent voice of that which escapes the possibility of totalization, the *singular-multiple event.*

3. A Question of Limits and Continuity: Aristotle, Epicureanism, and the Logic of Totality

In "The Nature of Language" Heidegger ponders Stefan George's poem "The Word," and specifically the last stanza: "So I renounced and sadly see: / Where word breaks off no thing may be." Language is the house of Being, such that "no thing is where the word is lacking. 'Thing' is here understood in the traditional broad sense, as anything that in any way *is*" (Heidegger 1971:61–62). Although the poet had "cherished the view that the poetic things, the wonders and dreams, had, even on their own, their well-attested standing within Being, and that no more was necessary than that his art now also find the word for them to describe and present them" (68), he now realizes that no thing can have being or specificity outside language. Nevertheless, Heidegger insists, what lies beyond the word "does in no way crumble away into a nothing that is good for nothing" (88).

Drawing on these Heideggerian themes, one might say that for Aristotle nothing exists outside the whole, the whole is whole, and therefore the nothing is good for nothing. Even though Aristotle admits diversity among the various sciences, all of them are governed by this same hierarchical logic, reflected in a metaphysics that gives supremacy to act over potency, a physics in which a hierarchy of the limit over the unlimited structures a universe of finite extension and spatio-temporal continuity, a political ideal of a sovereign state composed of interdependent parts, and an ethical ideal that defines the good in terms of wholeness and *eudaimonia* ("happiness") as a self-sufficient state that "makes life desirable and lacking in nothing" (Aristotle 1980:1097b15).[1] But Epicurus and Lucretius display entirely different priorities. Whereas Aristotle uses the limit as a simple determination separating a thing from what it is not, they treat it as an ambiguous site always invaded by a beyond disrupting the wholeness that the limit seeks to establish; whereas Aristotle insists on the continuity of time, space, and movement, they locate another realm of the *clinamen* in a time and space smaller than any continuous minimum. Although Epicurus and Lucretius may not entirely follow this path away from metaphysics, ultimately reinstating it in the form of a faith, they nonetheless move far enough to provide both an ethical and an ontological critique of metaphysical thought.

Aristotle and the Demand for Wholeness

Aristotle marks his distinction from Plato by opposing a philosophy of transcendence with one of totality. This enables him to critique his mentor while ensuring that his turn to empiricism retains the universality required by speculative thought. Plato, according to Aristotle, cannot provide a proper determination of sameness and difference. Plato's principle of sameness is the Form, but the Forms cannot accommodate the diverse meanings of the terms they are supposed to define and so relate to them only by analogy. Even without this difficulty, however, there is still no way to limit the number of Forms: there should be Forms for individuals as well as species and parts of individuals, Forms of Forms, Forms of Forms of Forms, and so on ad infinitum. Difference is determined by the dialectic of division, but this process remains haphazard and nominal because it cannot distinguish essential from unessential predicates and so cannot order differences. As a result, neither Platonic strategy suffices to define and therefore know a thing.[2]

To surmount these problems, Aristotle posits telos as an alternative principle of intelligibility. A telos is an end or limit, and a limit makes something whole and complete. Since the whole is logically prior to its parts, to locate the end enables one to account for the placement of parts within this whole, as well as the movement by which a thing becomes what it is at its best. Here it can be seen that even though Aristotle admonishes Plato for collapsing together the logical and conceptual orders, he still draws a correspondence between them: the whole that the mind grasps as universal knowledge reflects nothing other than the direction of particular movements in the domain of physical becoming. In the study of nature, therefore, where different states are seen as moments in a passage toward actualization, the final cause assumes supremacy; whereas in the realm of definition, the essence of a thing is known by the predications that establish a substantial and unified form finding its place within a larger category. On the latter point Deleuze is correct to say that the Platonic project is misunderstood if subsumed into the Aristotelian scheme of dividing a genus into contrary species; it is really one of selecting lineages, of separating true copy from false pretender (see Deleuze 1994:59–64; Deleuze 1990:253–56). But this caveat only highlights the essential distinction between the two thinkers in terms of their treatment of difference: Plato seeks to tame difference through a transcendent One serving as its cause and measure; Aristotle aspires to reduce it to the role of specification within a totality.

Building this totality is Aristotle's central task. It is necessary in this regard to rest the plurality of existence on boundaries that are carefully constructed and fiercely maintained. The result is a series of hierarchies privileging determinacy over indeterminacy; intention over accident; formal, efficient, and final causes over material cause; space over time; and being over nonbeing. Aristotle does not pursue these orderings with the obstinacy of the Christian thinkers who will later adopt him, but this consideration nonetheless establishes the horizon of his thought. Nevertheless, Aristotle's thinking does not remain blind to resistances within his orderly ideal. He continually encounters disruptions, ambiguities, and paradoxes even while proceeding toward a fixed and closed system. The further Aristotle advances, the more disruptive possibilities emerge, and the more alternative avenues he must close off. He must devise strategies to contain the indeterminate, unlimited, and contingent within his determinate whole while admitting them as fundamental principles. Yet the terms through which he displaces the absolute primacy of the indeterminate—the metaphysics of potency and act—also undermine the position he assigns to it. The resulting tension that runs through Aristotle's thought both provides the foundations for metaphysics and points toward a direction antimetaphysical thought must take.

The Closed Universe

The first book of the *Physics* addresses the feasibility of change: how can a thing become what it is not? Aristotle's answer is tied to the irreducible plurality of existence. Change is possible because Being is plural, so that a thing can first have certain qualities and then others while remaining fundamentally the same. Every concrete entity has a variety of relations, qualities, and attributes, so that the same subject is both a unity and a multiplicity. The chief criticism against the Eleatics, who deny that change is possible, is that they fail to theorize the multiplicity of being and the plurality of meanings for the words *one* and *is*. These thinkers must conceive Being as singular and rigid, and this leads them to hopeless contradictions.

Plurality follows from the separation between subject and predicate. When saying "X is white," for example, "there remains a conceptual distinction between the subject in which the whiteness is seated, and the qualification of 'being white'" (Aristotle 1934–57:186a28). To say Being is one—or, in Parmenides' words, "Only the One Being is"—would require closing this subject-predicate gap. It would demand, Aristotle says, that *is* mean "is identical-with-Being." Being or existence would no longer be an attribute of a thing: one could not say "X has being"; rather, one could say only "X *is* (or *is identical to*) Being." But the separation between subject and predicate means that neither is capable of being on its own. If the predicate is the One that *is,* the result is a nonbeing: "For an attribute is ascribed to some subject (other than itself); consequently, the subject to which 'being' (supposing it to be an attribute) is ascribed will have no being at all; for it will be other than 'being' (the attribute ascribed to it) and so will be something which (simply) is not" (186a35–b2). Conversely, if it is the subject that is identical-with-Being, the result is also a nonbeing, for a subject lacking attributes would have no being itself.

> For suppose the thing which is identical-with-Being also has the attribute "white," and that "being white" is not identical-with-Being—(the only sense in which it can "be" at all), for it cannot even have "being" as an attribute, because (*ex hypothesi*) nothing except what is identical-with-Being has any being at all—then it follows that white *is not,* and that not merely in the sense that it *is not this or that,* but in the sense of an absolute nonentity. Accordingly, that which is identical-with-Being (our subject) will be a nonentity; for (we assumed that) it is true to say of it that it is white, and this means it is a nonentity. (186b6–11)

Because a subject cannot *be* without predication, only a pluralist conception of Being makes any sense. Aristotle thus articulates Being as a multiplicity of categories such as substance, quantity, quality, time, position, and relation. Moreover, even if Being is unified in the sense of being a totality, "why should unity involve rigidity?" (186a16). If Being is plural and fluid in this manner, then change is feasible.

Those thinkers who believe change is impossible find it equally impossible to maintain a unitary conception of Being. The Physicists and Platonists, who recognize change, differ over its mechanisms, but both structure change around antitheses that are counterpossibilities within a material base. Although Aristotle offers a distinct alternative, his system shares this general structure (see 1934–57: bk. 1, ch. 5). Any concrete substance, he maintains, contains an undetermined material principle and a determinate formal principle. Change is the movement between formal antithetical principles acting not on themselves but on a material subject that can admit them and hence is indeterminate between them. Insofar as a substance maintains its essential being—defined by its essential as opposed to accidental predicates— it persists through the movement between antitheses and so changes while remaining the same. If its essence changes, however, it ceases to be what it is and becomes another being.

Book 1 of the *Physics* forms the high point of Aristotelian natural pluralism. The universe is presented as a multiplicity of substances governed by a plurality of principles, each substance having essential attributes but also capable of receiving changes while remaining the same. The fact of change— drawn not from sense data but from the conceptual impossibility of monistic Being[3]—introduces plurality into indeterminate materials capable of determination by varying forms. But change and difference threaten to spin out of control unless determinations are established. Aristotle thus proceeds to erect a series of boundaries and hierarchies whose effect is to domesticate both the plurality of Being and the flux of becoming through the institution of governable relations, causes, and limits.

Becoming is only as intelligible as the moments through which it passes. To ensure that these points can be traced, Aristotle argues that change takes place between *contrary* rather than *contradictory* antitheses. Both poles of a contrary antithesis can be given positive terms, whereas contradictories must be defined negatively, so that they necessarily "destroy or obstruct one another" (Aristotle 1934–57:262a11). A transformation, say, from cold to not cold invokes contradictory terms of change, but a move from cold to warm or hot invokes only contrary ones. Of course, a contradictory element exists even between hot and cold, since "X is hot" contradicts "X is cold," but Aristotle defines contradictories as pairs in which one term must *always* be true and the other false. If the substance in question did not exist, for example, neither "X is hot" nor "X is cold" would be true—although "X is not cold" would be true (see Aristotle 1984a: bk. 10). No privation of a quality of being, then, can be simply negative. But the contrary of being itself, or being as substance to which qualities adhere, is nothing, which means that being has no contrary. Unqualified being and nonbeing are therefore contradictories, and thus no change from one to the other can occur, since there is no passive term to receive both. The only possible term, formless or indeterminate matter, is already one element of the dichotomy.

> If we are considering it [formless matter] as the potentiality of receiving forms, it cannot perish, as such, but must necessarily be ex-

empt both from destruction and genesis. For if it "came to be," there must have been some subject already there for it to proceed from, and just "being there as the subject" is precisely what constitutes the nature of "matter" itself, so that it must have been before it came to be. For what I mean by matter is precisely the ultimate underlying subject, common to all things of Nature, presupposed as their substantive, not incidental, constituent. (Aristotle 1934–57:192a28–33)

Nonbeing is thereby reduced to the negation of being. Since change must occur between existents, there can be no absolute genesis or perishing: "Nor can we make 'natural existence' the term of an antithesis, for things move from one term of an antithesis to the other, and since nothing 'exists in Nature' that is contrasted with 'natural existence,' how could any such existent move out of what is not there for it to move out of? Or how could such a non-existent be a presupposition of the existent?" (189a33–34).

Contrariety "alone expresses the capacity of a subject to bear opposites while remaining substantially the same" (Deleuze 1994:30). A ground thus exists for change between contraries, but not between contradictories. This ground is delimited by an absolute separation of being and nonbeing. As with Parmenides, there are two roads but only one path, for the second route simply *is not*. The limitation of natural change to movement between contraries marks the first step in the domestication of plurality, removing the radicality of change by reducing the distance between opposite states in the defense of essence. Movement between contradictories would be groundless and therefore thoroughly contingent. It is not surprising, then, that Aristotle in every case—including that of Being, knowledge, and ethics as well as becoming—treats contrariety as the greatest form of difference, for only contrariety can be encapsulated in a determinate whole.[4] Nevertheless, it is also clear that contrariety is maximal only with respect to ground or essence. Indeed, the very use of contradiction as an insurmountable limit to change, knowledge, Being, and the good indicates it to be greater.

Contrariety, however, only sets the initial conditions by which change can be known. A sufficient grasp of becoming requires an account of its causes, and this necessitates privileging determinate over indeterminate causality. Initially, however, the opposite seems to be the case. Aristotle does not arbitrarily list the material cause as the first of the four types of causation, for he argues that the indeterminate, unlimited, and infinite—which are in various ways equated (see 1934–57: bk. 3, chs. 4–6)—are prior to the determinate, limited, and finite. The unlimited is "analogous to formless matter" (206b15); it is "really the 'material' from which a magnitude is completed, and is the potential, though not the realized, whole. It . . . is not any determined whole in itself, but only as the unlimited and 'material' factor of the whole which is constituted as such by the limiting and 'formal' factor" (207a21–23). The material and indeterminate are antecedent, for they are unconditional necessities of determinate forms. First substance, as formless matter or substrate, is exempt from genesis and annihilation and is the absolute precondition for change. It seems unclear, however, whether Aristotle has this firmly in mind when he states: "But in the production of things for a purpose (of art or of Nature), the necessity works the other way: the assumption is that the *end* is to exist or does exist, and this necessitates that the antecedents shall exist or do exist; otherwise, as in mathematics the failure of the conclusion necessitates the non-existence of the premiss we start from. . . . here the non-existence of the end or purpose will be necessitated" (200a19–22; alternative translation on pp, 182–83, note a). How docs thc final cause—the end or telos—displace the priority of the material and indeterminate? It does so through Aristotle's multifarious use of the term *prior*. Although the material indeterminate is prior in respect to order ("for the elements are prior in order to the constructions") and even in terms of implication of existence (for "that from which the implication of existence does not hold reciprocally is thought to be prior" [Aristotle 1984a:14b1, 14a35]), everything changes when the distinction of potentiality and actuality is introduced: "*e.g.*, potentially the half-line is prior to the whole, or the part to the whole, or the matter to the substance; but actually it is posterior, because it is only upon dissolution that it will actually exist" (Aristotle 1933–35:1019a8–10). A priority of part to whole remains in terms of potential, but "it is obvious that actuality is prior to potentiality" (1049b5) in formula, substance, and even time, since a potential can be actualized only by an existing being (see bk. 9, ch. 8). Since the actual existence of the end implies or necessitates the actual existence of the material constituents—as well as the agent of change and the form—but that of the constituents does not necessitate the existence of any end or purpose, the latter, in the higher sense of actuality, is prior (Aristotle 1934–57: bk. 2, ch. 9).

To seek the origin (*archē*) of a thing is to inquire into the mechanisms by which it arises and is dominated in its being.[5] Only the final cause answers both questions, and so it attains priority: "Though the physicist has to deal with both material and purpose, he is more deeply concerned with the latter; for purpose directs the moving causes that act upon the material, not the reverse" (Aristotle 1934–57:200a32–33). The natural scientist's primary interest in the *movement* of beings is sufficient to shift the meaning of nature (*phusis*) from unchanging substrate to developing form,[6] while the power of telos makes this change intelligible. An end is a limit, and a limit makes a thing or a process whole. The whole, as the unity of parts, is logically prior to the parts, which do not contain within themselves their unity with other parts. But this unity, which makes the whole greater than the mere sum of its parts, is achieved only by a shift onto the terrain of purposeful action and determinate movement. Once this is done, what comes into being last—the end—is prior, for it constitutes the precondition of what comes before.[7] A heterogeneous plurality that includes material constituents, processes of becoming, and motor forces that compel them is thereby organized by the final cause: "In this way, the end of becoming is its incipience. . . . How, then, does *archē* dominate? In anticipating *telos*" (Schürmann 1987:102, 104).

It is no surprise that although the material cause is listed first, it is investigated last. Aristotle examines it only after he restricts its field of operation by the space allotted to the determinate causes (see Aristotle 1934–57: bk. 2, chs. 3–9); after he has defined nature as a teleological realm through comparison with human fabrication and art (bk. 2, ch. 8);[8] after he links purposeful action to the existence of "the prime, conscious or unconscious, agent that produces the effect and starts the material on its way to the product, changing it from what it is to what it is to be" (bk. 2, ch. 3); and after he has explored and confined the "agency" of chance or luck—which is equated with the indeterminate (bk. 2, ch. 5)—by holding that accidental or chance events can always occur otherwise than by chance and in any case presuppose prior purposeful activity: "And since the results of *automaton* and *tyche* are always such as might have been aimed at by mind or Nature, though in fact they emerged incidentally, and since there can be nothing incidental unless there is something primary for it to be incidental to, it follows that there can be no incidental causation except as incident to direct causation. Chance and fortune, therefore, imply the antecedent activity of mind and Nature as causes" (198a6–11). All these moves restrict the function of indeterminacy before the one indeterminate cause is examined. Once the formal, efficient, and final causes are defined, the only role left to the material factor in change is that of passively receiving determinate forces. Becoming is thereby rendered a determinate movement, even while the continuation of chance and accident resists this reduction.

These moves establish the priority of the limit, but they do not remove the need to account for the principle that has been displaced: the indeterminate or unlimited. And so, although the unlimited or infinite is undeniably a first principle, its domain must be carefully circumscribed: "For everything is either determined by some principle or is a principle itself, and the undetermined cannot be determined at all, and so cannot depend upon anything else as its principle. . . . So the 'unlimited' cannot be derived from any other principle, but is itself regarded as the principle of the other things, 'embracing and governing all' . . . *unless indeed they accept other [determinate] principles alongside of it,* such as 'Intelligence' or 'Amity'" (Aristotle 1934–57:203b6–13, emphasis added). The coexistence of determinate first principles supplants the unlimited as a principle "embracing and governing all." If indeterminacy were absolutely prior, it would have to embrace all other things, "for everything is either determined by some principle or is a principle itself." Alongside other determinate first principles, however, the unlimited "is embraced and not embracing. Therefore *qua* unlimited it is unknowable . . . but it is contradictory and impossible that the unknowable and undefined should embrace and define anything" (207a24–32).

Aristotle thus concludes that the unlimited is embraced by and so contained *within* the limited. It exists as the potentially infinite divisibility of time, space, and matter, the limitless partition of the whole—which is bounded and limited—rather than limitless *extension* beyond all boundaries.[9] Although an infinite magnitude may be conceivable, in reality the infinite "cannot exceed all magnitude, but depends on the principle of division; for since it is analogous to the 'material' it is contained, whereas it is the 'form' that is the continent" (Aristotle 1934–57:207a33–b1). The infinite extension of time forward and backward is not a genuine exception, because time measures and is measured by movement, which is itself always determinate (bk. 4, ch. 12). Other thinkers, Aristotle holds, mistakenly treat the infinite as "that 'beyond which there is nothing'" when it is really "what is always beyond" (207a1–2). The absence of limit "may be regarded as the open 'possibility of more,' the 'more' that is actually taken being always limited, but always different" (206a27–28), so that it is a move "not only to 'more,' but to what you had never gone over or done before" (207a5). This "open possibility of more" must have some existential status, but Aristotle cannot allow it to interfere with the notion of determination via telos or limit. The unlimited must therefore "depend on the principle of division."

This allows the limit to be narrowly conceived as nonrelational. Only in the case of the unlimited is there a necessity to go beyond, while what remains beyond a limit can be nothing at all—otherwise the hierarchy would be inverted, and the limit would be only an ephemeral determination within the unlimited. Thus contraries and contradictories, which provide limits, are not relations, although relations, contraries, and contradictories are all forms of opposition; all relations are oppositions, but not all oppositions are relational (see Aristotle 1984a: bks. 7, 10). Since a relation requires two existents—contraries require two existents as well; contradictories do not—a limited thing will only incidentally be in contact with something else: "Again, being in contact and being limited are different things. Contact is a relation with something else, for there must be something to touch the touched; and this may happen to something limited incidentally; but 'being limited' is not a relation. Also a limited thing need not be touched by a thing homogeneous with itself and cannot be touched by any other" (Aristotle 1934–57:208a11– 14). This point is the core of the justification of the closed structure of the universe, for "universe" means "whole," and "the Whole is that outside which there is nothing whatsoever; whereas that from which something, no matter what, is missing and left outside is not 'All.' And 'whole' and 'complete,' if not absolutely the same, are very closely akin, and nothing is complete (*teleios*) unless it has an end (*telos*); but an end is a limit" (207a11–15).

This account leaves us with a closed universe, then, but one full of incongruities, several of which revolve around the concept of place. In an analysis filled with revealing tensions, Aristotle ultimately holds a body's proper place to be defined by the material continent surrounding it. For example, the proper place of a body of water is the inside surface of the jug that holds it, with the proper place of the jug defined by what its outer surface touches. If the jug is moved, then its place changes, *but the proper place of the water does not*. Aristotle in this way denies the possibility of absolute place or place as a dimensional entity—of a defined length, width, and height that may or may not be occupied by a body. He does this despite the fact that his universe is a closed sphere with a defined center and so can be mapped without reference to the bodies within it. Although he allows terms such as *being* and *prior* to have multiple, heterogeneous meanings, he insists on a singular meaning for *place*. He cannot treat place as both that which a body occupies and that which is potentially occupiable but not necessarily occupied, in one sense an attribute of bodies but in another sense not.[10] The result is that all bodies exist in a place for Aristotle, yet the universe itself—which is a closed and determined body—paradoxically has no place, for it is surrounded by nothing. Yet if the universe were infinite, another predicament would arise, for then the whole would be unlimited. Either approach leads to impasse, so that Aristotle's choice of one route over the other expresses little more than an ungrounded insistence on giving priority to determinacy, wholeness, and closure, regardless of the predicaments this engenders.

But an even deeper tension is found in the terms that establish this determinate whole. On one hand, confining the unlimited within the limit follows from the primacy of act over potency; on the other, the status of the infinite as a principle of divisibility rests on a manifest and unexplained deviation from the rule that potency presupposes a prior actuality, for the infinite *can never become actual:* "But how are we to understand 'potentiality' here? Not in the sense in which we say that the potentiality of the statue exists in the bronze; for that implies that the whole of the bronze may actually become the statue, whereas it is not so with an illimitable potentiality, since it can never become an unlimited actuality" (Aristotle 1934–57:206a19–21). Aristotle provides a solution to this problem, but it is inadequate. He suggests that "the only sense in which the unlimited is actualized at all is the sense in which we say that it 'actually is' such and such a day of the month, or that the games 'actually are' on; for in these cases, too, the period of time or the succession of events in question is not (like the statue-potentialities of the bronze) all actualized at once, but is in course of transit as long as it lasts. The Olympic games, *as-a-whole,* are a potentiality only, even when they are in process of actualization" (206a21–25). The analogy here is obviously tenuous, since a day and the Olympic games do in fact reach completion.[11] Moreover, conceiving of the infinite's actuality as its endless coming to be (an argument made by Hintikka 1979) secures at best only the infinite extension of time, but not the infinite divisibility of time and space: even though time may be said to exhibit an actual infinity in the sense that there will necessarily be future days and moments, Aristotle never claims there will actually be further and further divisions.[12]

Although the material substrate must retain its own actuality—for it persists through all change even while remaining potential with respect to being a component of a determinate being—the infinite cannot enjoy this status without disrupting the place of determinate principles. This gap between the material and the unlimited, which are otherwise equated, points to an indeterminacy in excess of any that Aristotle's physics can negotiate—an indeterminacy, in short, surpassing that of an already domesticated potentiality. The infinite that Aristotle struggles to fit into his schema of potency and act is in fact not a potentiality at all but a fully real virtuality. It is an immanent excess that must be abstracted away for determinate order to be established.

The ambiguity of the infinite enables Aristotle to answer Zeno's paradoxes purporting to show that movement is impossible because a moving object must always first traverse half a given distance and thus cross an actual infinity of points to reach its final destination (see Aristotle 1934–57: bk. 8, ch. 8). Moreover, it is central to the arguments for the continuity of time, space, and motion. An actual infinity would entail the absurdity of an extended magnitude composed of nothing but unextended parts, but an actual limit to division would lead to quandaries regarding atomic units of time and space, the most poignant being that the notion of presence would become untenable: it would be impossible to say that a thing *is* moving; instead, we could say only that it *has moved.* Such movement "would consist not in experiencing motions, but in having experienced them, and that which never was in motion would have accomplished the movement; for without ever passing through A, it would have passed through it. It would then be possible for our walker to have finished his walk without ever taking it: he would have walked this distance without walking *over* it" (232a11–13). Further, insofar as limited division might also entail physical atomism, and therefore the existence of void, it would risk dissolving the all-important barrier between being and nothingness: the error of Leucippus and Democritus is that "they hold that what is not is no less real than what is, because Void is as real as Body" (Aristotle 1933–35:985b9–10). Continuity can thus be saved from senselessness only by remaining in the realm of the purely potential infinite, constituted by elements that are not quite either solid or fluid. "If a succession of indivisibles could make up a continuum either of magnitude or time, that continuum could be resolved into its indivisible constituents" (Aristotle 1934–57:231b10), so that a continuous extension must instead be constituted by extended parts that are themselves divisible in the same way. Therefore, in the case of the limited, it is only incidental that there is a beyond related to it, while with the unlimited, what is beyond is always of the same order. Determinate totality and continuity are thereby established. Nonetheless, the same division of potency and act that makes this solution possible threatens it as well.

And the other inconsistencies of the settlement remain: the oblique way in which contradiction appears as a difference greater than the maximal difference of contrariety, the existence of indeterminacy as a persistent remainder after determinate principles are given, and the paradox of a universe that exists nowhere. In each case an indeterminacy presses against limits, presenting a nothingness that refuses to fade away and that imperils the logic of both totality and continuity. The true intertwining of the limit and continuity is here visible: on one level, the limit is a container, and the continuum is its filling; but, more profoundly, continuity is itself a limit, both to thought and to what may become actual, and the limit, as that which separates being from a nothingness that must be mere absence, is continuous with what it contains and organizes. Yet if this beyond were recognized as something that is both "more than nothing" and discontinuous from what is separated from it, the project itself would falter. Wholeness could not mean what Aristotle wants and needs it to mean, nor could telos perform the same function. The divisions and hierarchies established to tame plurality would be jeopardized; the boundaries Aristotle fights so valiantly to defend would be threatened.

It is necessary therefore to go beyond the limit, to displace it, and to show how it is not a first principle but a product of a more primordial difference and indeterminacy always heterogeneous to it. This inversion is carried out by Epicureanism, which in doing so reveals unethical implications in the demand for wholeness that Aristotle insists is a necessary foundation for just politics and morality. In the hands of Epicurus and Lucretius, the indeterminate is not simply a passive receptor of determinate factors but an active force in nature. The result is pluralism in the most genuine sense: a multiplicity no longer accepted with lament by a thinking driven toward closure, continuity, and limitation.

Substance and Singularity

Against Parmenides' proclamation that "only the One Being is," Aristotle responds with the statement, "X is white," asking which is the one that is, X or white. If either one is while the other in the strictest sense is not, the result is a nonbeing. The univocity of Parmenidean Being is thus replaced by Aristotelian plurality. Being must be plural if anything is to be at all, because a subject can be only through a predicatory act occurring beyond it.

Nonetheless, Aristotle defines Being qua Being as essence and essence as form or formula—that is, the set of necessary rather than accidental predicates adhering to the subject. The dilemma is obvious: essence is not what a subject *has* but what it *is*, even though Aristotle, in refuting Parmenides, draws on the separation of subject and predicate. If predicates are external to their subject, however, the subject's essence is no longer internal but invested in an outside, and the distinction between internal essence and external accident collapses, together with the differences between determinate and indeterminate and knowable form and unknowable matter, on which Aristotelian metaphysics depends. The gap between subject and predicate is coordinate with that between a thing's existence and its essence or being. Aristotle must maintain the separation of the former pair while repairing the rift between the latter if knowledge is to be successfully invested in individuals rather than transcendent Forms.

Hence Aristotle persistently equivocates on the meaning of *substance:* on the one hand, it is the ultimate subject, which is "not predicated of any substrate, but other things are predicated of [it]" (Aristotle 1933–35:1017b13–14); on the other, it is "the *essence,* whose formula is the definition" (1017b22–23), and adheres to the subject. Sometimes he portrays formless matter as being "precisely the ultimate underlying subject, common to all things of Nature, presupposed as their substantive, not incidental, constituent" (Aristotle 1934–

57:192a32–34); other times he says it is "that which in itself is neither a particular thing nor a quantity nor designated by any of the categories which define Being" (Aristotle 1933–35:1029a20–21)—but clearly if matter falls outside the categories of Being, it must be a nonbeing and so cannot be substantial.

Aristotle seeks to negotiate this impasse with a promise of reciprocal sufficiency: when predication completely defines the nature of its subject such that a subject and its predicates are interchangeable—when, for example, one can say both "Man is a two-footed rational animal" and "A two-footed rational animal is a man"—the subject can be equated with its essence, securing knowledge and its universality. The predicates that define a subject are those that identify the general class to which it belongs and the differentia that specify it within this group. To this end, Aristotle requires a hierarchical system of predication to organize particulars into differential species, genera, and categories.[13] But this schema can reach neither the truly particular nor the truly universal. It must instead always operate within the middle regions, dealing with species such as "man" and genera such as "animal." The result is that knowledge, as the mutual and complete imbrication of subject and essence, never reaches the level of concrete existence, nor can conceptual knowledge wrap itself into a closed totality.

Essence and definition clearly operate best at the level of species. Aristotle states: "The essence of each thing is that which it is said to be *per se*. 'To be you' is not 'to be cultured,' because you are not of your own nature cultured. Your essence, then, is that which you are said to be of your own nature. But not even all of this is the essence" (1933–35:1029b14–15). Further, "The essence is an individual type . . . [, and] essence belongs to all things the account of which is a definition. We have a definition, not if the name and the account signify the same (for then all accounts would be definitions . . .), but if the account is of something primary" (1030a3–10). Everything hinges on the nature of essential predicates and how they can be "primary." They can be primary, Aristotle insists, only at the level of a genus divided into species: "Hence essence will belong to nothing except species of a genus, but to these only; for in these the predicate is not considered to be related to the subject by participation or affectation, nor as an accident" (1030a12–14). Only predicates that divide a genus into species, as attributes such as winged or bipedal divide the genus "animal," can be primary, for they *specify* and individuate the genus by altering and shaping essence. Predicates that further divide a species into individuals also differentiate, but only through accidental traits and affectations, and so do not delineate essence: Socrates is distinguished from other men by his height, hair color, personal history, and so on, but these are merely contingent qualities, in no way modifying his nature as a man and therefore always appearing to be added to something that is already substantial (bk. 7, ch. 4; see also Hare 1979). Conversely, those attributes above the level of specific difference are too large: having color or having mass are essential traits, but they are generic and so do not specify. To be primary is literally to "make a difference" in terms of essence. Everything that has a name can be given a formula that describes it, but only at the level of species can this formula be a definition.

But there is a further difficulty in reaching the particular. The irreducible particularity or "thisness" of any individual renders knowledge of concrete entities impossible. Even if all essential and accidental attributes of Socrates could be listed and organized, the definition would still require reference to, for example, his materiality: one would have to say that Socrates is a man with these characteristics *who is made of this particular material*.[14] This last predication of Socrates is not a general category,[15] and it makes the definition redundant: Socrates is *this* man because he is made of the particular material of which Socrates is made. Matter, because it is formless and particular, is itself unknowable. Hence there is no definition of Socrates but only a designation. As a result, one can have knowledge of more general species but only *recognition* of particulars: "But when we come to the concrete thing, *e.g. this* circle—which is a particular individual, either sensible or intelligible . . .— of these individuals there is no definition; we apprehend them by intelligence or perception; and when they have passed from the sphere of actuality it is uncertain whether they exist or not, but they are always spoken of and apprehended by the universal formula. But the matter is in itself unknowable" (Aristotle 1933–35:1036a2–9).

Not only does an opacity prevent knowledge from reaching primary substance; it is likewise impossible to totalize the hierarchy of conceptual predicates that enable knowledge at the level of secondary substance. One moves from species to genera to the most general categories, such as substance, quantity, quality, and time, but nothing encompasses these highest classifications: there is no highest genus. Neither of the possible candidates, being and unity, can function in this way because each is predicated of specific differences. In other words, while the genus "animal" is predicated of species such as "man" and "bird," it is not predicated of specific differences such as winged or rational: we say, "Man is an animal," but not, "Winged is an animal." This difference obtains because the genus signifies what is common among its members, not what differentiates them. But being and unity are predicated of specific differences—they signify both identity and difference— precisely because terms such as *winged* are equivocal, functioning both as differentia of a genus and as subjects predicated of other genera and categories incommensurable with the first, which they divide. And so we do say "winged is": "But it is impossible for either Unity or Being to be one genus of existing things. For there must *be* differentiae of each genus, and each differentia must be *one;* but it is impossible either for the species of the genus to be predicated of the specific differentiae, or for the genus to be predicated without its species. Hence if Unity or Being is a genus, there will be no differentia Being or Unity" (Aristotle 1933–35:998b21–27; see also 1059b32–34). The primacy given to substance over the other categories adhering to it— regardless of whether this primacy is part of an analogical or univocal conception of being[16]—may rescue the theory of the categories from metaphysical dissolution on one level, but it does nothing for the problem of definition insofar as the latter rests on a logic of simple identity and difference, a logic that arises largely from the equivocation over the meaning of substance itself. Being and unity remain the most common attributes, applying to all beings, but neither is the highest set, and so the hierarchy of conceptual predicates cannot refer to an ultimate totality that it divides and categorizes, undermining its role in definition and knowledge at all levels.

Accounting for the particular and the universal, which Aristotle can never quite reach, requires adding an element that overturns the logic of identity and difference he employs. In other words, it compels the introduction of the difference that is the event. The particular would not be particular if it did not contain a difference that escapes the universal, and this difference is the event, whose identity can only be as that which differs from itself. Conversely, that something escapes the universal explains why it cannot be a closed totality, or rather, can be so only by drawing the event into a representational schema. The event thus holds an ontological priority over both the particular and the universal by providing their conditions of possibility. But the event also carries the conditions of impossibility for the schema of particular and universal by forever deferring their reconciliation.

In Aristotle's discourse the sites of this difference are the material, indeterminate, and infinite—the opaque first principles he struggles to displace. If the failure to close the gap between essence and existence signals the return of formless matter, however, such matter cannot remain a pliable clay, indeterminate among possible forms. It must instead take on a more active role, embodying a becoming, but not one that is uniform or unidirectional, which could be resolved into a category or telos, for then its nature as that which escapes form, telos, or general categories would be forgotten. Matter must instead embody the anarchic becoming characteristic of the event. The atomism of Epicurus and Lucretius illustrates how this is accomplished.

Epicurean Reduction and Inversion

Epicureanism not only reverses key Aristotelian metaphysical categories but also creates new concepts that do not fit the ancient ontological framework. But this process is continued only up to a point, after which there is only a reduction or minimization of ancient ontological assumptions that nonetheless maintains their dominance. These features place Epicurus and Lucretius within a tradition of antimetaphysical thought yet prevent them from truly moving away from metaphysics.

The Infinite, the Limit, the Atom

We will never escape the logic of a determinate totality without rethinking the nature of first beginnings. Lucretius is clear on this point. Earlier thinkers, he maintains, reduced first beginnings to one or more of the four elements, held substances to contain minute quantities of all things (Anaxagoras's *homoeomeria*), or treated formless matter as an indeterminate, infinitely divisible substrate assuming various forms. These theories, however, either make something come from nothing or make everything come from everything.[17] If fire is the first beginning of all things, it must change into something else and hence be destructible—but a permanent substrate must remain, or something will come from nothing. If all things are made of and can return to the four elements, it is unclear which are the first beginnings, the elements or the things. If first beginnings are simply minute amounts of things, then there are no first beginnings at all. Finally, if matter is infinitely divisible, it is again reducible to nothing (Lucretius 1992:1.483–920).

First beginnings must be permanent and heterogeneous with respect to their products if the idea of imperishable foundation is to be taken seriously (Lucretius 1992:2.730–1010).[18] They must remain essentially hidden and not given over to some determinate and knowable form that is their product and not their cause: "The first-beginnings in begetting things ought to bring with them a nature secret and unseen, that nothing may be prominent to thwart and hinder from its proper being each thing which is being made" (1.778–81). The atom thus expresses the proper understanding of first beginnings. It is an invisible, indestructible chunk of plenum whose only qualities are shape, extension, and weight—the minimum of essential attributes—and that, through combination with other atoms, produces all sensible objects and their qualities, including color, smell, feeling, and even sentience.

Atomism further necessitates a redefinition of the infinite and the limit.[19] The limit is a boundary, but one always affected by its beyond. It is never a simple determination but a site of paradox. Conversely, what has nothing beyond to disrupt it is not closed but open and unlimited. The universe is therefore infinite: "Clearly nothing can have an extremity unless there be something beyond to bound it, so that something can be seen, beyond which our sense can follow the object no further. Now since we must confess that there is nothing beyond the sum of things, it has no extremity, and therefore it is without end or limit" (Lucretius 1992:1.960–64; see also ibid.:951–1051 generally; Epicurus 1993:41–42).[20] This boundless space must contain unlimited atoms and void through which they move.[21] The variety of atoms is "incomprehensible" but not "absolutely infinite," for the latter possibility would entail some atoms large enough to be visible. However, an infinite number of each type of atom is required; otherwise, in a truly infinite void, they could not combine (Epicurus 1993:41–42; Lucretius 1992:2.478–580). Atoms join to form self-contained worlds that, as a logical consequence of unlimited void and atoms, are also infinite in number. Anything that is possible thus exists somewhere, in one world or another.

What are limitless in this sense are number, time, and space. The infinite here relates to a maximum of extension; the limit, to a minimum. For this reason, however, what is beyond the limit—beyond the minimum—always inheres *within* the limited thing. It is not a beyond that is an *outside*. We are thus presented with a second infinity, not of endless extension and continuity, but of discontinuity within any continuum. The limit here does not separate inside from outside along a common smooth space; rather, it divides one level from another, creating worlds within worlds. In this way Epicurus can hold, against the Aristotelian notion of continuous divisibility, that space and time are divided into minimal quanta while also maintaining the existence of another, virtual order exceeding these absolutes.

Beyond the sensible is the thinkable. We reach the atom only by going beyond the limits of the sensible realm. Below the world of becoming—of creation and destruction—must lie a minimum of plenum persisting through change. The atom is thus a thinkable minimum and can indeed only be thought. That the atom is paradoxically made of parts that have no subdivisions is not surprising, since the thought of the atom follows only by analogy from sensible phenomena made of divisible parts. The parts of the atom must be understood to share something with sensible parts but not to be identical to them. Epicurus can thereby maintain both the physical indivisibility of the atom and the theoretical indivisibility of its parts.[22] The atom is of a fundamentally different order existing within becoming as its condition of possibility, but it is found by locating the limit of the realm of sensuous becoming in the form of a necessary limit to the divisibility of matter:

to say matter is infinitely divisible amounts to claiming that something can come from nothing, for what is the infinitely small if not nothing at all (Epicurus 1993:56–57)?

The majority of interpreters hold Epicurus strictly to a theory of minimum magnitudes, such that space and time are composed of discrete segments.[23] It is well known that this position leads to geometrical quandaries, the most obvious being that such real spatial minima would have to be three-dimensional cubes of the same minimum extension in length, width, and depth, but then the length of any diagonal of this cube would be incommensurable with the minimum distance just postulated. More than this, however, this position leaves the atom completely determined within thought, destroying its hidden character. A deeper indeterminacy must therefore be installed within it. This is the *clinamen*, and it is derived from an analysis of the way atoms must interact. Material objects consist of atoms constantly vibrating and colliding. These movements are imperceptible yet thinkable, but they are also secondary and unessential. Without them atoms naturally fall downward along straight paths through infinite space.[24] This situation leaves nothing within the thinkable realm relating atoms to one another essentially and therefore offers no account of the secondary collisions that produce a cosmos and its material compounds. Weight differentials cannot cause collisions, for atoms of different weights fall with equal velocity through void. What is required is an indeterminate atomic swerve—the *clinamen*.[25] This swerve is not a secondary determination of the atom's movement that, like the posterior movements caused by collisions, is unnecessary or accidental. It is as requisite an attribute as the downward fall, as much an essential quality of Epicurean atoms as gravitational attraction is of the atoms of modern physics,[26] so that strictly speaking it is incorrect to speak of a "beginning" or "origin" of the atomic collisions (see Rist 1972:49–51). Moreover, the swerve necessarily takes place beyond the minimum of thinkable space and time: "The bodies must incline a little; and not more than the least possible, or we shall seem to assume oblique movements, and thus be refuted by the facts . . . but who is there who can perceive that they never swerve ever so little from the straight undeviating course?" (Lucretius 1992:2.243–50).[27]

As an indeterminate first cause, the *clinamen* provides the conditions of possibility and impossibility for causality (see Deleuze 1990:270). Nothing occurs without cause, so that atoms must relate to one another, but the *clinamen* prevents the fall into determinism. It is thus tied to free will,[28] which does not result from an unmoved first mover or an immaterial spirit beyond all causality; rather, "what keeps the mind itself from having necessity within it in all actions, and from being as it were mastered and forced to endure and to suffer, is the minute swerving of the first-beginnings at no fixed place and at no fixed time" (Lucretius 1992:2.289–93).[29] Free will results from an internal cleft in causality related to an essential indeterminacy in first beginnings. Consequently, there is no contradiction between Lucretius's insistence on the primacy of natural law, such that "each thing has its power limited and its deep-set boundary mark" (1.76–77, repeated at 1.595–96, 5.89–90, and 6.65–66), and his appeal to an indeterminate swerve nourishing and corrupting these limits. The limit, again, is always permeated by a heterogeneous but immanent beyond; the *clinamen* is an immanent excess of movement of the atom. It is a necessary but undetermined attribute rather than mere accident or chance over essence, the latter being among the classical distinctions that Epicureanism maintains (Epicurus 1993:68–71; Lucretius 1992:1.449–82). As such, the *clinamen* represents an early formulation of the singular-multiple event, a micromovement that gives rise to a contingent, macroscopic order.

We can therefore move across a spatial hierarchy of limits, from sensible object, to thinkable atom, to the *clinamen* occurring beyond the minimum of thought: becoming, the ground of being, and a deeper indeterminacy both stitching together the first two but also subverting their bond. There is also a corresponding temporal hierarchy: "In one moment of time perceived by us, that is, while one word is being uttered, many times are lurking which reason understands to be there" (Lucretius 1992:4.794–96). Atomic vibration occurs in a time that can only be thought: "Even in the least period of continuous time, the atoms are moving in clusters toward one place. However, in a passage of time perceptible only to the mind, they move not in one direction, but are constantly colliding with one another until the constancy of their motion comes under the scrutiny of the senses. . . . This visible motion will be the result of internal collision even if up to the visible level we admit that the speed of its motion meets no resistance from collision" (Epicurus 1993:62). Although time, like space, is continuous, there are times beyond the limit of the sensible. Movements occurring in this beyond *seem* to take no time at all. When Epicurus declares that atoms move "as swift as thought" (61), he means that these movements occur so quickly that they can be perceived only as instantaneous.

Atomic collisions produce constant streams of atomic films emanating from objects. They enable perception at a distance—seeing, hearing, and smelling. The latter two perceptions are produced by larger, slower atoms coming from deep within objects; these atoms encounter more resistance, travel limited distances, and move in perceptible amounts of time. But the films that produce sight—"images" or "simulacra"—"have unsurpassable fineness and subtlety" and move "with the speed of thought" (Epicurus

1993:47–48). They "run through space inexpressible by words in a moment of time" (Lucretius 1992:4.191–93), appearing to be immediate. Images "flit about hither and thither through the air" (4.32), and different images, emerging consecutively in different places, give the impression of movement (4.768–76).

Perception of simulacra and other emanations grounds all truth and knowledge, because "it is from the senses in the first instance that the concept of truth has come, and . . . the senses cannot be refuted. . . . For unless they be true, all reasoning is false" (Lucretius 1992:4.478–85; see also Epicurus 1993:85–88). Thus, "whatever image we receive by direct apprehension of our mind or our sense organs, whether of shape or of essential properties, that is the true shape of the solid object, since it is created by the constant repetition of the image or the impression it has left behind" (Epicurus 1993:50). But these same atomic films also produce illusion and falsity. Because of their fineness, simulacra "easily unite in the air when they meet, being like spider's web or leaf of gold" (Lucretius 1992:4.726–27), producing phantasms. The mind usually ignores such images but is susceptible to them during sleep, when they "penetrate through the interstices of the body, and awake the substance of the mind within, and assail the sense" (4.730–31). Thus humans dream of mythical creatures, vengeful gods, or their own spirits suffering eternal torture. These manifestations are false: mythical creatures such as centaurs cannot exist because the bodies and spirits of humans and horses are incompatible, vengefulness is beneath truly divine beings, and the soul is mortal (3.417–829, 5.878–924, 6.50–89; see also Epicurus 1993:123–25). In a time shorter than the minimum of perceptible time, atomic movements provide the conditions for both true knowledge and false myth.

This account of a primordial indeterminacy underpins an antiteleological stance. Whereas Aristotle derived natural telos through analogy to human fabrication and art, Lucretius explicitly contests this: human instruments are created for use, but natural forms "were produced before any conception of their usefulness" (1992:4.853–54). Explanations of natural entities in terms of the purposes they serve "put effect for cause and are based on perverted reasoning; since nothing is born in us simply in order that we may use it, but that which is born creates the use" (4.832–35). But teleology is ultimately subverted by an excessive difference and a corresponding pluralism incapable of totalization. This open pluralism does not mean "anything goes." On the contrary, atoms join only in certain combinations, uniting under specific circumstances based on shape and collision: natural law limits the possible, and divine intervention is not a legitimate causal explanation. Rather, openness arises from a rift internal to natural law that makes it impossible to gather laws and causes into a whole.

Hence the analysis of natural phenomena always demands a multiplicity of causal explanations: "Everything occurs without disturbance in accordance with what admits a variety of explanations that are in accordance with observed phenomena, whenever we admit—as we must—a probable explanation for them; but whenever we admit one explanation but reject another that agrees equally well with the evidence, it is clear that we fall short in every way of true scientific inquiry and resort instead to myth" (Epicurus 1993:87). This is not merely epistemological pluralism, which would suggest that one truth lies beneath many possible interpretations. Lucretius twice states that the philosopher must provide many causal possibilities, "but which may be the true one, is not his to lay down who proceeds step by step" (1992:5.532–33; see also ibid.:6.703–4). Nonetheless, these passages are not unambiguous: "If you should yourself see some man's body lying lifeless at a distance, you may perhaps think proper to name all the causes of death in order that the one true cause of the man's death may be named. For you could not prove that steel or cold had been the death of him, or disease, or it may be poison, but we know that what has happened to him is something of this sort. Even so in many cases we have the like to say" (6.705–11). With discrete incidents, one explanation must be correct. However, *repetitions* of these events may each have different causes, so that it is not impossible that "a new moon should not be always created with a fixed succession of phases in fixed shapes" or that "every single day the one which has been made should not vanish and another be restored in its place and station" (5.731–36). Everything obeys natural law, but repetition exceeds law. Cycles and repetitions do not presuppose an identity of causes. In this way the indeterminate *clinamen* demands not only the structural incompleteness of causality but also the uniqueness of each event and therefore a difference internal to repetitions of the same. There is an epistemological aspect obliging the plurality of explanations (the limitations of sensory evidence), but this plurality is not restricted to it.

The contingency of the *clinamen* leads Lucretius to hold that historical events, being irreducibly particular, are always accidental attributes of a thing (1992:1.449–82). It also leads him to describe the interaction of atoms not in terms of an abstract law given from above but rather in the language of power, struggle, and pact or contract. These associations are produced by the atoms themselves, but always in accordance with the dictates of their independent natures and limits (*foedera natura*). It is an order arising from and returning to chaos.[30]

Aristotle sought a clean pluralism by displacing indeterminacy as a first principle. Epicurean thought employs originary indeterminacy to theorize an open and incomplete natural plurality. Indeed, "with Epicurus and Lucretius the real noble acts of philosophical pluralism begin" (Deleuze 1990:267). And it is through the thought of this pluralism that Epicureanism locates unethical implications in those philosophies driven toward determinate closure.

Ethics and Ontology

Cicero reproaches Epicurus for advocating restraint while counseling pleasure as the standard for action: "If I listen to him, he says many things in many places about self-control and restraint; but 'the water sticks,' as the saying goes. For how can a man praise restraint when he places the highest good in pleasure? For restraint is hostile to the passions; but the passions are pleasure's adherents" (Cicero 1991:3.117). According to Cicero, Epicurus lacks a theory of virtue that would justify moral limitations, leaving him to rest justice, law, and morality on nothing more than convention and the egoistic logic of self-advantage (see, for example, Epicurus 1993:150n.31). From an Epicurean perspective, however, the problem of ethics is not solved by a search for excellences that are grounded in human nature and orient human life toward a cosmic order. Such a pursuit is a symptom of the problem, not its solution.

The demands of teleological philosophies stem from a moral framework expressing a negative attitude toward death and pain. Suffering occurs on two levels: physical suffering, involving the sometimes unavoidable pain that befalls humans, and existential suffering—a mental anguish demanding the explanation of suffering and resulting from anxiety about death. Aristotle conspicuously ignores the latter theme in his ethical writings, but Lucretius cites it as the cause of evil: "These sores of life [avarice, ambition, and cruelty] in no small degree are fed by the fear of death" (1992:3.63–64). Existential anxiety robs life of potential happiness by making "anticipation of [death] painful" (Epicurus 1993:125). Anyone is susceptible to resentment, and it is not surprising, given this point, that Epicurus's school, the Garden, admitted both men and women, free and slave (see Diogenes Laertius 1965:10.3–26; Epicurus 1993:122). The role of philosophy, insofar as it seeks to cultivate a life of happiness, is to dispel the fear of death and promote appreciation of life. Epicurean philosophy, as Nietzsche says, becomes the art of living rather than the search for truth.[31]

From an Epicurean perspective, existential resentment underpins teleological thought. Fear of death promotes the belief in an immortal soul and the concomitant possibility of eternal suffering, while the demand to explain suffering gives rise to images of vengeful gods intervening in worldly affairs. Aristotle—certainly in his later years, after Plato's death—does not present such a theology,[32] but his calls for determinate causality in nature still betray an anxiety concerning contingency, uncertainty, and openness. Teleology, regardless of its guise, embodies a demand for justification stemming from and promoting bitterness toward life. Despite its opposition to metaphor and mysticism, Aristotle's scientism is really another form of myth—a single truth elevated over equally plausible alternatives that shrouds the plural, contingent nature of existence, thereby devaluing life. The rationalist astral religions of Plato and Aristotle are therefore no better than the traditional doctrines they seek to replace (see Festugière 1956).

Thus philosophy's initial task is to discredit teleology and its accompanying mysticisms. Teleological and theological interpretations must be replaced with naturalistic ones. Responsibility for the creation or administration of the world must not be attributed to the gods, whose serene existence is antithetical to such obligations. The demand for human or cosmic telos produces only anxiety.

> Unless you spew all these errors out of your mind, and put far from you thoughts unworthy of the gods and alien to their peace, their holy divinity, impaired by you, will often do you harm . . . you yourself will imagine that they, who are quiet in their placid peace, are rolling great billows of wrath, you will not be able to approach their shrines with placid heart, you will not have the strength to receive with tranquil peace of spirit the images which are carried to men's minds from their holy bodies, declaring what the divine shapes are. What kind of a life follows at once from that error, it is easy to see. (Lucretius 1992:6.68–79)

But the temptation to elevate one explanation above others that agree equally with the evidence must also be avoided. Demands for a single naturalist explanation are a theological remnant. The answer to mysticism, then, is the affirmation of an irreducible plurality of explanations. Happiness and self-sufficiency then follow from a tranquillity of mind that is tied to affirmation and demystification through naturalism. This makes physics, rather than metaphysics, the first philosophy of Epicureanism.

Proper orientation to death is also requisite: "Grow accustomed to the belief that death is nothing to us, since every good and evil lie in sensation. However, death is the deprivation of sensation. . . . while we exist, death is

not present, and whenever death is present, we do not exist" (Epicurus
1993:124–25). Cultivation of this understanding "makes a mortal life enjoy-
able, not by adding an endless span of time but by taking away the longing
for immortality" (ibid.). The demand for immortality produces a vicious
circle, leading to the invention of an immortal soul and opening the possibility of eternal anguish.

> For when anyone in life anticipates that birds and beasts will man-
> gle his body after death, he pities himself; for he does not distinguish
> himself from that thing, he does not separate himself sufficiently
> from the body there cast out, he imagines himself to be that and,
> standing beside it, infects it with his own feeling. Hence he resents
> that he was born mortal, and does not see that in real death there
> will be no other self that could live to bewail his perished self, or
> stand by to feel pain that he lay there lacerated or burning. (Lucre-
> tius 1992:3.879–87)

The correct attitude toward death provides first and foremost an appreciation of life, because "the training for living well and dying well is the same"
(Epicurus 1993:126). Affirmation of life and its contingencies follows from
affirmation of the necessity of death: "I have anticipated you, Fortune, and
have barred your means of entry. Neither to you nor to any other circumstance shall we hand ourselves over as captives. But when necessity compels
us, we shall depart from life, spitting on it and on those who vainly cling to
it, declaring in a beautiful song of triumph how well we have lived" (Epicurus 1993: *Vatican Sayings,* no. 47). As the absolute negation of life, death negates even its own meaning in relation to life. Hence it is to be neither feared
nor welcomed, and life is not to be judged in terms of its inevitability: "Much
worse is he who says that it is good not to be born and 'once born to pass
through the gates of death as quickly as possible'" (Epicurus 1993:126–27). It
is from the meaninglessness of death that life can be affirmed.

The immortal Epicurean gods, who play no part in worldly affairs, are models for human well-being. Their indifference to humanity implies that humanity's own indifference to the disenchanted world is a precondition for its happiness. Participation in public religion is therefore required not to gain divine
favor but to celebrate divine happiness and thereby partake in it (see Epicurus 1993: *Fragments,* no. 57; Festugière 1956:62). Neither mortality nor immortality, divine concern nor indifference, plays a role in human contentment.
Happiness and tranquillity of mind (*ataraxia*) result only from increasing
pleasure and decreasing pain. The two requirements turn into one, however,
for the highest pleasure is achieved in equilibrium rather than restlessness,[33]

and this is maximized by eliminating pain. Sensual pleasures are ephemeral and call only for the alleviation of want (see Epicurus 1993: *Vatican Sayings*, no. 33). Once this is achieved, pleasures may be modified, but not increased: "The pleasure in the flesh will not be increased when once the pain resulting from want is taken away, but only varied. The limit of understanding as regards pleasure is obtained by a reflection on these same pleasures and the sensations akin to them, which used to furnish the mind with its greatest fears" (Epicurus 1993:144n.18). Luxuries are empty cravings, and the desire for extravagances is directly linked to the demand for immortality and the fear of eternal damnation: "The fear of infinite punishment is the natural price to be paid for having unlimited desires" (Deleuze 1990:273). Attaining happiness, then, requires reducing desires to the fulfillment of natural and necessary wants.

All this constitutes the Epicurean "care of the self,"[34] in which friendship forms an indispensable support against existential resentment: "The same knowledge that makes one confident that nothing dreadful is eternal or long-lasting, also recognizes in the face of these limited evils the security afforded by friendship" (Epicurus 1993:148n.28). Moreover, "we do not need the help of our friends so much as the confidence that our friends will help us" (ibid.: *Vatican Sayings*, no. 34). A life without friends is filled with risks and anxieties, and so the benefits of friendship outweigh its accompanying difficulties: "It is necessary even to run risks for friendship's sake" (no. 28). For these reasons, "The noble man is most concerned with wisdom and friendship. Of these one is a mortal good, the other immortal" (no. 78).

Epicureanism does not present a political theory, but it does locate existential issues that any political ideal must address. Indeed, the denial or neglect of these matters signals resentment. As a result, political theory is not so much a matter of theorizing an "ideal state," for the problem of politics is no longer simply the rational harmonization of parts. The ideal state now appears as a yearning for certainty and harmony grounded in fear of death.[35] The search for a single truth, Form, or telos of human life and society emerges as a product and continuation of resentment toward life. The question for a political theory, then, is how social arrangements might best combat existential fear and anxiety in order to produce affirmation of life, contingency, and multiplicity.

Epicurus and Nietzsche

Nietzsche gives high praise to Epicurus yet strongly criticizes him as well. These divergent appraisals stem from Epicureanism's ultimate failure to escape ancient ontology and metaphysics. Although many Epicurean moves subvert metaphysical presumptions, they ultimately only minimize, rather than reject, metaphysical categories.

On the one hand, Nietzsche commends Epicurus for rejecting unitary truths and pre-Christian salvation doctrines.

> *Why we look like Epicureans.*—We are cautious, we modern men, about ultimate convictions. Our mistrust lies in wait for the enchantments and deceptions of the conscience that are involved in every strong faith, every unconditional Yes and No. . . . Thus an almost Epicurean bent for knowledge develops that will not easily let go of the questionable character of things; also an aversion to big moral words and gestures; a taste that rejects all crude, four-square opposites and is proudly conscious of its practice in having reservations. (Nietzsche 1974: §375)

Further: "One must read Lucretius to understand *what* it was Epicurus opposed: *not* paganism but 'Christianity,' which is to say the corruption of souls through the concept of guilt, punishment and immortality.—He opposed the subterranean cults, the whole of latent Christianity—to deny immortality was already in those days a real *redemption*.—And Epicurus would have won, every mind of any account in the Roman Empire was an Epicurean: *then Paul appeared*" (Nietzsche 1990:191). These are the areas where Epicurean antitheology and antimetaphysics shine: the rejection of telos; naturalism as a doctrine of plurality; and the identification of resentment and sadness in both the demand for salvation and the constitution of an ethics of responsibility, guilt, and punishment. Other times, however, Nietzsche calls Epicurus "the soul-soother of later antiquity" (1986: "The Wanderer and His Shadow," §7), a carrier of Christian pacification, decadence, and ressentiment suffering from "the *impoverishment of life*" and seeking "rest, stillness, calm seas, redemption from themselves through art and knowledge, or intoxication, convulsions, anaesthesia, and madness" (1974: §370).

A covert Epicurean reliance on telos, providence, and theology is the target here. Even in an uncaring, purposeless world, Epicurus bases his contention that happiness can be achieved through the satisfaction of necessary wants on a belief that these needs can be fulfilled without great exertion: "Thanks be to blessed nature for making the necessary easy to secure and the unnecessary difficult to supply" (Epicurus 1993: *Fragments*, no. 67; see also ibid.:130). There is also a theological anthropomorphism in the reliance on the human form of the gods, which allows Epicurus to draw from their existence an ethic and lifestyle (see Blumenberg 1983:145–79, 263–67). Lucretius himself states that the man who has purged his mind of fears is "accustomed to discourse often in good and godlike fashion about the immortal gods themselves" (1992:5.52–53), implying the need for an extensive theology and not merely public participation in religious activities (5.165; see also Summers 1995). Finally, the very metaphysical philosophy Epicurus criticizes is reinstated in the idea of the atom. Despite its generally heterogeneous nature, the atom is ultimately defined by size, shape, and weight, attributes that are homogeneous with its products. Despite the strategies to interrelate them, atoms retain a primary independence because of their "hardness" (see Deleuze 1994:184). Epicureanism thus shrinks from a philosophy of difference in favor of stability and identity. It emphasizes one aspect of contingency—indeterminacy—but forgets another—dependence and relationality—even though both are necessary components of the event. Although Lucretius insists on the atom's being a permanent substrate on grounds of conceptual necessity, this clearly exhibits the very resentment that Epicureanism opposes in metaphysical philosophies (Blumenberg 1983:167–68). Permanence is the demand of those unable to affirm contingency and the possibility of nonexistence.

Despite pushing beyond the Aristotelian limit and continuum, opening thought to a discontinuous infinity, Epicureanism ultimately fails to dispense with metaphysics but rather rests on a minimum of ontotheological assumptions, a modicum of permanence and providence that allows Epicurus to soothe anxieties and relieve existential suffering.[36] Such minima are insufficient, however, and hence Nietzsche proclaims: "I have presented such terrible images to knowledge that any 'Epicurean delight' is out of the question. . . . Even resignation is *not* a lesson of tragedy, but a misunderstanding of it! Yearning for nothing is a *denial* of tragic wisdom, its opposite!" (1967a: §1029). Nevertheless, Epicureanism sets the direction for a philosophy of difference through its affirmation of originary indeterminacy coupled with an ethical critique of the demand for wholeness.

4. The One and the Many: Augustine and Gnosticism

In fact, the problem of the origin of evil pursued me even as a boy
of thirteen: at an age in which you have "half childish trifles, half
God in your heart," I devoted to it my first childish literary trifle,
my first philosophical effort—and as for the "solution" of the
problem I posed at that time, well, I gave the honor to God, as was
only fair, and made him the *father* of evil.

—Friedrich Nietzsche, *On the Genealogy of Morals*

THE INABILITY TO SECURE totality might lead thought toward a groundless difference that accounts for this failure. Alternatively, the failure could
be attributed to human deficiency, in order to resecure and reinvest self-identity in a higher source. In Christian thought God limits the universe by creating, comprehending, and exceeding it. Knowledge of particulars is also en-
trusted to him: Augustine calls it "the depths of blasphemy . . . to allege that
God does not know all numbers" (Augustine 1984:12.19). Whole and complete unto himself, God is Being pure, simple, and transcendent, grounding
a hierarchy of beings, from angels to formless matter, that are created from
nothing.

What appears, then, is a differential system produced by a fully positive
source. But questions then arise regarding the status of the negative. Such
difficulties also confront Neoplatonic thought generally. At issue is how the
negative—a difference that does not participate in and through the source
and so cannot be affirmed—can arise within this fully positive process of
production.[1] Plotinus subsumes negation under the degradation of entities
emanating from the One, so that evil is the faintest image of authentic Being and equated with matter. Evil, as nonbeing, cannot be mere nothingness;
as the corruption of form, it cannot be a formal principle itself, for this would
violate the law of noncontradiction. But evil is also not any particular pol-
lution of form; it is necessarily a *principle* of negation. The matter into which

form is invested thereby becomes the essence of evil. It is the measureless, the formless, lacking all quality (Plotinus 1956:1.8). Negation, then, is a correlate to the positive, the one increasing as the other decreases.

This solution is clearly unacceptable to Christian thought. Although difference emanates from a fully positive source, the last term in the series is a negation refusing to fade into nothingness, making evil the ultimate product of the good. Hence arises Plotinus's ambivalence toward matter and evil: although he insists that emanation is a faultless and necessary overflow from the One, its final result is a fall that implicates negation within the origin itself.[2]

The orthodox Christian Neoplatonism[3] examined in this chapter thus requires a more radical separation of being and nonbeing, alongside a promise of final victory over the negative. In doing so, it recognizes far more explicitly than Aristotle a heterogeneous difference that differs from the One and the Many but can acknowledge this difference only as a simulacrum of the good, a sinfulness to be eliminated. It falls to Augustine to secure this interpretation and safeguard the goodness of God and his creation. The surviving texts of the Valentinian and Sethian Gnostics, however, highlight another route. What is normally interpreted as their dualism is not the brute opposition of metaphysics but rather a reversal of the priorities governing orthodox Christianity that no longer reduces excessive difference to a sin or fault. For the Gnostics, the evil that mimics the good is the hierarchy of the One and the Many itself, which shows itself to be a deficient copy of a genuine plurality that is not defined by any fixed center or limit. In this way a multiplicity that illuminates the inadequacies of metaphysical thought gains supremacy.

Augustine and the Origins of Evil

In his *Confessions* Augustine admits to having once considered Epicureanism: "In my judgement Epicurus would have won all the honours, were it not that I believed that the soul lived on after death and received the reward or punishment which it deserved. Epicurus had refused to believe this" (Augustine 1961:6.16; see also Simpson 1985). The story of sin, promise of judgment, and hope of redemption are crucial aspects of Augustinian Christianity that must prove their efficacy against established pagan doctrines and Gnostic teachings. Each facet depends on the credibility of a sole omnipotent and benevolent deity and, concomitantly, a doctrine of human will at once capable of evil and dependent on God, split within itself and in need of repair.

These elements do not fit together easily. Indeed, each component, while indispensable, ultimately corrodes the ground underlying the others. The result is a series of vacillations by which Augustine seeks to secure the unity and consistency of Christian faith and the purity of the One against a groundless difference threatening to corrupt it.

Augustine certainly holds belief to be a prerequisite for knowledge (*credo ut intelligam*). Indeed, he claims that he began to prefer the teachings of the Church because of its integrity regarding the powers of reason (Augustine 1961:6.5). This does not make him a theologian who rejects philosophy, however, for he took his adoption of Christianity to be the completion of his earlier philosophical ideas (see Rist 1994: chs. 1, 3), with his discovery of Neoplatonism being the penultimate step of his conversion (see Bonner 1986:80–88). Nor does the status of faith reduce the role of reason to judging among a select number of interpretations accepted within the framework of doctrine. Rather, in rejecting the Christian anti-intellectualism mocked by many of the ancients, Augustine extends the employment of rational argument against those philosophies and religions sufficiently oriented to the appropriate concerns. On this terrain, reason may not be able to confirm belief, but it can eliminate incoherent pretenders. Thus, while it is paramount for Augustine to discredit paganism, he largely ignores atheism and the Epicurean belief in deities unconcerned with worldly affairs, because neither shares the necessary assumptions concerning the purposes of religion (Augustine 1984:10.18). But insofar as it can be maintained that religion's function is to secure human happiness, Augustine holds paganism to be caught in irreconcilable inconsistencies and redundancies. The multiplicity of limited gods, given overlapping responsibilities that often trump one another and organized by a hierarchy conforming to no rationale, produces a cacophony of divine chaos from which no credible faith can issue.

The sheer number of gods involved in any event or activity leads to immense absurdity: "If anyone engaged two nurses for a child, one to give him solid food only, the other to give him nothing but drink, we should think him a clown, putting on a kind of farcical performance in his own home. But the Romans employ two divinities for these purposes, Educa and Potina!" (Augustine 1984:6.9). Different deities care for the countryside, mountains, hills, and valleys, while others watch over separate crops during planting, sowing, and storage. "Each man appoints one door-keeper for his house and that one, being a man, is enough. But the Romans appointed three gods; Forculus to guard the doors (*fores*); Cardea the hinges (*cardo*); Limentinus the threshold (*limen*). So Forculus could not guard both hinges and threshold at the same time!" (4.8). Three gods protect a woman after she gives birth, another joins couples in marriage, yet another escorts the bride home, and several more participate in the first night: "If there is any modesty in human beings (there seems to be none in the gods!), I feel sure that the belief in the presence of so many divinities of both sexes to urge on the business in hand would so embarrass the couple as to quench the enthusiasm of the one and stiffen the reluctance of the other!" (6.9).

Given this multitude, many gods are simply superfluous. Jupiter is credited with the empire's growth, yet there is also a goddess, Victory: "Why should Jupiter himself be needed in this matter, if Victory is favourable and propitious, and always comes to those whom she wishes to be conquerors? Given her favour and sympathy, what nations would have remained unconquered, even though Jupiter had taken a holiday, or had been otherwise employed?" (Augustine 1984:4.14). Faith is a subset of virtue, yet it is deified whereas other virtues are not. And why not simply worship Virtue? "Surely, where Virtue is, there Faith is also? . . . In any case, faith and modesty are included in virtue; yet Faith and Modesty have been deemed worthy of altars in their special shrines, independent of Virtue" (4.20). The goddesses Felicity and Fortuna appear indistinguishable: "Is there any difference between felicity and fortune? Yes, there is: fortune may be good or bad; but felicity could not be bad, without ceasing to be felicity. But surely we ought to believe that all the gods . . . are good without exception!" (4.18). A tiny group of "select" gods "operate on a footing of equality, like a senate in conjunction with the plebs," yet "some of the gods who have not been considered at all worthy of selection are in charge of more important and dignified functions than those performed by gods entitled 'select'" (7.3). Felicity is not "select," yet she seems to supersede all other deities, "for who but Felicity gave Jupiter his kingship—assuming, that is, that he was happy in his reign?" (4.23). Moreover, "if Felicity had granted perpetual peace, Mars would be out of employment" (7.14). In any event, those who refused to accept one god ought to be satisfied with Virtue and Felicity: "Bearing in mind the functions of all those gods and goddesses, which the pagans have whimsically invented according to their fancy, let them see if they can discover anything which any god could supply to a man who possesses virtue and felicity" (4.21).

Some polytheists tried to avoid such difficulties by treating the various gods as moments or parts of Jupiter, but this move simply reproduces the same problem in different form, for it is senseless to worship each component independently.

If it should be feared that the omitted or neglected aspects of Jupiter might be angry, the inference would be that here there is not (as they would have it) one whole life of one Living Being, containing in itself all gods as its powers or members or aspects, but rather, each aspect has a life distinct from the others, if one aspect can be angry independently of another, if one can be appeased while another is irritated. If, on the other hand, it is asserted that all the aspects together, that is the whole of Jupiter himself, could have been offended if his aspects were not worshipped individually and separately, this assertion is the merest folly. None of them could have been neglected while the god himself, who in himself possesses them all, was being worshipped. (Augustine 1984:4.11)

Even with their sovereign god, the pagans multiplied him into many gods unnecessarily: "Jupiter is entitled Victor, Invictus, Opitulus, Impulsor, Stator, Centumpeda, Supinalis, Tigillus, Almus, Ruminus—it would be tedious to go through the whole list. These titles have been bestowed on one god for various causes on account of different powers. The existence of many activities in Jupiter does not compel him to turn into an equal number of gods" (7.11).

Paganism, according to Augustine, presents a hierarchy of limited gods with heterogeneous functions. Hierarchy is required to prevent divine anarchy, but this ordering must then resolve all differences into a single deity. For it remains undisputed within the circles of debate Augustine inhabits that the gods are good, and if the purpose of religion is happiness ("Human nature in its weakness has already felt that happiness can only be given by a god" [1984:4.25]) then the entire mass of gods becomes useless, if only for reason of "economical procedure" (4.11). If religion seeks a divine power to secure human happiness—which for Augustine has at once an emotional content (joy) and a theoretical one (truth) (see Gilson 1960: intro., ch. 1)—then the heterogeneous multiplicity of paganism becomes a mere multitude that necessarily resolves itself into Oneness: "If Felicity is not a goddess, because she is, in truth, a gift of God, we should seek the God who can bestow that gift and abandon the pernicious mob of false gods to which the silly mob of fools attach themselves" (Augustine 1984:4.23). Happiness is quickly defined as the attainment of eternal life, "which is, without any doubt, incomparably to be preferred to all earthly kingdoms" (6.1). Here, too, the pagan gods fail to fulfill what religious faith demands: "It is . . . a mark of the most unconscionable folly to ask or hope for eternal life from such divinities. Even supposing they are concerned with supporting and propping up this brief life of care, they watch over its particular departments, so it is asserted, in such a way that if anything belonging to one god's sphere of responsibility is sought from another god, a ridiculous anomaly arises, like some farcical situation in a mime" (ibid.).

The human requirement of happiness not only delegitimates paganism but also shifts the balance of reason toward the Christian faith. Here, the interrelation of belief, reason, and understanding becomes clear. Reason achieves nothing without faith, but it must recognize only true belief, and this move itself requires rational activity: "Even granting that reason has decided to follow the lead of faith, it still has to know what faith is, and here too a rational effort is required. . . . Prior to faith there is some understanding of the things one should and would believe, and man cannot dispense with this" (Gilson 1960:30; see also Ramirez 1982). This prior understanding is the eudaemonic goal that joins reason to faith. It gives the Christian leap its superiority over others: it is an eminently *reasonable* move necessary to attain a pregiven goal.

The shift in the character of the ground that follows is thus quite in keeping with the spirit of rationalism. Aristotle insists on a finite foundation, for only the limited is knowable and hence good, and tries to ignore or suppress the gaps within this whole. But Augustine treats these gaps as lacunae that point toward God, holding them to indicate the limits of human understanding without precluding the existence of a supreme divinity who overcomes them. The ground is now an infinite being and so can be grasped only by itself. Augustine's God presents an unlimited that is nonetheless determinate—a self-determined infinity partially open to human cognition but fully available only through grace, uniting being, truth, and goodness. He is therefore both an omnipotent God capable of ensuring human salvation and a loving God who cares to grant it. Omnipotence requires that God create heaven and earth not from any prior material but from nothing; that his creation not be the instantiation of a world of (Platonic) Forms separate from him, forms being merely ideas within his divine intellect; that there be no time before God, but that God exist *before* time;[4] that he remain unchanging even while causing change in the world (Augustine 1984:7.7); and that all future events be already known as part of his providential plan (12.28). Benevolence demands that God be pure and uncontaminated by evil, that he be just, and that he deliver judgment against those who turn from him. The corequirements of absolute love and sovereignty form the core around which the question of evil assumes a centrality absent in pagan doctrines installed with heterogeneity and strife.[5] Having radicalized the demand for a unified ground, Augustine must contend with anything appearing to disrupt or decompose the purity of his divinity.

Against the Manichean belief in an evil force coexisting with the god of Christ,[6] Augustine takes evil to be nothing but a lack or deficiency of good. Since God created all beings and their natures, evil must be the perversion of nature, a corrosive nonbeing within beings. The evil forsake the light of God in favor of themselves—hence pride is the first sin (1984:12.16)—while the good cling to divine illumination. Sometimes Augustine maintains that a remnant of good must always remain to be corrupted, such that "not even the nature of the Devil himself is evil, in so far as it is a nature; it is perversion that makes it evil" (19.13). Other times he insists that "evil is nothing but the removal of good until finally no good remains" (Augustine 1961:3.7). Still, evil must have some existential status, for if it were merely nothingness, then God, in creating all being from nothing, would have created everything from evil.[7] Nor can evil be a lack corresponding to the distance between a created being and its Creator, for then evil would be a necessary condition of creation itself. Augustine argues, "Can it be that there simply is no evil? If so, why do we fear and guard against something which is not there? If our fear is unfounded, it is itself an evil, because it stabs and wrings our hearts for nothing" (7.5). Further, "even what is perverted must of necessity be in, or derived from, or associated with—that is, in a sense, at peace with—some part of the order of things among which it has its being or of which it consists. Otherwise it would not exist at all" (Augustine 1984:19.12). Evil must exist, but not as a necessary or positive condition. So Augustine enacts a cleavage between nonbeing, or the negation of being, and nothingness: the latter is the absence of being (*deprivatio*) without implication of lack or incompleteness; the former is a corruption or lack of fullness of being (*depravatio*). The seductive power of evil lies in this distinction, even though to love evil is to love what is trivial and ultimately nothing.[8]

Augustine thereby attempts to resolve the problem of evil facing Neoplatonism by separating difference from negation. A new line intersects Plato's, opening being onto a multidimensional plane. One axis runs from being to nothing; the other, from being to nonbeing. Those beings organized along the former have differential degrees of perfection. All are contingent on God for their being (Augustine 1993:2.17), but none contains any lack or negation. Augustine insists that "the universe would not be perfect unless the greater things were present in such a way that lesser things are not excluded" (3.9) and that any failure to accept this denigrates the lesser orders of being for their mediocrity. Existential resentment is the result of a refusal to appreciate the goodness of all God's creations: "Whatever might rightly occur to you as being better, you may be sure that God, as the Creator of all good things, has made that too. When you think that something better should have been made, it is not right reason, but grudging weakness, to will that nothing lower had been made, as if you looked upon the heavens and wished that the earth had not been made. Such a wish is utterly unjust" (3.5). Lack is instead found along the line from being to nonbeing, from good to evil. A man who sins does not fall lower on the order of creation but rather maintains his place while becoming sickly. As a result, he loses his (internal) resemblance to God but maintains his (external) image. One must therefore hate the corruption within this man but not the man himself (see Augustine 1984:14.6).[9] This de-limitation, however, requires Augustine to maintain nonbeing as absolute negativity and simulacrum cut off from the creation. If nonbeing were to attain the status of substance, it would either challenge God's omnipotence or undermine his benevolence.

But the problem of the origin of perversion remains: how can an almighty God not bear responsibility for evil? Augustine suggests that corruption is possible in any nature created from nothing, since "no existence which came from nothing can claim to be equal to [God]" (1984:12.5), meaning that such a being must be subject to change. This is clearly an inadequate response, given Augustine's own distinction between the becoming of the cycles of the creat-ed universe and the becoming corrupt of evil; moreover, even to the degree that it does explain the possibility of evil—while seeming to limit God's pow-er[10]—it does not answer the question of its genesis. Augustine initially re-sponds to this last issue by shifting the locus away from Adam's original sin to the prior fall of the angels. Their evil choice, he says, can be traced to their evil will, but the origin of this will confounds the logic of causality.

> If you try to find the efficient cause of this evil choice, there is none to be found. For nothing causes an evil will, since it is the evil will itself which causes the evil act; and that means that the evil choice is the efficient cause of an evil act, whereas there is no efficient cause of an evil choice; since if anything exists, it either has, or has not, a will. If it has, that will is either good or bad; and if it is good, will anyone be fool enough to say that a good will causes an evil will? If it does, it follows that a good will is the cause of sin; and a more absurd conclusion cannot be imagined. (12.6)

An evil act may be traced to an evil will, and such a will can be explained on the basis of prior evil acts and wills, but the first evil will cannot be caused in this manner and certainly cannot come from a good will or act. Augus-tine thus concludes that this first evil will must be a first cause: it "is that which has no cause, since cause precedes effect" (ibid.). But this is the very definition of God: a *causa sui*, for "the cause which is cause only, and not effect, is God" (5.9). Augustine can still maintain that evil, as corruption, remains parasitical on a prior good nature, but this only reinforces the way evil originates *within* creation. Manichean dualism reappears: evil attains positive status as an existent containing its own conditions of being.[11]

Since this self-created evil cannot be another deity, it must be invested in the only site available: human or angelic will attempting to be godlike. The will thus becomes the locus of paradox. Because good must have its source in God, the will cannot produce good autonomously,[12] but it must still have sufficient power to assume sole liability for evil. In goodness, the will is contingent; in evil, it is self-sufficient—otherwise, one could assert the Pelagian heresy that "the choice of the will is so free that [there is] no room for God's grace" (Augustine 1993: "Reconsiderations," 1.9.3). Further, however, the complete separation of God from sin must not disrupt divine providence, which guarantees judgment against sinners and eternal bliss for the city of God.

God's prescience must not preclude the voluntary nature of sin. It need not do so, Augustine contends, because precognition does not imply any responsibility of the seer: "Simply because God foreknows your future happiness—and nothing can happen except as God foreknows it, since otherwise it would not be foreknowledge—it does not follow that you will be happy against your will. . . . It follows, then, that his foreknowledge does not take away my power; in fact, it is all the more certain that I will have that power, since he whose foreknowledge never errs foreknows that I will have it" (1993:3.3). Providence here becomes a third option between the dichotomy of free will and destiny. Destiny or fate implies the unity of causes, but free will itself is part of the causal chain. Augustine opposes this schema to the Stoic cleavage between necessity and fate (Augustine 1984:5.9). There is only efficient causality, he argues, produced by human, angelic, or divine will. Causes beyond human control appear natural, fortuitous, or necessary, but they do not eliminate the role of human volitions and so do not reduce causality to determinism.

> Against such profane and irreverent impudence we assert both that God knows all things before they happen and that we do by our free will everything that we feel and know would not happen without our volition. We do not say that everything is fated; in fact we deny that anything happens by destiny. . . . Now if there is for God a fixed order of all causes, it does not follow that nothing depends on our free choice. Our wills themselves are in the order of causes,

which is, for God, fixed, and is contained in his foreknowledge, since human acts of will are the causes of human activities. . . . Just as he is the creator of all natures, so he is the giver of all power of achievement, but not of all acts of will. Evil wills do not proceed from him because they are contrary to the nature which proceeds from him. (5.9)

But the adequacy of this response depends on the vitality Augustine can instill in human will. Without sufficient internal strength it cannot be separated from the external causes surrounding it to shoulder independent culpability. Adam's original sin, as the foundation for the Fall, is the most salient, for Adam had *pure* free will, in which "desire was not yet in opposition to the will. That opposition [divided will] came later as a result of the punishment of the transgression" (14.12). Disobedience of a rule "so easy to observe, so brief to remember" (ibid.), justifies the severe punishments inflicted. Yet only after the act can Adam and Eve "distinguish the good which they had lost and the evil into which they had fallen. Hence the tree itself, which was to make this distinction for them if they laid hands on it to eat the fruit in defiance of the prohibition, got its name from that event, and was called 'the tree of the knowledge of good and evil'" (14.17). Although the first humans are aware of the ability to choose, they lack a prior knowledge of good and evil and thus cannot understand the nature of vice; consequently, they cannot competently decide to abandon God. The dilemma arises from the demand that no corruption exist prior to the crime, yet "the transgression of eating the forbidden fruit, was . . . committed only when those who did it were already evil" (14.13). The origin of this evil, like that of the angels, is inexplicable.

> The pair lived in a partnership of unalloyed felicity; their love for God and for each other was undisturbed. This love was the source of immense gladness, since the beloved object was always at hand for their enjoyment. There was a serene avoidance of sin; and as long as this continued, there was no encroachment of any kind of evil, from any quarter, to bring them sadness. Or could it have been that they desired to lay hands on the forbidden tree, so as to eat its fruit, but that they were afraid of dying? In that case both desire and fear was already disturbing them, even in that place. But never let us imagine that this should have happened where there was no sin of any kind. . . . Never let us suppose, I repeat, that before all sin there already existed such a sin. (14.10)

Adam must sin freely to remove blame from God, yet his free will is distinguished by its chastity and naïveté, making it unclear how he could voluntarily lose his innocence and abandon God.

Augustine tries to rescue the substantiality of free will by shifting from the terrain of free will/destiny/providence to that of free will/divided will. Divided will is the painful experience in which the mind, while easily commanding the body and its limbs, is powerless to control itself: "The mind gives an order to the body and is at once obeyed, but when it gives an order to itself, it is resisted" (Augustine 1961:8.9). The will finds itself overwhelmed by its own illicit desires, a phenomenon that explains humans' persistent incapacity to fully grasp what is closest to them—their own souls and the language they create and use to express themselves (see Rist 1994: ch. 2)—and the confused way in which they seek after a happiness they only dimly remember. Divided will creates a being unable on its own to rise above bodily sensations and toward genuine spiritual truths. These failures signal that the will is not whole and complete. Its commands to itself are not obeyed because they are "not given with the full will. For if the will were full, it would not command itself to be full, since it would be so already" (Augustine 1961:8.9). Divided will is thus "a disease of the mind, which does not wholly rise to the heights where it is lifted by the truth" (ibid.).

The chronic rift in the will compels the self to seek unity beyond itself and so indirectly establishes the existence of God. Human judgment, Augustine argues, would be impossible without such an unchanging source for a stable truth (1961:7.16). Furthermore, divided will negatively secures the existence of free will by implying a primordial time of purity and health lost through sin. No other possibility is conceivable, given a benevolent, omnipotent God. Such a being is too compassionate to have created humanity in this sickly condition, and his responsibility for the fall into illness is incongruent with his love and power. Moreover, the punishment of divided will perfectly fits the alleged crime: "In the punishment of that sin the retribution for disobedience is simply disobedience itself. For man's wretchedness is nothing but his own disobedience to himself, so that because he would not do what he could, he now wills to do what he cannot" (Augustine 1984:14.15). But God is also the source of healing, mending the will through his undeserved and predetermined grace. Repairing the will thereby becomes the highest good: "But what in fact, do we want to achieve, when we desire to be made perfect by the Highest Good? It can, surely, only be a situation where the desires of the flesh do not oppose the spirit, and where there is in us no vice for the spirit to oppose with its desires. Now we cannot achieve this in our present life, for all our wishing" (19.4). Health results when God helps us turn toward him and raises us to participate in his timeless purity.

The focus on divided will allows Augustine to reconnect humanity's free will to original sin while maintaining God's benevolence, supremacy, and providence. Nevertheless, this resolution is limited. It succeeds only by defining a state of perfection through reference to a present condition presumed to be faulted, and this ideal cannot sustain itself against a rigorous examination of its qualities. Augustine is necessarily vague about the postapocalyptic condition. The blessed, he says, will be incapable of sin, although "the fact that they will be unable to delight in sin does not entail that they will have no free will. In fact, the will will be the freer in that it is freed from a delight in sin and immovably fixed in a delight in not sinning" (Augustine 1984: 22.30). But this reopens the previous quandary of the will's having substantiality only in sin and begs the question of why God allowed evil to occur in the first place. A final set of shifts appears in the closing pages of the *City of God*. Sin, fall, and redemption are now necessary components whose order "had to be preserved" so that the redeemed soul "will not forget its own liberation, nor be ungrateful to its liberator. It will remember even its past evils as far as intellectual knowledge is concerned; but it will utterly forget them as far as sense experience is concerned" (ibid.). Evil now becomes a temporary fault serving a greater good. The damned, being necessary ingredients for the bliss of a minority of saved souls, become the real martyrs of Christian theology. The final conquest of evil safeguards God's omnipotence even while the requisite sin appears to undermine it.

Ironically, although Augustine deploys reason to show the inconsistencies of polytheism, he ultimately appeals to faith in seeking to protect Christianity from its own rational incoherences. Initially he offers the Christian notion of God because of the paradoxes found in pagan philosophy. But since these paradoxes are internal to reason, it is no more rational to posit an infinite God who resolves them than not to do so. Reason may be impotent without some sort of belief accepted on faith, but this does not justify Christian doctrine in particular, especially when it cannot intelligibly guarantee the eudaemonic conditions reason seeks. Augustine's only response is to argue that the limitations of reason make the aporias encountered in understanding God's Word inevitable, and this means only that we should cling more tightly to faith. Unable to show the rational inferiority of the pagan belief in infinite cycles of time, for example, he contends that "faith ought to laugh at these theories, even if reason could not refute them" (Augustine 1984:12.18). Room for this faith is carved from the disagreements among philosophers, whose quarrels resulted "because they sought the answers to these questions as men relying on human senses and human powers of reasoning" (18.41) and because of the restriction of human viewpoints: "The observer who cannot view the whole is offended by what seems the deformity of a part, since he does not know how it fits in, or how it is related to the rest" (16.8). Hence, "when we fail to find the answer, either through deficiency of insight or of staying power, we should believe that the purpose is hidden from us, as it was in many cases where we had great difficulty in discovering it" (11.22). Evil here assumes the very role Augustine had earlier rejected: an illusion resulting from human finitude.

Given a supreme and loving divinity, several responses are possible regarding the origin of evil: it may be treated as a simple lack of good or as a positive condition, its fault may be displaced onto humanity or the Devil, it may be considered illusory or necessary to a higher perfection, the issue may be buried in the name of a being whose dominion remains mysterious to those of limited vision, or it may be resolved through a final judgment or a promise of moral improvement or perfection through work on earth. Augustine submits each of these possibilities, including the last when he gives the Church an earthly project of receiving pagan converts.[13] No solution, however, is sufficient to make evil an unnecessary deviation from an incorruptible good, and so Augustine must constantly shuffle among them. Augustine may extend the metaphysical search for a unitary ground, but he certainly also magnifies the paradoxes within this demand. His failure to unite being, truth, and goodness, even within a supreme divinity, brings back to the fore a groundless difference *within* the origin. The negative can no longer be considered a difference that corrupts the purity of the origin, for difference and impurity are themselves conditions of the origin. It becomes necessary again to consider the possibility that unity is not primordial and examine alternative organizations of Being.

Gnostic Immanence

What is a heretic? The Church Fathers, including Irenaeus, Hippolytus, Tertullian, and Augustine, agree that not blasphemy but a mode of interrogation defines Gnostic heresy. Rejecting orthodox strictures of faith, the Gnostic asks subversive questions but stubbornly refuses to provide alternative answers. Such inquiries ultimately corrode faith itself. Tertullian writes: "Away with the person who is seeking where he never finds; for he seeks where nothing can be found. Away with him who is always knocking; because it will never be opened to him, for he knocks where there is no one to open. Away with the one who is always asking, because he will never be heard, for he asks of one who does not hear" (in Pagels 1979:114). Irenaeus similarly argues that "according to this course of procedure, one would be always inquiring but never finding, because he has rejected the very method of discovery" (in ibid.). The Gnostic heretic, then, commits a performative contradiction, undermining the very ground on which he stands. Such questions should not be asked in the first place, for they threaten the faith. But surely, if these individuals are caught in such a trap, they cannot be a real threat to the Church. Further, as Tertullian notes, "'the heretics and the philosophers' both ask the same questions" (Pagels 1979:113). How, then, are the two distinguished? And if these questions are truly self-undermining, why are they dangerous?

The situation becomes more clear when we realize that the orthodoxy tries to answer the very questions it maintains should not be asked. The Church Fathers thereby become heretics themselves, and it should not be surprising that when the Church fractures, the new heretics of the Reformation look to the early Church for justification. The doctrine of predestination in Augustine is only the most obvious example. So perhaps heresy is defined by an aura of irresistibility that entices the orthodoxy into an alien territory and subjects it to a disconcerting cross-examination. But pagans ask the same questions, and some pagans, as Augustine notes with Platonism, are all too close to the Christian faith. Why is the heretic treated differently?

The pagans offer systems alternative to the Church's, so they can be presented as "external Others" whose answers to existential questions can be criticized to secure the supremacy of the Christian faith. But Gnostics refuse this status; they consider themselves the "true" church within the Church but nonetheless have "tended to regard all doctrines, speculations, and myths— their own as well as others'—only as approaches to truth" (Pagels 1979:114).[14] This is consistent with their subversion of the ground of faith, but it also gives them a distinctively threatening status. Always marginalized, they perpetually reappear within the heart of the Church. Always self-subverting, they nonetheless are not self-destructive. The Gnostic heretic, then, is a nomad who survives on the very terrain that ought to devour him, a being who finds a mode of living on a groundless ground.[15]

Positivity Must Be Multiplicity

From a Gnostic perspective,[16] only one caught in the ignorance of the negative could conduct the search for heresy. It is from the vantage point of the negative that positivity appears as Oneness, requiring any difference incompatible with this Oneness to be labeled evil and expunged. The philosophy of the negative is one of barriers separating inside from outside and of the reduction of difference to determination by the One. The negative is not a pale image of the One and its hierarchy, however; rather, the latter is the negative image of a truly multiple positivity. The heretic is the "insider" who exposes the former image as false. The "Gnostic heretic" achieves this through gnosis.

As with knowledge of Epicurean atoms, the search for gnosis begins with the realization that other philosophies and religions remain trapped in positing something existent as the supreme God, never reaching the preexistent origin. The *Tripartite Tractate* traces the development of these false theologies. The first group "have reached as far as the visible elements" but "do not know anything more than them" (*Tripartite Tractate, Nag Hammadi Library* [hereinafter *NHL*] 1.5.109.22–24).[17] They seek the origin of existing things in providence, cyclical theories of time, or nature but cannot in turn account for these origins themselves. The second group of "those who were wise among the Greeks and the barbarians" reached a crude level of the intellectual realm (1.5.109.24–110.22). The third group, the Jews, established a "unified harmony . . . by the confession of the one more exalted than they" (1.5.111.17–23) but did not realize that this unity "exists as a representation of the representation of the Father. It is not invisible in its nature, but a wisdom envelops it" (1.5.110.35–111.2; see also Perkins 1992:278–79). For this reason, Jewish prophets could predict the coming of a savior but no details of his nature. They did not realize that "the one who exists is not a seed of the things which exist. . . . His Father is . . . the invisible, unknowable, the incomprehensible in his nature, who alone is God in his will and his form, who has granted that he might be seen, known and comprehended" (*Tri. Trac., NHL* 1.5.114.15–30).

The hidden nature of God requires a refusal to reduce him to human representations, which are at best oblique analogies with limited function.

> Names given to the worldly are very deceptive, for they divert our thoughts from what is correct to what is incorrect. Thus one who hears the word "God" does not perceive what is correct, but perceives what is incorrect. So also with "the father" and "the son" and "the holy spirit" and "life" and "light" and "resurrection" and "the church" and all the rest—people do not perceive what is correct but they perceive what is incorrect, [unless] they have come to know what is correct. The [names which are heard] are in the world. (*The Gospel of Philip, NHL* 2.3.53.23–37)

But a full appreciation of the nominal character of these titles fundamentally challenges the character of the ground. This is undoubtedly what Irenaeus finds dangerous in Valentinian Gnosticism, for the orthodox Church had always secured its ecclesiastical hierarchy by reference to a divine order created and governed by a single being (see Pagels 1979: ch. 2). The Gnostic demand exceeds the negative theology both Plotinus and Christianity can accept, threatening to divide the origin from its products so deeply that no determinate order may be established.[18] For the Gnostics, however, the ground must be truly heterogeneous if it is to function at all.

Given all this, it is odd that ancient and contemporary interpreters of Gnosticism commonly reinscribe this demand for heterogeneity within a model of emanationism found in Neoplatonic thought generally.[19] A transcendent and unrepresentable origin is held to radiate aeons, which in turn produce lesser aeons, angels, and glories, creating the divine and fully positive constellation of the Pleroma. At the edge of the Pleroma, the distance and progressive loss are sufficient for the sin of Sophia to produce an evil demiurge, who creates the world and imprisons part of the pleromic light within the human souls to be redeemed.[20] From rather different perspectives, Irenaeus and Plotinus both recount this ontology in order to ridicule it. Irenaeus maintains that if there is a limit to the Pleroma, it must be finite, and whatever lies beyond it must necessarily encompass the Pleroma and surpass it, thereby being the true God. If this other is said to be held at an infinite distance from the Pleroma, then a third principle must surround the Pleroma and its other, and this must be the true God (Irenaeus, *Against Heresies* 2.1.1–3, in Grant 1997:107–8). From a Christian perspective, then, Gnosticism suffers from the same criticisms that threaten other emanationist theories: as the successive emanations degrade, the surrounding darkness triumphs (see Perkins 1986). Plotinus attacks the discontinuity the Gnostics establish between the evil physical world and the Pleroma, arguing that it undermines any relation between humanity and its savior. A God absent from the world would simultaneously be absent from the soul, leaving no possibility of gnosis (Plotinus 1956:2.9.16). It is therefore necessary, Plotinus concludes, to insist on a harmonious and beautiful world containing within it a beauty of a higher order, so that the self may seek, through a movement of ecstasy and contemplation, a living One that differentiates itself without losing its absolute simplicity.

Nevertheless, by ascribing to Gnosticism an attempt to show how the One can give itself over to the Many, such interpretations portray the very type of inherently negative philosophy that is being opposed. Consequently, despite some articulations that seem to fit this conventional reading, the Gnostics must be seen to present a far more radical rethinking of the origin. They express a theory not of emanation but of immanence—that is, a positive,

virtual movement of differentiation in which successive differences are not
related in terms of loss.[21] Instead of a hierarchy based on the distance between
created product and origin, there is a sameness resulting from a univocal voice
speaking within all aeons. Against Irenaeus, it can be seen that although the
physical world created by the demiurge lies "outside" the Pleroma, it is never something placed beyond a limit or a boundary. It is rather outside by
virtue of having lost the immanent folding required to make it a positive
member of the pleromic universe. The negatively constructed world, based
on hierarchy and unity, is a bad image or copy of a fully positive and multiple movement. And so, against Plotinus, if a divine component remains in
humanity despite our separation from the Pleroma, it is precisely as an anarchic element exceeding any unity or order.

   Zostrianos, in the tractate of the same name, seeks to understand the production of that which truly exists:

   (About) existence: how do those who exist, being from the aeon
   of those who exist, (come) from an invisible, undivided and self-
   begotten spirit? Are they three unborn images having an origin better than existence, existing prior [to] all [these], yet having become
   the [world ...]? . . . What is that one's place? What is his origin? How
   does the one from him exist for him and all these? How [does he
   come into existence] as a simple one, differing [from] himself? Does
   he exist as existence, form and blessedness? By giving strength is he
   alive with life? How has the existence which does not exist appeared
   from an existing power? (*NHL* 8.1.2.24–3.13)

The answers come through a journey in which Zostrianos passes over various heavenly aeons and undergoes several ritual baptisms. On reaching the
level of all-perfect aeons, he sees how each aeon produces lesser aeons that
are its parts yet individual and complete in themselves: "The Autogenes is
the chief archon of his own aeons and angels as his parts, for those who are
the four individuals belong to him; they belong to the fifth aeon together. The
fifth exists in one; the four [are] the fifth, part by part. But these [four] are
complete individually" (8.1.19.6–16). These individual parts also infinitely give
rise to subparts: "Indeed, each of the aeons has ten thousand aeons in himself, so that by existing together he may become a perfect aeon" (8.1.123.12–
17). Although this organization begins with the first, perfect aeons, it is not
hierarchical. Protophanes, for example, comes from Kalyptos: "He is his
image, equal to him in power and glory but with respect to order higher than
him (yet not higher) in aeon" (8.1.125.1–5). The aeons "are not crowded

against one another, but to the contrary they are alive, existing in themselves and agreeing with one another, as they are from a single origin. . . . All of them exist in one, dwelling together and perfected individually in fellowship and filled with the aeon which really exists" (8.1.115.2–7, 116.1–6). Gnosis is knowledge of this interrelationship between part and whole, individual and the All, and of the principle of its genesis: "When one knows how he exists for him and (how) he has fellowship with their companions, one has washed in the washing of Protophanes. And if in understanding the origin of these, how they all appear from a single origin, how all who are joined come to be divided, how those who are divided join again, and how the parts [join with] the alls and the species and [kinds—if] one understands these things, one has washed in the washing of Kalyptos" (8.1.23.2–17).

If this is the form of pleromic life, then how it is generated? By what principle can the aeons remain complete individuals while nonetheless referring to a common origin from which they emerge and a greater whole of which they form parts? If the principle is one of identity, the result will be a unity. The aeons must rather relate to one another through a foundational difference.

In *The Three Steles of Seth,* the invisible Father is characterized as "the one who truly pre-exists because he is a non-being" (*NHL* 7.5.121.26–27). Similar descriptions are found in *Marsanes* (*NHL* 10.1.13.15–19) and *Allogenes.* The latter describes the origin of being as "[One] who subsists as a [cause] and source [of Being] and [an] immaterial [material and an] innumerable [number and a formless] form and a [shapeless] shape and a powerlessness and a power and an insubstantial substance and a motionless motion and an inactive activity" (*NHL* 11.3.48.19–29). Further, "he is neither boundless, nor is he bounded by another. Rather he is something [superior]. He is not corporeal. He is not incorporeal. He is not great. [He is not] small" (11.3.63.1–7). This paradoxical source, incomprehensible by virtue of being absolutely primordial, is revealed only indirectly (see 11.3.48.9–13, 53.21–22) as an excess of energies flowing through all beings and containing them. The *Trimorphic Protennoia* describes it as "the movement that dwells in the [All, she in whom the] All takes its stand . . . I move in every creature . . . I am the Invisible One within the All. It is I who counsel those who are hidden, since I know the All that exists in it. I am numberless beyond everyone. I am immeasurable, ineffable, yet whenever I [wish, I shall] reveal myself of my own accord. I [am the head of] the All. I exist before the [All, and] I am the All, since I [exist in] everyone" (*NHL* 13.1.35.2–32). Other tractates describe "[a] gushing [spring]" (*A Valentinian Exposition, NHL* 11.2.23.18) and "a fountain bubbling with life. . . . Language is not able to reveal this" (*Discourse on the Eighth and Ninth, NHL* 6.6.58.13–17). As the paradoxes surrounding it make clear, this is a virtual energy and movement implicated in all things: "The male father of all (who are) in thought, perception, (in) form, race, [region . . .], (in) an All which restrains and is restrained, (in) a body yet without a body, (in) essence, matter and [those that] belong to all these. It is with them and the god of the unborn Kalyptos and the power [in] them all that existence is mixed" (*Zost., NHL* 8.1.2.13–24).

In theories of emanation effects or products are externalized from their source, such that the origin remains transcendent. Conversely, an immanent causality maintains the internalization of an effect within its heterogeneous cause (see Deleuze 1992:171–72). Gnostic ontologies clearly adopt the latter approach: "The emanation of the Totalities, which exist from the one who exists, did not occur according to a separation from one another, as something cast off from the one who begets them. Rather, their begetting is like a process of extension, as the Father extends himself to those whom he loves, so that those who have come forth from him might become him as well" (*Tri. Trac., NHL* 1.5.73.18–28). Each aeon contains the other aeons it produces as its parts (*Allog., NHL* 11.3.51.12–28), and the invisible origin contains the entirety of aeons: "He contains them all within [himself], for [they] all exist because of [him]" (11.3.47.11–14). Indeed, the aeons are essentially various modes of the divine origin, independent but joined: "Each one of the aeons is a name, <that is>, each of the properties and powers of the Father, since he exists in many names, which are intermingled and harmonious with one another" (*Tri. Trac., NHL* 1.5.73.8–12). Also: "The Church exists in the dispositions and properties in which the Father and the Son exist, as I have said from the start. Therefore, it subsists in the procreations of innumerable aeons. Also in an uncountable way [they] too beget, by [the] properties [and] the dispositions in which it (the Church) [exists]" (1.5.59.2–15). The Father is said to have "stretched himself out and it was that which he stretched out which gave a foundation and a space and a dwelling place for the universe" (1.5.65.4–9). He creates a surface on which the aeons emerge, each in its own space. Each "exists as a perfect one because he is undivided with his own region" (*Zost., NHL* 8.1.68.21–23). It is as though the aeons were Leibnizian monads, an infinite number of individuals enveloping particular regions of an infinite surface (see *Tri. Trac., NHL* 1.5.67.19–26), each containing and expressing the whole (see *Zost., NHL* 8.1.48.3–26; Dillon 1992:103–4) from a particular perspective: "As for the parts in which he exists in his own manner and form and greatness, it is possible for <them> to see him and speak about that which they know of him, since they wear him while he wears them, [because] it is possible for them to comprehend him. He, however, is as he is, incomparable" (*Tri. Trac., NHL* 1.5.63.7–14).

The aeons are in this way both complete individuals and interrelated. They are connected by virtue of their common origin, but this cannot be understood as a unity, for unity, again, is a mere representation of the divine. The origin is not a center, and the Pleroma is not a closed totality, so that the aeons "belong together" in a Heideggerian fashion rather than in the manner of an identity. For this reason, although the language echoes Plotinus's description of the noetic realm in which all Forms are at once different and completely interpenetrated,[22] the two accounts must not be confused. The Gnostic aeons do not emanate from a central point but spread rhizomatically across a plane. This plane does not preexist them; they arise with its extension, and its extension is no more than the genesis of new aeons. Each forms a new center: "He creates the aeons as roots and springs and fathers" (*Tri. Trac.*, NHL 1.5.68.8–10). The aeons are contained within the Father, and the Father remains in the aeons as a trace (see *The Interpretation of Knowledge*, NHL 11.1.2.28–38). Aeonic life is thus the eternal production of new centers, of new positive differences. The aeons are unified by a univocal being speaking through all of them: "They are in the single name, and are all speaking in it" (*Tri. Trac.*, NHL 1.5.67.28–30). This voice is not the equivocal one of an analogical being that would retain a hierarchy among those that participate in it but an immanent, energetic movement within beings and overflowing them. It is a groundless ground relating beings through a primary, virtual dispersion.

The Gnostics describe this production as "begetting," opposing it to "creation." The former is an internal repetition that invokes the power of the entire Pleroma to engender a new difference within it: "All those who glorify the Father have their begetting eternally,—they beget in the act of assisting one another—since the emanations are limitless and immeasurable and since there is no envy on the part of the Father toward those who came forth from him in regard to their begetting something equal or similar to him, since he is the one who exists in the Totalities, begetting and revealing himself" (*Tri. Trac.*, NHL 1.5.70.21–30). But further, as an internal repetition begetting is essentially hidden. This is the significance of the bridal chamber: "Redemption (takes place) in the bridal chamber" (*Gos. Phil.*, NHL 2.3.69.26–27). It is a private realm, hidden from the ignorant, where male and female participate equally.

> For when the semen reaches the climax, it leaps forth. In that moment the female receives the strength of the male; the male for his part receives the strength of the female, while the semen does this. . . . Therefore the mystery of intercourse is performed in secret, in

order that the two sexes might not disgrace themselves in front of many who do not experience that reality. For each of them (the sexes) contributes its (own part in) begetting. For if it happens in the presence of those who do not understand the reality, (it is) laughable and unbelievable. (*Alcepius, NHL* 6.8.65.19–34)[23]

In contrast, creation is an external production, the manufacture of a copy from an original, with no need for secrecy: "He who creates works openly and he himself is visible. He who begets begets in [private] and he himself is hidden" (*Gos. Phil., NHL* 2.3.81.28–31; see also *The Teaching of Silvanus, NHL* 7.4.100.13–14). But creation is also a false genesis opposed to the truth of begetting: "At the present time we have the manifest things of creation. We say, 'The strong who are held in high regard are great people. And the weak who are despised are the obscure.' Contrast the manifest things of truth: they are weak and despised, while the hidden things are strong and held in high regard. The mysteries of truth are revealed, though in type and image. The bridal chamber, however, remains hidden. It is the holy in the holy" (*Gos. Phil., NHL* 2.3.84.14–23).[24]

Physical man and his world are creations of a demiurgic god arrogant enough to believe he is the only god (see *The Apocryphon of John, NHL* 2.1.11.18–22). The demiurge results from Sophia's sin, which is not an evil act but an error, "more contemptible than sinister" (Jonas 1970:133).[25] Whether Sophia tries to beget on her own (the Sethian myth) or tries to know the Father perspicuously (the Valentinian myth),[26] the sin is essentially one of turning away from pleromic life, losing sight of the true nature of genesis in terms of its hidden nature and its relation to the All. The demiurge emerges either as an aborted fetus expelled from the Pleroma or as part of Sophia that falls away. He creates the physical universe from the image of the Pleroma above him, but it lacks the internal energy of the original. It is a flattened, lifeless copy, a penumbra: "For everything which is visible is a copy of that which is hidden" (*Teach. Silv., NHL* 7.4.99.5–7). As opposed to a begotten offspring, "the creature is a shadow of pre-existing things" (*Val. Exp., NHL* 11.2.35.28–30). The mortal body "came to be from a misrepresentation, from the semblance which had emerged" (*Letter of Peter to Philip, NHL* 8.2.136.13–15). As a result, physical humans are left as sick beings.

[He who] has been created is [beautiful, but] you (sg.) would <not> find his sons noble creations. If he were not created but begotten, you (sg.) would find that his seed was noble. But now he was created, (and) he begot. What nobility is this? First adultery came

into being, afterward murder. And he was begotten in adultery, for
he was the child of the serpent. So he became a murderer, just like
his father, and he killed his brother. Indeed every act of sexual in-
tercourse which has occurred between those unlike one another is
adultery. (*Gos. Phil.*, NHL 2.3.60.34–61.12)

It is as though the fall "outside" the Pleroma amounted to a loss of dimension. The demiurge plummets into the depths of darkness, but it is a false
depth that amounts to no more than an erasure of the original depth of the
Father. It is not a spatial outside, which would indicate, as Irenaeus maintains, the finitude of the Pleroma. Just as depth is always distorted when an
object is projected onto a flat surface, so too is the depth of the Pleroma perverted by its negative image. On a two-dimensional surface, depth is por-
trayed through a line that indicates an edge or a cut.[27] Depth is thus misunderstood as a division, not as a virtual, differential folding within beings and
the infinitely folding field on which beings emerge. The "outside" is thus the
loss of inflection found in this misrepresentation and resulting from ignorance that has "no root. . . . Oblivion did not come into existence from the
Father, although it did indeed come into existence because of him" (*Gospel
of Truth*, NHL 1.3.17.30, 18.1–4).

Enormous consequences follow from this error.[28] Positivity is mistaken for
a unitary source reducing all centers to a single Creator and understanding
difference through a created hierarchy. Cause and effect are externalized, so
that the relations between creatures are those of limitation and contradiction, both logical and existential (see *The Book of Thomas the Contender*, NHL
2.7.139.2–11). Two creatures can be affirmed simultaneously only through the
identity of their Creator, and the Creator is affirmed only as the transcendent apex of its hierarchy. The fullness of the Pleroma is distorted into a
determinate totality in which the Creator rules through a Law of retributive
justice.[29] The result is a deficient and dead world in which the positive difference of the Pleroma can appear only as a threat to the demiurge's hierarchy. The vestige of pleromic light within human souls must therefore be
buried: humanity is thrust into a mundane world, blamed for its condition,[30]
and then given a moral system that implicates it more deeply within the cosmic order (see *The Testimony of Truth*, NHL 9.3.29.22–30.17). Despite these
efforts, however, this difference consistently eludes all attempts to contain it,
mocking the demiurge and his archons.[31]

The attainment of gnosis awakens this pleromic element, lifting the veil
of ignorance and exposing the negative nature of the limit and the One. The
philosophy of the One now seems only to implicate its followers more deeply

in the negative, who then struggle against all that threatens to expose its fallacies. The idea of positivity as a One that grounds a Many is but an error of the negative; the limits and determinations established within this philosophy are pale images of the true difference understood through gnosis. It is not surprising that Gnostic practices were largely nonhierarchical, operating on principles of equal access and participation and even allowing women to preach (see Filoramo 1990: ch. 11; Pagels 1979: chs. 2–3), nor that Gnostic ethics reject the moral alternatives offered by philosophies of the negative.

The Ethics of Excess

Gnostic ethics have generally been framed in binary terms, with the Gnostic depreciation of the cosmos yielding a choice between a libertine attitude rejecting all law as a creation of the demiurge and an asceticism hoping to shield the soul from the material world (see Filoramo 1990: ch. 11; Jonas 1970: ch. 11; and Williams 1996: chs. 7–8, which argues against such a classification). Given the Gnostic revaluation of the origin, however, these characterizations are too restrictive, for both choices are sunk in the negative logic of the limit. In rejecting moral restraints, the libertinism of which Plotinus and the heresiologists accuse Gnosticism sanctions moral nihilism, while the ascetic position apparently counseled by certain Gnostic tractates clings ever more tightly to the limit. These interpretations, then, reinscribe Gnosticism within the very philosophy it opposes. The Gnostics offer neither an uncontrolled libertinism nor an ascetic moralism but an ethical sensibility based on the fugitive, differential energies tapped through gnosis.

Plotinus's attack is instructive. Without specifying any immoral practices by the Gnostics, he declares them to be "more wanton" than the Epicureans, who deny providence, and maintains that Gnosticism "scorns every law known to us; immemorial virtue and all restraint it makes into a laughing stock, lest any loveliness be seen on earth; it cuts at the root of all orderly living, and of the righteousness which, innate in the moral sense, is made perfect by thought and by self-discipline: all that would give us a noble human being is gone. What is left for them . . . comes to pleasure, self-seeking, the grudge of any share with one's fellows, the pursuit of advantage" (1956:2.9.15).

> This school, in fact, is convicted by its neglect of all mention of virtue: any discussion of such matters is missing utterly: we are not told what virtue is or under what different kinds it appears; there is no word of all the numerous and noble reflections upon it that have come down to us from the ancients; we do not learn what constitutes it or how it is acquired, how the Soul is tended, how it is

cleaned. For to say "Look to God" is not helpful without some in-
struction as to what this looking imports: it might very well be said
that one can "look" and still sacrifice no pleasure, still be the slave
of impulse, repeating the word "God" but held in the grip of every
passion and making no effort to master any. Virtue, advancing to-
wards the Term and, linked with thought, occupying a soul, makes
God manifest: "God" on the lips without a good conduct of life, is
a word. (Ibid.)

The charge, then, concerns a refusal to cultivate a hierarchy of excellences to
bring the soul into harmony with the divine. Without virtues "setting bound
and measure to our desires and to our entire sensibility, and dispelling false
judgement" (1.2.2), self-control is impossible. The Gnostics, denigrating the
world order, must therefore be immoralists.

But one must consider the problem of desire from a Gnostic viewpoint
to see why moral law is a mistaken solution. With the fall into the negative,
fullness is equated with completeness, and incompleteness is concomitantly
felt as a deficiency or lack to be filled. On this terrain desire seeks fullness
through external objects, making the flesh a site of envy and lust. Once the
divine element within the human soul has been separated from the Pleroma and imprisoned in the material world, with the consequent rise of error,
ignorance, and oblivion, humans assume an animal nature. They seek fullness in material goods, moving from one desire to another: "And he goes the
ways of the desire of every passion. He swims in the desires of life and has
sunk. To be sure, he thinks that he finds profit when he does all the things
which are without profit" (*Teach. Silv.*, NHL 7.4.90.3–9). *The Exegesis on the
Soul* describes the soul's journey to the world and how it is defiled by "men
of great flesh . . . receiving bread from them, as well as wine, oil, clothing, and
the other external nonsense surrounding the body—the things she [the soul]
thinks she needs" (*NHL* 2.6.130.21–28). Similarly, *The Book of Thomas the
Contender* describes the ignorant as those "with a bitterness of the bondage
of lust for those visible things that will decay and change and swerve by impulse" (*NHL* 2.7.140.33–34). In *The Gospel of Thomas* Jesus counsels his followers: "There was a rich man who had much money. He said, 'I shall put
my money to use so that I may sow, reap, plant, and fill my storehouse with
produce, with the result that I shall lack nothing.' Such were his intentions,
but that same night he died. Let him who has ears hear" (*NHL* 2.2.44.2–10).
Such statements hardly look libertine or nihilistic. But if restraint is not
established through a moral law or the cultivation of virtue, how is ethical
behavior attained? It is not that infinite desire must be tempered by limits—

desire seems boundless only because no object can ever bring completeness. But fullness does not come from completeness, and so the search for limits only recreates the same error of the negative. What is instead required is gnosis—the fugitive experience of excess within the self.

One is counseled to "light the light within you" (*Teach. Silv., NHL* 7.4.106.14) because "the kingdom is inside of you, and it is outside of you. When you come to know yourselves, then you will become known, and you will realize that it is you who are the sons of the living father" (*Gos. Thomas, NHL* 2.2.32.25–33.2). Gnosis is not a rationally based self-knowledge[32] but a spiritual sensibility resting on ecstatic experience and an appreciation of the nature of origins and energies flowing beneath consciousness (see Filoramo 1990:32, 38–46; Jonas 1970:165–66). Put differently, gnosis is an experience of the singular-multiple event. It is a sense of the internal difference and distance from oneself and of "an activity that is at rest and silent" (*Allog., NHL* 11.3.53.33–35) within the self but also of the interrelationality of the self and its connection with the divine: "[He has come to] know [the Son of Man], that [is, he has come to] know [himself. This] is the perfect life, [that] man know [himself] by means of the All" (*Testim. Truth, NHL* 9.3.36.23–27). Self-knowledge is thus also knowledge of the Father as the principle of production, individuation, and dispersion. But this knowledge is always revealed only indirectly: "Truth did not come into the world naked, but it came in types and images. The world will not receive truth in any other way" (*Gos. Phil., NHL* 2.3.67.9–12). Because it is extrarational, it is both comprehensible and incomprehensible (see *Teach. Silv., NHL* 7.4.99.29–102.7), and paradoxically it is known only through ignorance: "If you should know him, be ignorant of him. . . . Do not [know] him, for it is impossible; but if by means of an enlightened thought you should know him, be ignorant of him" (*Allog., NHL* 11.3.59.30–32). It is always disclosed as that which is truly hidden: "This is the way it is: it is revealed to him alone, not hidden in the darkness and the night, but hidden in a perfect day and a holy light" (*Gos. Phil., NHL* 2.3.86.15–18). To achieve gnosis is to find repose in the Father, but this rest is a state of wakefulness compared with the oblivious condition of actual life (see, for example, *Gos. Truth, NHL* 1.3).

The ethical promise of gnosis is that recognition of the divine within the self will temper lustful desire: "When you will care for it, will request of it that you remain pure, and will become self-controlled in your soul and body, you will become a throne of wisdom and one belonging to God's household" (*Teach. Silv., NHL* 7.4.92.2–8). Care of the self both follows from and leads to a form of fullness that is not one of completeness. The experience of excess cannot be cultivated through a moral philosophy that seeks the good life through virtues developed so that an individual is complete and lacking in nothing. It is not surprising that certain Gnostic sects encouraged experimental modes in living that Irenaeus, for example, condemns as immoral[33] or that Valentinian Christians would incense orthodox leaders by accepting a wide variety of divergent ethical positions within their single sect (Pagels 1988:70–72).

Self-control does not come from asceticism, because one learns to lead a pure life from gnosis, not the reverse. Oblique references to the orthodox Church accuse it of relying on ascetic rituals instead of gnosis to attain salvation: "Jesus said to them, 'If you fast, you will give rise to sin for yourselves; and if you pray, you will be condemned; and if you give alms, you will do harm to your spirits. When you go into any land and walk about in the districts, if they receive you, eat what they will set before you, and heal the sick among them. For what goes into your mouth will not defile you, but that which issues from your mouth—it is that which will defile you'" (*Gos. Thomas, NHL* 2.2.35.15–27). Seeking purification through external acts, asceticism fails to attack the heart of the problem of desire—its mistaken understanding of deficiency—and promises a false salvation to those willing to martyr themselves.

> The foolish—thinking [in] their heart [that] if they confess, "We are Christians," in word only (but) not with power, while giving themselves over to ignorance, to a human death, not knowing where they are going nor who Christ is, thinking that they will live, when they are (really) in error—Hasten towards the principalities and the authorities. They fall into their clutches because of the ignorance that is in them. For (if) only words which bear testimony were effecting salvation, the whole world would endure this thing [and] would be saved. [But it is in this way that they drew] error to themselves. [. . . they do] not [know] that they [will destroy] themselves. If the [Father were to] desire a human sacrifice, he would become [vainglorious]. (*Test. Truth, NHL* 9.3.31.22–32.21)

The result is that ascetic Christians, because they neither "seek after God" nor "inquire about their dwelling-place, which exists in rest," become "more wicked than the pagans," and "if they find someone else who asks about his salvation, their hardness of heart sets to work upon that man. And if he does not stop asking, they kill him by their cruelty, thinking that they have done a good thing for themselves" (*Authoritative Teaching, NHL* 6.3.33.5–25). "On account of his senselessness, then, he is worse than a pagan, for the pagans know the way to go to their stone temple, which will perish, and they worship their idol, while their hearts are set on it because it is their hope" (6.3.34.10–17). These senseless men weary themselves, having learned to "seek and inquire about the ways [they] should go, since there is nothing else that is as good as this thing" (6.3.34.20–23). But the rational soul has "learned about God" (6.3.35.2). Such a soul has learned not a set of practices but rather gnosis—not a morality but an ethical sensibility.

In this way, the Gnostic survives upon a groundless ground. It is by affirming not limits but an immanent excess transgressing and annihilating boundaries that positive ethical practices can develop. The heretic is therefore not one who threatens to destroy unity and bring about nihilism but rather one who locates the ressentiment and nihilism underpinning the demand for unity. In this way, the Gnostic heretic develops thought in the direction of a philosophy of difference.

5. Reason and Faith: Aquinas, Duns Scotus, and Ockham

> You see what it was that really triumphed over the Christian
> god: Christian morality itself, the concept of truthfulness that was
> understood ever more rigorously, the father confessor's refinement
> of the Christian conscience, translated and sublimated into a
> scientific conscience, into intellectual cleanliness at any price.
> Looking at nature as if it were proof of the goodness and
> governance of a god; interpreting history in honor of some divine
> reason, as a continual testimony of a moral world order and
> ultimate moral purposes.
>
> —Friedrich Nietzsche, *The Gay Science*

As is well known, the reintroduction of Aristotle's full corpus to the Latin West fomented a crisis in both philosophy and theology, challenging the command that the latter held over the former. For those who were not resigned to stand solely on either reason or faith, the task was to develop a new fusion of pagan philosophy and Christian doctrine. This fusion needed to recognize the independence of each but still retain the fundamental unity of knowledge. The truths of reason could therefore not conflict with those of Scripture. Aquinas registers this requirement by insisting that there cannot be two separate truths; rather, a hierarchy must place one over the other, so that reason brings humans toward divine truth, which nevertheless is reached only through grace.

Although the truth of the Christian faith exceeds the capacity of human reason, truths that reason is fitted by nature to know cannot be contrary to the truth of faith. The things that reason is fitted by nature to know are clearly most true, and it would be impossible to think of them as false. It is also wrong to think that something that is held by faith could be false since it is clearly confirmed by God. Since we know by definition that what is false is contrary to the truth, it is impossible for the principles that reason knows by nature to be contrary to the truth of faith. (*Summa Contra Gentiles* 1.7, in Aquinas 1988:4)

The impossibility of confirming a precept held by faith seems not to bother Aquinas here, but it does illuminate a central dilemma both he and his successors face. The attempt to make philosophy a handmaiden of theology calls for concessions on both sides, and it becomes impossible to maintain a dual loyalty. The demand to be true to both reason and faith ultimately undermines both. Hence, as Nietzsche declares, the Christian God is killed by the Christian will to truth itself.

The distinction between reason and faith corresponds to that between finite and infinite, so that reconciling them requires linking irreducible domains of being. Here Aristotle's thought provides useful material through his discussion of the way being relates to the categories without being a common identity over them. Analogy and univocity emerge as the possible answers to the problem of the categories and are extended in one direction toward the problem of individuation and in the other toward the relation between God and his creatures. Here too difficulties arise, since analogy fails to account for individuation, while univocity threatens to demolish divine transcendence unless strict limitations are imposed. Ultimately, however, these limitations rest on the very faith that is precariously tied to and supported by reason.

Regarding both these issues, the differences between Platonist/Augustinian and Aristotelian-inspired theologies give way to a common goal of synthesis while revealing the difficulties in combining not only the philosophical schools but the differing attributes of God that each emphasizes. Aquinas, one of the first Dominicans to adopt an Aristotelian empiricist epistemology, accepts that knowledge begins with sense experience in order to proceed analogically from creatures to God. Applying a metaphysics of causality, he accounts for both divine transcendence and immanence, but only by attributing to creatures an autonomy that undermines God's absolute power over them and merely asserting safeguards that secure a deficient knowledge of the divine by making the mundane harmony of the world reflect the divine essence. Duns Scotus, a Franciscan thoroughly trained in Augustinian theology, modifies this theology in several respects to promote a harmony with Thomism while seeking to overcome the deficiencies of both schools of thought. After the Subtle Doctor's therapy, the route to God still passes through creatures, from which concepts are abstracted; now, however, its starting point is neither empirical reality nor divine illumination but a univocal concept of being, and it traces the path of an essential order designed to ensure an absolute dependence on the first cause. Nonetheless, this solution reproduces its predecessor's need to restrict divine power so as to secure some degree of rational knowledge, even as it attempts to safeguard the order reason traces by also asserting that nothing can escape divine control. Ockham uses Aristotelian logic and epistemology to sever the connection between existing individuals and the concepts through which they are cognized, razing the capacities of reason in order to reassert an Augustinian emphasis on transcendence, but this reestablishes God's omnipotence by removing the mechanisms necessary for knowledge of him, so that the synthesis of reason and faith leaves neither able to support the other. What remains, however, is the possibility of a new synthesis not subordinated to the logic of identity. Here Scotus's analysis of individuation provides the direction by locating in each being an excess that cannot be grasped by any schema of representation. This haecceity, when freed from the requirements governing Christian thought, usurps the divine ground through a movement of groundless difference.

Aquinas and the Ladder of Being

God has created a universe of diverse beings, each moving toward its end. The end of any creature is its most perfect state, or what it is at its best. In moving toward its own fulfillment, however, it simultaneously comes nearer to the perfection that is God. This progression thus suggests a hierarchy based on the degree of perfection each being can attain, providing an order that humans can trace using reason and sense knowledge to move closer to knowledge of God, although this final end is attained only with grace. Reason therefore does not conflict with faith but rather constitutes one of two ways to know about God. In this way a natural theology is possible (*Summa Contra Gentiles* 1.3, in Aquinas 1988:3).

But God is not the apex of this order of being. Rather, he transcends it, which indicates a radical difference between divine and created, such that the former cannot be known through the latter. No created thing, no matter how perfect, can be anything but infinitely distant from this Creator. It seems, then, that natural knowledge, beginning with the senses, cannot be led to this being, which remains heterogeneous with respect to any experienced being: "Our natural knowledge starts from sense-perception and reaches only as far as things so perceived can lead us, which is not far enough to see God in himself" (Aquinas 1989:29). Here, this Christianized Aristotelianism encounters a dilemma similar to that of Plato's Form of the Good. For Plato, the Forms can be known, and thus an order of physical objects can be determined based on degrees of participation. But the Form of the Forms, the Good, remains opaque, because it is not an object of knowledge but rather the source and medium for knowledge, as light is the medium for vision (see Plato 1974: 506d–511). Since knowledge of this medium would require another medium, and so on ad infinitum, the Form of the Good is unknowable, and as a result there is no basis for the order of Plato's divided line, which it supposedly orients. In the same way, there can be no grounds for establishing an order of beings according to their differing distances from a God infinitely removed from all of them. Reason should be incapable of even a deficient knowledge of God's essence, of what he is, leaving it with only a negative rather than a natural theology.

Such resignation is unacceptable: "Faith can't profess falsehood, yet it makes certain affirmations, as, for example, that God is three persons in one nature, and that he is almighty" (Aquinas 1993:228). If we say God is good, wise, and so on, these designations do not merely exclude something from him or express only that he is the source of creaturely qualities—for example, that God is good because he causes goodness in things. First, "neither view explains why certain words are not used of God: we don't say *God is a body* even though he causes bodies, and though it might be a way of denying that he is merely unformed matter" (Aquinas 1989:30). Moreover, these views fail to account for the sense intended for such claims: "People who speak of a living God want to say more than that he causes life and differs from non-living bodies" (ibid.). These propositions must be affirmative, even if they depict the divine substance inadequately. Certain words only negatively apply to God because his substance does not include them, but other words signify perfections "that he himself possesses . . . in a more excellent way" (32).

Thus, even though a discontinuity remains between the being of God and that of his creatures, the way certain predicates are affirmed of him still needs to be related to the way they are applied to worldly things. Aquinas argues that this can be accomplished through a logic of analogy drawn from Aristotle's analysis of the categories. Aristotle shows that being is not the highest genus, since it is predicated of specific differentia. Hence its universality must be understood differently from generic universality. A genus is univocal, retaining a single meaning across the differences it signifies. It can therefore be predicated only of terms that signify entirely the essences of the individuals and species classified under it, for it comprises what is common to all of them: "animal," for example, can be predicated of "man" or "Socrates" but not of terms signifying only parts of man's or Socrates' essence, such as "rational." The genus thereby contains its differentia within it, as a whole contains its parts, but is not predicated of them for the same reason that one cannot say "the part is the whole." These parts, however, are predicated of other genera—"rational," for example, is predicated as a quality—that are incommensurable with the first genus. Similarly, "body" belongs in one sense to the category of "substance" and in another to "quantity" (see Aquinas 1968:2.6–8). These terms thus exhibit an equivocation that is not resolved by a higher commonality, and so being, as their common predicate, cannot have the same sense or meaning when predicated of them. It must be not univocal but equivocal.

But being is also not homonymous. It is more than a common name whose various meanings are unconnected, such as the word *dog*, which signifies both a barking animal and a star.[1] In each case being evokes an understanding that includes, for example, the law of noncontradiction: nothing can both be and not be at the same time and under the same relation. Hence Aquinas maintains that *being* is an analogical term whose different modes are proportional to one another. Such a ratio is evident between substance and the other categories, for the latter are accidents whose being is sustained only through the former, making their being only analogous to that of substance. Similarly, a relation exists between God and his creatures, since the latter are effects of his power, so that every creature, being marked by its creator as the source of its being, maintains a deficient resemblance to God, although God need not resemble his creations: "And this is how everything that receives existence from God resembles him; precisely as existing it resembles the primary universal source of all existence. . . . But we would not say that God resembles creatures. *Mutual likeness obtains between things of the same order but not between cause and effect,* as pseudo-Denys says: a portrait can take after a man but a man does not take after his portrait" (Aquinas 1989:17–18).[2] The statements "God is" and "the world is" are equivocal and invoke different senses of being, since there is an infinite distance between God and his creation, and hence God's essence remains opaque. Nevertheless, some relation must obtain between the divine and the worldly, and so a pure equivocation cannot arise between the attributes affirmed of each. Aquinas thereby understands analogy as a middle between the extremes of commonality and indifference: "Words are used analogically of God and creatures, not purely equivocally and not purely univocally" (1993:225).

Through analogy it is possible to trace an attribute to its created perfection so as to assert it of God: "To affirm thus of God the perfections of creatures, but according to a mode that eludes us, is to be between the purely univocal and purely equivocal. Signs and effects of God, the perfections of things are not what God Himself is; but God Himself is, in an infinitely higher mode, what things are" (Gilson 1994:107). Wisdom, for example, is a perfection of creatures; God is wise, although in a radically different way—his wisdom is not an attribute, for his substance is simple. Analogy always contains this proviso, for one applies predicates to God even while recognizing that the traits in question remain unknowable in their divine form. Linking heterogeneous beings in an ontological hierarchy makes the analogy of being a metaphysical one rather than a logical analogy of attribution, in which a trait is held intrinsically by only one thing even though the intellect ascribes it to others—for example, we properly apply the word *healthy* to animals, but we also use it to describe medicine, which causes health, and urine, which can indicate health (Aquinas 1989:32)—or a physical analogy of inequality, in which beings intrinsically share the same trait in the same mode but differ in the degree of perfection: "Men and dogs, for example, are *equally* animals but they are not *equal* animals" (Phelan 1948:18).[3] This does not quite enable positive and essential knowledge of God, and Aquinas repeatedly denies such a possibility. Nonetheless, it does promise to go beyond a meager negative knowledge of the divine: "We cannot grasp what God is, but what He is not, and the relation other things have with Him" (Aquinas, in Gilson 1994:107).

It is now necessary to determine the criteria by which one being is ranked over another to compose this ladder of being. In doing so, the attributes to be analogically said of God cannot be assumed, for these are the conclusions of natural theology, not its axioms. It may be possible, however, to establish the standards on the basis of rationalist proofs for the existence of God— deriving what can be said of God from the fact that he is.[4] This is the role of Aquinas's five proofs in the second question of the *Summa Theologiae*. Sense knowledge makes evident that things change, moving from potentiality to actuality. No potential being, however, can cause its own actualization, so it must be moved by another thing; and this mover, if it is a changing being, must be moved by yet another. If the series were to continue forever, there would be no first cause of change. There must therefore be a first mover that is unmoved. Similarly, there must be a first efficient cause that is not caused, and a being that is necessary and not contingent, for if every being need not be, there must have been a time when there was nothing, but then no movement from nonbeing to being could be possible. The cause of a quality is that which holds the quality most fully—fire for example, is hottest, and therefore makes everything else hot—and so there must be some being that causes in all other things their being, goodness, and other perfections. Finally, all things tend toward an end or a goal, and if they lack awareness, they must be directed by something else. Nature, therefore, must be guided toward its goals by a being with understanding, and this being is God.

Aristotle's prime mover is an eternal motor force, but its causal power is not sequential. For Aristotle, time is infinite and formless matter is uncreated, so that the first cause is neither the first in a temporal sequence nor responsible for an absolute genesis. But Aquinas dissents.[5] Just as an analysis of movement indicates something outside all possible change, so too does it imply a power beyond all that is observed in nature. The ancient principle that nothing can come from nothing is "a general conception or opinion of natural philosophers because the agents they observe in nature act by causing change, and that needs a subject capable of changing. But . . . an agent outside nature doesn't need this" (Aquinas 1993:254–55). The capacities of an agent are determined by "the way it has actual existence" (253). A natural substance, composed with formed matter, is not fully actual but instead mixed with potentiality and furthermore does not contain every perfection within it. Such an agent "doesn't produce being without qualification but determines already existent being in this or that way" (254). Given an analogical relation between divine and natural, any being that exists without qualification is capable of producing without qualification and so can create ex nihilo.[6] God is therefore not simply a first cause existing simultaneously with those lesser causes beneath it; rather, he is prior to both them and the temporality in which they exist (265–68). This proves not that the world and time were created but only that this degree of omnipotence is attributable to God, which is sufficient at least to provide a rational opposition to Aristotle's position on the infinite duration of the world and move the question into the realm of faith.

From experience, then, it is possible to derive a being that is not caused or moved by another. It is eternal, unqualified, and therefore necessary, with eternity understood as existing as a simultaneous whole, without succession or parts (Aquinas 1989:23–24). The hierarchy of existence is oriented toward these traits. For example, those beings whose conditions of causality are more internal to them are more perfect: "Different kinds of things produce in different ways, those on a higher level producing in a more interior way" (Aquinas 1993:115). In the order of substances, "a wonderful linkage of things can be seen, for the lowest member of a higher classification (*genus*) is always found just above the highest member of a lower classification" (*Summa Contra Gentiles* 2.68, in Aquinas 1988:5). One can thus move from non-living bodies, which produce only by affecting other bodies and only when other bodies first move them; to plant life, which is capable of self-motion but produces something external to it (a fruit or seed); to animals capable of self-awareness but only of an external world; to humans, who can achieve self-reflection, although this still begins with sense knowledge of an external world; to angels, who have a purely internal self-reflection; and finally to God, whose existence is nothing but his infinite self-understanding (Aquinas 1993:115–17).[7]

Similarly, one can base an order on the composition or simplicity of essence. A composite substance, made of form and matter, is susceptible to classification into a species or genus through intellectual operations of abstraction that provide its intelligibility. Its existence correspondingly resides in the realm of becoming, and it moves from potency to the actualization of a nature common to itself and others of its species. Immaterial substances—human souls and angelic intellects—are incapable of such categorization because their essences cannot be signified in parts,[8] so that each is unique: "In these substances we cannot find many individuals in the same species; there are as many species among them as there are individuals" (Aquinas 1968:4.5). Further, by virtue of their incorporeality, intelligences have greater actuality and less potentiality than do composite beings. Nevertheless, they are not without potency and so are not absolutely simple: "There is in them a composition of form and being" (4.2). In other words, the essence (ens) of these substances does not necessitate their existence, or act-of-being (esse), nor can it provide them with existence, for then they would be the cause of themselves. It follows that even an incorporeal substance has its existence caused through another, producing a series that must ultimately refer back to a being in which, by virtue of being uncaused, its essence and existence are not distinct.[9]

This line of thought establishes a correspondence between the natural and divine, such that the diversity of the former refers back to the simplicity and unity of the latter. Every creature, as an effect of God, maintains a resemblance to him. The multiplicity of natural ends follows therefrom: "The perfect goodness that exists one and unbroken in God can exist in creatures only in a multitude of fragmented ways. Now variety in things comes from the different forms determining their species. So because of their goal things differ in form" (Aquinas 1993:271). The order of these forms demonstrates God's providence. Although the reasons behind God's will are inscrutable, for he is bound neither to create the universe nor to establish it in this particular form, it is evident that there are such reasons.

> God must love his own goodness, but from this it doesn't follow
> necessarily that creatures must exist to express it, since God's good-
> ness is perfect without that. So the coming to be of creatures, though
> it finds its first reason in God's goodness, nevertheless depends on
> a simple act of God's will. Given, however, that God does will to

share his goodness with creatures as far as that is possible by way of resemblance, then that gives the reason for the variety of creatures. But it doesn't necessitate this or that measure of perfection or this or that number of things. Given, however, that God by an act of will decides on this number of things and that measure of perfection for each thing, then that gives the reason for it having such a form and such matter. And so on in the same way down the list. . . . Clearly then the dispositions of providence have their reasons, but reasons that presuppose God's will. (274)

Providence does not mean that God wills every event in the cosmos; rather, it indicates that everything that happens has its ultimate source in God's will. Some things happen necessarily, and others by chance, but necessity and contingency are modes of being established by God (277–84). It is fallacious to assert either that arbitrary will, not reason, governs the universe or that this will determines all things, leaving no room for contingency or freedom. Nature operates in its own sphere, and each thing moves toward its distinctive telos, but its source is a being that transcends it. For natures of the higher orders, however, a return to this source is possible. This return would be a supernatural end, attained only through supernatural means.

Humankind thus has both a natural and a spiritual end. The first is the good life attainable on earth, and the second is everlasting bliss. Since "as ultimate goal we pursue what so fulfils our desire as to leave nothing else to be desired," and because "a drive of nature can't be pointless" (Aquinas 1989:174, 111), the natural human telos identified by Aristotle points to a higher, Christian end. The two are related insofar as God's grace does not destroy or undermine what nature achieves but instead perfects it. The pagan politics and ethics of virtue can thus be incorporated as a set of worldly goods remaining subordinate to theology.

Reason is therefore an important but insufficient capacity for the attainment of human ends. By pointing to a source beyond its capacities, however, it both justifies its own relevance and carves out room for faith as its supplement. Pagan philosophy can therefore be assimilated into Christian thought as long as it knows its limitations: "It is useful for the human mind to exercise its powers of reasoning, however weak, in this way provided that there is no presumption that it can comprehend or demonstrate [the substance of the divine]" (*Summa Contra Gentiles* 1.8, Aquinas 1988:5). Concomitantly, Christian theology can make a claim to an initial foundation in reason. Knowledge and belief thereby buttress each other, even while retaining their differences. Reason remains a superior cognitive faculty, whereas faith realizes a higher truth. Neither can convert the other to its form, but both act in harmony to develop each to its fullest (see Gilson 1994:15–25).

Nevertheless, this solution is problematic, for the rationalist project of partially tracing the ladder of being begins with a faith that the created universe exhibits a hierarchical order that can lead to partial knowledge of the divine. Herein lies the significance of the well-known criticism that Aquinas's five proofs are not demonstrations at all, since, to be convincing, they presuppose a belief in God. The absence of this conviction imperils the attempt to locate in nature an imperfect sign of God.

Gilson here poignantly notes the concession necessary for the Thomistic synthesis of faith and reason: "Looked at from within, St. Thomas's metaphysics seems . . . to extol a God whose principle attribute is not power, but goodness" (1994:183). This move is necessary to maintain a certain "right of creatures." Although all things seek to return to God, this is a move no less toward their own perfection than to the divine, and for this reason, one must never consider God the sole cause of becoming—the power of the secondary causes of nature must also be respected: "We must hold firmly to two apparently contradictory truths. God does whatever creatures do; and yet creatures themselves do whatever they do" (182). Aquinas tries to resolve this antinomy with the assurance that in creating beings with their own power, God glorifies himself by expressing his own excellence in that of his work. This, in turn, benefits faith by enabling it to find support through reason.

> If no philosophy was so constantly busy safeguarding the rights of creatures, it is because it saw in this the one means of safeguarding the rights of God. Far from encroaching upon the Creator's privileges, the perfections attributed to second causes can only increase His glory, since He is their first cause and since this is a new occasion for glorifying Him. It is because there is causality in nature that we can go back step by step to the first cause, God. In a universe stripped of second causes the most obvious proofs of the existence of God would remain impossible, and His highest metaphysical attributes would remain hidden from us. (184)

Yet it is also central to Thomism that God's glory be already sufficient unto itself and incapable of increase. It therefore cannot necessitate a subordination of one principle of faith (divine omnipotence) to another (benevolence). To refuse this maneuver will have significant consequences, as Ockham makes clear.

Duns Scotus and Univocal Being

For Aquinas, analogy is germane to the realm of judgment. In Aristotelian terms judgment is a form of understanding based on complex propositions such as "Socrates is white." Nevertheless, judgment, which assigns predicates to a subject—or quasi attributes in the case of the divine, since a purely simple being does not admit such an act of predication—refers back to apprehension as simple knowledge of being, and here there is no room for analogy: between the statements "God is [a being]" and "Socrates is [a being]" there can be only univocity or equivocity. Aquinas here accepts equivocity, maintaining that reason can demonstrate God's existence and analogically ascribe certain attributes to him but that the divine being remains opaque. This move functions on the division between essence and existence, and it forces Aquinas to admit that his demonstrations of God's existence do not live up to strict Aristotelian standards for demonstrative proof, which require a definition of the thing in question—that is, its essence—as a middle term in its syllogism. Aquinas maintains that Aristotle's requirement applies only when one argues from cause to effect, not from effect back to cause, where "the central link is not what the cause is (since we cannot even ask what a thing is until we know that it exists) but what the name of the cause is used to mean" (Aquinas 1989:12). To this Duns Scotus replies: "There is no point in distinguishing between a knowledge of His essence and a knowledge of His existence. . . . For I never know anything to exist unless I first have some concept of that of which existence is affirmed" (1987:16).

If attribution refers back to apprehension, then "we must look beyond all our ideas of attributes or quasi-attributes, in order to find a quidditative concept to which the former may be attributed" (Dun Scotus 1987:19). Here both analogy and equivocity fall into hopeless contradictions. If two separate concepts of being are ascribed to God and creatures, then it is impossible for one to be known through the other, and even if they are analogically related, "they are conceived as distinct either prior to or simultaneously with the comparison, and therefore they are not perceived as one concept" (21–22). Analogy certainly has a role to play in describing the relation of creatures to a God heterogeneous to them but serving as their common measure. But an analogical relation can be drawn only between two things that are already known and so complemented by a prior moment of univocity. It is therefore necessary to assert that being is a univocal concept if there is to be any natural knowledge of God.

Thus, against Thomists, who start with physical reality and proceed analogically up toward God, and Augustinians, who begin with God and descend analogically to creatures, Scotus maintains that a univocal concept of being qua being is the first object of the intellect.[10] Philosophy and theology thus overlap in metaphysics, which includes God within its purview, although, unlike theology, it does not make him its prime subject (Harris 1927: vol. 1, pp. 86–87). The univocal being of metaphysics "purdures in every object" as the "condition for the possibility of knowing objects in general" (Heidegger 1978:30). It signifies no commonality between God and creatures except insofar as both really exist and thereby arises from neither one nor the other but is instead the conceptual apparatus by which both can be known. Univocation designates a concept "which possesses sufficient unity in itself, so that to affirm and deny it of one and the same thing would be a contradiction. It also has sufficient unity to serve as the middle term of a syllogism, so that wherever two extremes are united by a middle term that is one in this way, we may conclude to the union of the two extremes among themselves" (Duns Scotus 1987:20). Univocal being is a quidditative concept, meaning that it is predicated *in quid,* signifying the entire essence of the subject it predicates. It therefore applies specifically to substances—to anything about which we can ask, "What is it?" with the answer ultimately being, "It is a being"—and so is predicated in common of both created and uncreated essences. There are, of course, other senses of being, for it is not predicated *in quid* either of specific or individual differentia or of accidental attributes. Nevertheless, although no one sense of being is common to all that is intelligible (4), Scotus holds the quidditative concept to be primary in two senses. The first is a direct primacy applied to all substances, which otherwise need share nothing in common. The second is a virtual primacy, whereby the other senses of being—*in quale* predications, which are modifications or qualifications of essence (see Wolter 1946:90–98)—are not included in or reducible to the quidditative concept but nonetheless refer to it through adherence to substances: they fall under the umbrella of substance, which has the power (*virtus*) to give them being.

Hence, all to which "being" is not univocal *in quid* are included in those to which "being" is univocal in this way. And so it is clear that "being" has a primacy of commonness in regard to the primary intelligibles, that is, to the quidditative concepts of the genera, species, individuals, and all their essential parts, and to the Uncreated Being. It has a virtual primacy in regard to the intelligible elements included in the first intelligibles, that is, in regard to the qualifying concepts of the ultimate differences and proper attributes. (Duns Scotus 1987:4)[11]

The being exceeding that given to the intellect can therefore be known not through an asserted analogy to what it exceeds but rather through a concept common to both: "In this life already, a man can be certain in his mind that God is a being and still be in doubt whether He is a finite or an infinite being, a created or an uncreated being. Consequently, the concept of 'being' as affirmed of God is different from the other two concepts but is included in both of them and therefore is univocal" (20).[12]

The univocity of being is not generic but rather indifferent. It is a transcendental, applying to both finite and infinite being without invoking an identity over them, whereas the univocity of the genus characterizes the ten categories and so applies solely to finite being: "Hence the Philosopher, in *III Metaphysics* [ch. 3, 998b22–27], does not show that being is not a genus because of any equivocation, but because it has a greater commonness and univocation than the commonness of a genus" (Duns Scotus, in Prentice 1970:54). Having established the status of being in this way, that of other concepts follows. Predicates that are similarly indifferent to the division of finite and infinite are also univocal and can be affirmatively said of God, or of God and some or all of his creatures, without invoking a generic unity and without requiring an analogical relation between the two beings.

> Whatever pertains to "being," then, in so far as it remains indifferent to finite and infinite, or as proper to the Infinite Being, does not belong to it as determined to a genus, but prior to any such determination, and therefore as transcendental outside any genus. Whatever [predicates] are common to God and creatures are of such kind, pertaining as they do to being in its indifference to what is infinite and finite. For in so far as they pertain to God they are infinite, whereas in so far as they belong to creatures they are finite. They belong to "being," then, prior to the division into the ten genera. Anything of this kind, consequently, is transcendental. (Duns Scotus 1987:2)

Such transcendentals need not be predicated of all things. It is sufficient that they are not subsumed by a genus: "Not to have any predicate above it except 'being' pertains to the very notion of a transcendental. That it be common to many inferior notions, however, is purely incidental" (3). From this, three classes of transcendentals can be derived. The first contains goodness, unity, and truth, which are convertible with being and thus certainly univocal, although they are not as primordial as being and function as its quasi properties.[13] The second class comprises disjunctive binaries such as necessary/possible or act/potency, which as pairs extend across the finite/infinite divide and so are coextensive with being. Even though one member of each pair, such as necessary or uncreated, properly applies only to infinite being, the statement "all beings are either necessary or contingent" applies to infinite and finite beings without establishing an identity over them.

The third group established by the principle of indifference consists of pure perfections that can be predicated of both God and some or all of his creatures but whose capacity for modal differentiation prevents these perfections from establishing an identity between them. Perfections such as wisdom and potency can exist in an infinite mode and in doing so express a plurality of formal distinctions within the divine essence that in no way compromises its absolute simplicity; in their finite modes, they apply to creatures according to varying degrees of intensity. These perfections, Scotus holds, differ qualitatively and heterogeneously but are nonetheless said univocally of the different beings they predicate, because their sense is modified only by the initial division of being into infinite and finite. Further, being itself is said univocally across their modal differentiations, because the infinite/finite division that separates them is not an external or quidditative difference that divides them into distinct types the way differentia divide a genus into species (see Gilson 1955:456–57; Harris 1927: vol. 2, pp. 64–68). The theological upshot of this is that one can say "God is wise" and "Socrates is wise" without invoking an identity between God and Socrates but also without wisdom's being said equivocally, even though God's infinite wisdom eludes human comprehension. "And so 'wisdom,' or anything else, for that matter, which is common to God and creatures, can be transcendental. A transcendental, however, may also be predicated of God alone, or again it may be predicated about God and some creature. It is not necessary, then, that a transcendental as transcendental be predicated of every being, unless it be coextensive with the first of the transcendentals, namely 'being'" (Duns Scotus 1987:3).

There is thus an alternative to the being of analogy, although it is based on nothing more than an asserted certainty that we can have natural knowledge of God. Further, since analogy is essentially a hierarchical conception, while univocity is not, the latter requires new methods to establish an order that reason can trace to move closer to the divine. In addition, these strategies bear limited scope and power because certain advantages gained from the analogical conception must be ruled out. Most important, God's power of absolute genesis cannot be derived through an analogy from the productive power of a qualified being to that of an unqualified one. The infinite and intrinsic perfection that such power implies cannot be inferred from the eternity of the first mover, for the perfection of a thing is not based on its duration (Duns Scotus 1987:63). Nor can it be deduced from the power to produce an infinity of effects when having infinite time to generate them. Even granting that this agent could accomplish an infinity of effects simultaneously,[14] it would be truly infinite only if it could cause these effects immediately and totally. But this degree of power does not follow from the need for a prime mover to prevent an infinite regress of causes, for this necessity does not indicate that the prime mover could bypass the intermediate causes to generate an effect on its own (62–65). Finally, even a capacity to create ex nihilo implies not an infinite power but rather one corresponding to the degree of perfection of the created thing. Since no being can confer more than it has, from a produced effect one can infer only an equal degree of being for its cause, not a greater degree, and no created being is infinitely perfect.[15] The Christian understanding of omnipotence can therefore be only an article of faith. It is possible to demonstrate God's absolute knowledge of all that can be produced from his status as the first efficient cause (68–70), but in terms of productive power, all that can be established is a formal infinity in the manner of a Plotinian model of emanation, in which secondary causes are immediately responsible for all beyond the first produced effect (178–79n.33).

This limitation, however, means that the power of secondary causes must be considered when deriving the existence and character of God. But doing this requires a more refined attitude toward causation. The divine may be understood as the first member of two essential orders, one of eminence and one of dependence. In an order of eminence, the prior is more perfect than the posterior. An order of dependence is one of cause and effect, in which the posterior cannot exist without the prior, although the prior can exist in itself without contradiction.[16] The unity of these two orders, whereby what is prior in terms of causality is also more perfect, requires that the series be essentially rather than accidentally ordered.[17] Among essentially ordered (*per se*) causes, the second cause depends on the first for its act of causation; with accidentally ordered causes (*per accidens*), the second may depend on the first for its existence, but not its causal power. The relation of a father and son is an incidental or accidental one, for the son owes his existence to his father but can act on his own after his father's death. Both are essentially ordered to the sun, however, since it is the source of energy making possible all life. Similarly, an efficient cause is essentially ordered to a final cause, for without the latter the former's action is impossible—an agent is moved to act by an end. Moreover, the formal and material causes are ordered to the efficient and final, since the former two lack sufficient efficacy to provide the unity of their composition, and hence they both refer to causes extrinsic to the thing moved (Duns Scotus 1966:2.9–34). As indicated by these examples, with essentially ordered causes the prior "is of another nature and order, inasmuch as the higher cause is more perfect . . . since no cause in the exercise of its causality is essentially dependent upon a cause of the same nature as itself, for to produce anything one cause of a given kind suffices" (Duns Scotus 1987:41). Further, an essentially ordered cause must exist simultaneously with its effect, because the latter relies on the former for its causal force. This need not be the case in accidentally ordered series, however. Only with essentially ordered causes is it possible to construct a scale of perfection leading toward God as an ultimate source, heterogeneous to all his effects and so equivocal in cause, although still univocal in being. But this ontological order is not a temporal sequence. Indeed, although it can be shown that a temporal order necessarily relies on an essential order culminating in a first cause, nothing logically prevents a temporal series from being infinite.[18]

From all this Scotus deduces God's triple primacy as first efficient cause, highest end, and most perfect being. All other agents refer to prior efficient causes for their own capacities to act but ultimately to an agent that is simply first. That nothing can come from nothing implies that what comes into being must be moved by another with the power to cause effectively. If there is no order among these beings, "then this nature capable of causing does not cause in virtue of some other cause, and even if we assume that in one individual it is caused, nevertheless in some other it will not be caused" (Duns Scotus 1987:44). Denying an essential order therefore leads to the conclusion that at least one uncaused cause exists; if such an order obtains, however, then each cause is contingent on another for its efficiency, which leads to either an infinite regress or, again, a first efficient cause. Unlike the first cause of a temporal order, which is part of its sequence, the first efficient cause must lie outside the series. If it were part of its chain of effects, it would be the cause of its own efficacy and so would paradoxically come before itself: "The series as a whole, then, is dependent on something which does not pertain to the group that is caused, and this I call the first efficient cause. Even if the group of beings caused were infinite, they would still depend upon something outside the group" (42). Nonetheless, the nature of an essential order means the series cannot be infinite, for this would indicate an infinite number of causes existing simultaneously to produce an effect, which is absurd (ibid.). An infinity of accidentally ordered causes—say, from parent to child across an eternity of generations—is possible, but not without presupposing an eternal and static essentially ordered series standing above it, for "no change of form is perpetuated save in virtue of something permanent which is not a part of the succession."

> And the reason for this is that everything of this succession which is in flux, is of the same nature and no part thereof can be coexistent with the entire series for the simple reason that it would no longer be a part of the latter. Something essentially prior to the series then exists, for everything that is part of the succession depends upon it, and this dependence is of a different order from that by which it depends upon the immediately preceding cause where the latter is part of the succession. . . . Indeed, to deny the essential order is to deny the accidental order also, since accidents do not have any order save in virtue of what is fixed and permanent. (43)

The actual existence of the first cause follows from its unconditional nature: if it did not exist, it could not be brought into being either by itself or another; if another could bring it into existence, it would no longer be God. Yet it must exist by virtue of the impossibility of an infinity of essentially ordered causes. It therefore has not merely possible but necessary existence (48).[19]

The existence of a highest final cause is derived similarly and is additionally based on the essential order of the four causes. The formal and material causes are less perfect than the efficient and final causes because they are part of an entity moved by another (see Duns Scotus 1987:45–46). A *per se* efficient cause, in turn, is moved by its end, and whatever exists as an effect must be ordered toward such an end.[20] But the first efficient cause cannot be moved by an end above it. It therefore can act only for itself, and, being the ultimate end, it must be the most eminent: "Now the first efficient cause does not act primarily or ultimately for the sake of anything distinct from itself; hence, it must act for itself as an end; therefore, the first efficient cause is the ultimate end. . . . The first efficient cause is not a univocal cause with reference to the other efficient causes but rather an equivocal cause. Such a cause, therefore, is more excellent and noble than they. Consequently, the first efficient cause is the most excellent" (49). As an agent acting toward an end, the first cause is also a voluntary and intellectual will. An efficient cause acting solely of necessity cannot propose an end to itself in order to move toward it and so must depend on a prior agent consciously moved by such an end, but there can be no agent prior to God. His essence is therefore nothing other than his self-knowledge and volition, for he is moved only by himself. His knowledge extends to a full understanding of all its effects, for there is no higher agent with such knowledge for which he would act. Precisely because he is not moved necessarily, he must cause voluntarily and contingently.

Divine infinity is not extensive, for if it were, God could not coexist with a multitude of other, finite beings. Nonetheless, no second infinite and necessary being can exist. First, if two such beings existed, neither would be able to know the other, for the knowledge of a being's essence is prior to its existence and this would place the knowing God above its counterpart. But the ignorance of each to the other would also compromise the infinity of both. This problem cannot be resolved by each knowing the other through the similarity between them, for then it would be a general and not perfect knowledge (Duns Scotus 1987:85–86). Second, similar reasons require a single infinite will, goodness, and power, since the existence of a second would limit the first. Third, because the infinity of such a being necessitates its existence, if more than one were possible, these others would have to exist, too; since there is no essential limit to the number of individuals of any species, an infinite number of gods would result. Finally, if there were two necessary beings, then they would be necessary either by virtue of what they had in common or on the basis of their differences. If their necessity rested on their shared nature, then they would not be necessary, for each would include extraneous elements (their differentia); if it rested on their differences as well as their shared nature,[21] then each being would be necessary by virtue of two things, so that if one were removed, it would paradoxically still be necessary (88–89). Moreover, since nothing can be essentially ordered to two ultimate ends, if two such infinite beings existed, "they would not form one universe" (52). Following Aristotle, however, Scotus holds it to be improper to introduce superfluous multiplicities.

Reason thus demonstrates not only the existence of a single first mover—on which all effects ultimately depend, either by being part of an essential order or by presupposing it—but also its perfect knowledge and voluntary will. This last trait does not undermine the certainty of God's order but rather confirms it. There is an essential order between will and intellect, the latter being prior to the former: although knowledge does not necessitate action, a voluntary act presupposes knowledge (see Bettoni 1978:82; Gilson 1955:463–64). Truth is in this way grounded prior to any arbitrary act of divine will, so that the latter is bound by conformity with divine self-knowledge. God has perfect knowledge of all essences, for their being is measured by their participation in him, and he creates them in an order that reflects his own perfection. Although humans cannot comprehend the infinite wisdom of the existing order, and God is in no way bound to it—he need not create any universe and chooses to do so from an infinity of possible ones—what he has chosen is indeed ordered fully and completely: "Even those things and events which appear to us as negligible and meaningless enter into God's absolutely perfect design and are parts of it. They are like individual notes in the immense harmony of the universe" (Bettoni 1978:164). Otherwise the will of God would manifest contradiction: willing disorder would mean that despite his own self-love, God would will that creatures turn from him.[22]

It may seem that Scotus has overcome the Thomistic choice to privilege divine benevolence over power while sustaining both the total freedom of God's will and the order that human reason can partially trace. In doing so, however, he has illicitly introduced the very point that he holds cannot be demonstrated: God's absolute omnipotence. This is implied by the way the independence of secondary causes—which was initially given in conformity with the accepted formal infinity of the first being and which was necessary to establish the existence of this first being—is evacuated in the articulation of a God who with infinite knowledge orders the world totally, allowing nothing to escape his control, once reason demonstrates his existence. The question of the creation of the world and time may be left as a matter of faith, given that a temporal sequence may conceivably be infinite, but this does nothing to diminish God's de facto mastery over all things, since the impossibility of proving total efficient causality is not allowed to create any possibility that something might escape the divine ordering. A central feature of Plotinian emanation theory, which presents the type of formal infinity Scotus holds to be rationally demonstrable, is that successive productions are ordered less and less to their first cause. But this consequence is ignored. Scotus initially denies the theological conception of God so that reason has room to operate and establish a natural theology, but he later affirms this conception within and through this natural theology to guarantee its findings. The truths of reason require an order of secondary causes that humans can trace, but it is necessary first to deny the certainty of God's absolute and immediate domination to begin this journey and then to grant it to ensure that such a hierarchy exists.[23]

The synthesis of reason and faith therefore depends on an ambiguity in this key component of Christian thought, jeopardizing the modicum of knowledge to which human reason may aspire. Although starting with a restriction on reason greater than that which Aquinas imposes, Scotus ultimately imports an assumption in its favor that is both necessary and fatal. The initial position follows not from divine goodness but rather from the impossibility of rationally demonstrating God's total domination. Strictly speaking, however, the rational undecidability concerning God's power does not justify this position over one that privileges the truths of faith tout court—

and the latter view threatens to destroy the truths of reason that Christian scholasticism seeks to incorporate.

Ockham and the Rights of Divine Omnipotence

As Ockham sees it, if his Scholastic predecessors make unjustified compromises with regard to faith, they are no less guilty of overextending the powers of reason. Specifically, they take categorical distinctions that are only products of thought and treat them as either real or formal extramental differences. The moderate realisms of Scotus and Aquinas are lesser culprits than some others, but both illegitimately separate common nature and individual difference, essence and existence, to derive hierarchies leading toward God, seeking demonstrations of his existence that also provide insight into his perfection. From a nominalist or conceptualist position insisting on the distinction between human knowledge and natural reality,[24] this is unquestionably excessive. Moreover, it is incompatible with aspects of Christian doctrine emphasizing a transcendent and mysterious being.

Against essentialist ontologies Ockham maintains that only substances and accidents exist, either individually or in aggregates. Any logical or epistemological priority of universals is irrelevant, for knowledge is easily grounded in the experience of a plurality of singulars from which concepts are abstracted: "A universal is the first object in the order of adequacy [i.e., of adequacy as object of the intellect], but not in the order of origin of cognition" (Ockham 1990:32). It is unnecessary even to posit intelligible species in order to connect intuitive cognition of individuals to abstract categories, because such categories are simply a different way of knowing the same singular things and result from habitual exposure to them.[25] Since universality is a characteristic only of signs, "the problem of individuation is effectively a logical one of showing how general terms used in propositions refer to individuals signified by them" (Coleman 1992:503). It is therefore unnecessary, and indeed untenable, to follow Scotus in holding an actually existing common form to be instantiated through an individuating haecceity that is not really but only formally distinct from it. This position asserts a common nature individualized by some additional "contraction." To say the two components are only *formally* distinct, however, implies that they are *really* the same and invokes the contradictory and absurd proposition that the same thing is both individual and universal: "Therefore we must say with the Philosopher [Aristotle] that in a particular substance nothing whatsoever is substantial except the particular form and the particular matter or a compound of matter and form" (Ockham 1990:40; the full argument against Scotus is found in Ockham 1994: question 6; the argument between Scotus and Ockham is examined later in this chapter).

Similarly, any extramental distinction between essence and existence—between something's "existing" and "being a thing"—is erroneous. Only singular things exist, and anything that does not exist does not retain a real "thingness." Essence and existence cannot be distinguished according to the terms for substance (matter, particular form, or their combination) or accident (quantity and quality) or by the division of potentiality and actuality. If they were truly distinct, it would not be contradictory to preserve an existence without an essence or vice versa, but such scenarios are impossible (Ockham 1990:92–93). The only alternative is that both terms refer to the same thing, one in the form of a noun signifying real existence and the other as a copula in a purely mental act of predicating abstracted attributes.

> We have to say, therefore, that essence (*entitas*) and existence (*existentia*) are not two things. On the contrary, the words "thing" and "to be" (*esse*) signify one and the same thing, but the one in the manner of a noun and the other in the manner of a verb. For that reason, the one cannot be suitably substituted for the other, because they do not have the same function. Hence the verb "to be" can be put between two terms by saying "Man is (*est*) an animal," but the same cannot be done with the noun "thing" or "essence" (*entitas*). (93)

Again, what exists must be separated from the way it is cognized. Certainly existence as predicated of God differs from that predicated of his creatures, for he exists necessarily and they do not: "For that reason, there is no distinction in God between 'that which is' and 'that in virtue of which it is,' because there is not anything different from God in virtue of which God is. But in a creature there is a distinction, because that which a creature is and that in virtue of which a creature is are simply distinct, just as God and a creature are distinct" (95). This does not, however, establish a real distinction within either being, as though essence were what the thing is and existence were that by virtue of which it is. It is thus fallacious to derive the existence of God from his essence, for this is to demonstrate something on the basis of itself. It is also impossible to establish a hierarchy based on the increasing convergence of essence and existence, since all beings are equal in their dependence on God for existence (93–94).[26]

In these ways Ockham's razor limits the resources reason can rightly use to demonstrate the existence and character of God. Clearly Ockham's criti-

cisms of Scotus seriously distort the latter's understanding of essential order, consistently treating sequentially ordered causes as essentially ordered
(see Ockham 1990:115), but they are consistent with the constraints he has
developed. First, the categorical distinctions necessary for establishing such
an order as static are only mental constructions. There can be no real ordering among the four types of cause, for example, because the supremacy giv-
en to telos rests on the logic that the whole is greater than the sum of its parts
and therefore prior to them, but Ockham views a whole as nothing more than
an aggregate. Similarly, the argument that an accidental order of causes must
refer to a permanent order because change takes place only in virtue of something unchanging illicitly invokes a real universal. No hierarchical order can
be established among the partial causes of an effect, since nothing makes "one
cause more dependent on the other than conversely. For instance, the object
and the intellect are partial causes for the act of knowing, but neither one
depends on the other, either for its existence or for its conservation" (115).
Finally, it is not necessary that a partial cause be universally more perfect than
its effect, and even if this cause must exist simultaneously with its effect, it is
not necessarily more perfect than those causes that need not coexist. This is
proven by a simple example: the generation of humans is essentially ordered
toward the sun, but the sun is not a more perfect cause of a child than is its
father, who is an intellectual being. The sun is superior only in the degree of
independence in causality: "For though Socrates cannot naturally produce
a man without the sun, the sun, however, can produce a man without Socrates, because it can do it by means of Plato. Consequently, the superior cause
is more independent in its causality than the inferior cause. But independent
causality is an aspect of perfection" (116). A partial cause is superior only in
the sense that "a more perfect condition or predicate belongs to it" (ibid.).
Only a total higher cause could be absolutely more perfect than any partial
cause—although even a total cause need not be higher than its effect. Thus
no scale of perfection can be mapped onto a causal order to bring reason
closer to knowledge of God. His absolute perfection is fundamentally different from the partial perfections of the causes that follow him.

Even without this mediating order, one can still argue from the impossibility of an infinite regress of causes, but the demonstration can be effective
only if it forecloses the possibility of a total cause other than God. Here one
cannot establish a first efficient cause on the basis of production, for an eternal sequence of beings, with each being produced by something before and
none being the cause of itself or dependent on itself, is logically possible. Even
if this order does depend on something that exists continuously, the latter
need not be more perfect, as has already been shown. Solely on the basis of

production, however, there is no justification for asserting with Scotus that this order exists only with reference to something permanent: "For it cannot be sufficiently proved as regards production, that one man cannot be produced by another as his total cause. In this case it would be said that one man is totally dependent on another man, and he again on another, and so on, *ad infinitum;* but he would not be dependent on something with an infinite duration" (Ockham 1990:121–22).[27] From production, therefore, the possibility of an ephemeral total cause remains. Nonetheless, the existence of a permanent cause can be demonstrated on the basis of conservation. An effect that changes and hence is produced by another is also dependent on some other for its continued existence. But a cause can continue to preserve an effect by only coexisting with it, and if it is itself produced, it must refer to a prior coexistent cause for its own continuation. Without a first cause, the absurd result is an infinite number of simultaneously existing beings: "Hence, though it is possible to admit that we go on *ad infinitum* in the order of productive causes without an actual infinity, nevertheless going on *ad infinitum* cannot be admitted in the order of conservation without an actual infinity" (123; see also Adams 1987:966–72).

This first cause must indeed stand outside all that is conserved, or it would be the cause of itself. Stripped of any accompanying ontological order, however, this demonstration reveals very little about the divine apart from its heterogeneity. Further rational demonstration is generally irrelevant, though, being inapplicable to the Christian concept of God. If reason is to be put in the service of faith, it is first necessary to explicate the differences between the two modes of thought. Above all, we must not confuse the metaphysician's notion of God with the theologian's.

> A theologian understands by the term "God" an infinite being which is nobler than an infinity of beings of a different type; if these were coexistent, it would be nobler than all of them, not only taken separately, but even taken together. . . . If we understand "God" in this sense, then the existence of God is not naturally known. The inference is clearly valid. The antecedent is proved thus: It is not naturally evident that something infinite exists, except from motion or from causality; but in this way it can only be proved that something infinite exists which is better than each one of an infinity of beings taken separately, not better than all taken together. (Ockham 1990: 98)[28]

It is not naturally evident that the God of theology, who is both three and one and absolutely perfect and omnipotent, actually exists or that he is good

or wise, although "from this it does not follow that we cannot prove another conclusion in which 'good' or 'wise' is predicated of a concept of God, if
by 'God' we understand 'something to which nothing is superior in perfection or prior.' For the existence of God in this sense can be demonstrated"
(100). Philosophy's use to theology therefore rests on its ability to demonstrate conclusions of the same type as theology produces using a different
middle term (98–102). Nevertheless, to the degree that reason is stripped of
the tools used for explicating these traits, its applications are minimal. It is
not even possible to follow Scotus in demonstrating the existence of only one
God, let alone show whether any being could be infinite in the theological
sense. Reason can show that a being to which nothing else is more noble must
exist, but it cannot say that only one such being exists (125–26; see also Adams 1987:972–75).

In any event, since the God of theology trumps that of reason, limiting the
scope and relevance of reason is consistent with faith. It is a central article
of faith that "whatever God can produce by means of secondary causes, He
can directly produce and preserve without them" (Ockham 1990:25). Theological omnipotence thereby goes beyond the formal infinity demonstrable
by reason, to the point where "anything is to be attributed to the divine power,
when it does not contain a manifest contradiction" (ibid.). It is not enough,
therefore, to affirm God's voluntary will but remain self-assured that he allows humans to know his traits through the mediation of his creation. It
cannot be assumed that he chooses to limit his *potentia absoluta* to a *potentia ordinata* for us. Clearly God is not known intuitively, for he is not immediately present in this life, and so he also cannot be known abstractly or in
terms of a simple concept proper to him. Nor can we obtain knowledge of
him through something else, for noncomplex knowledge (apprehension) of
one thing cannot cause noncomplex knowledge of another: one cannot know
God from knowing a creature any more than one can know a lion from knowing a horse. Rather, God can be known only through a composite of concepts
proper to himself and creatures—univocal concepts that do not invoke a
generic unity among the beings predicated of them (102–6; on the differences
from Scotus's univocal being, see Leff 1975: ch. 5). Noncomplex knowledge
of God is attained by reaching an appropriate level of indifference through
an extreme abstraction of traits proper to creatures.

> In this manner I concede that non-complex cognition of some crea-
> ture in itself leads to the non-complex cognition of another in a
> common concept. For instance, through non-complex cognition of
> a whiteness that I have seen I am led to the cognition of another

whiteness which I have never seen, since I abstract from the former whiteness a concept of whiteness which indifferently refers to the one or the other whiteness. In like manner, from an accident that I have seen I abstract the concept of a being (*ens*), which does not refer more to this accident than to substance, nor more to a creature than to God. . . . In the same manner the other argument holds, about removing imperfection from the wisdom of a creature and attributing to it what belongs to perfection. This just means abstracting from created wisdom a concept of wisdom which does not mention either a created or an uncreated thing, since mention of a created thing brings in imperfection. (Ockham 1990:111–12)

This process is possible only with certain predicates; for example, one can never the attribute the quality of "stoneness" to God because it implies the imperfection of materiality. Further, univocal concepts are still predicated equivocally of God and creatures, since they are attributive and denominative for the latter but quidditative for the former: God *is* wisdom, whereas a creature *has* wisdom (see Ockham, in Adams 1987:948). Intellectual powers, together with the proof of a first mover, thereby establish minimally the same affirmative traits also sought by Aquinas and Scotus. Nonetheless, these traits are not confirmed by any observable cosmic order. Rather, humans live in a contingent world and use contingent facts to attain at best probable knowledge. Both reason and faith demand this: their ground must move to the furthest reaches of comprehensibility.

If this condition does not disturb Ockham, it is because he makes up for the uncertainty of the world by simplifying the rules of the game. An economy of terms replaces an ontological or existential order. Nominal signs are subordinate to conceptual ones, which arise naturally and are common to more or less all human minds,[29] while written signs are subordinate to spoken. All signify real objects, directly or indirectly, even if they do not mirror them. Terms are also categorized as absolute or connotative (the latter indirectly signifying other objects in addition to that which is directly signified) and categorematic or syncategorematic (the latter signifying only in conjunction with the former). Second-order terms, either imposed (nominal) or intentioned (mental), refer to those of the first order. The theory of suppositio determines the meaning and truth value of propositions through the status of their subject: the truth of "man is an animal," for example, depends on whether the species has a personal suppositio (referring to a real being), a simple suppositio (signifying the concept of that being), or a material suppositio (the term itself taken as a material sign) (see Ockham 1990:47–74).

Once the meaning of imposed signs is determined by convention, propositions are evaluated solely in terms of internal consistency. Their formal composition need not reflect any real distinctions in the world.

> For instance, for the truth of the proposition "This is an angel" it is
> not required that this common term "angel" be really the same with
> that which has the position of subject in the proposition, or that it
> be really in it, or anything of the sort; but it is sufficient and neces-
> sary that subject and predicate should stand for the same thing. If,
> therefore, in the proposition "This is an angel" subject and predi-
> cate stand for the same thing, the proposition is true. Hence it is not
> denoted, by this proposition, that this [individual] has "angelity,"
> or that "angelity" is in him, or something of that kind, but it is de-
> noted that this [individual] is truly an angel. Not indeed that he is
> this predicate ['angel'], but that he is that for which the predicate
> stands. (76)

From this, Ockham asserts both that no one has special authority to interpret Scripture and that the Word of God nonetheless has only one true meaning: "Scripture is a set of propositions whose coherence depends on any reader
at any time analysing the meaning of its propositions in the light of his individual experience based on his intuitive knowledge of terms" (Coleman
1992:532). The world is hardly certain, but divine laws are clear. Their commands must be obeyed for no reason beyond the fact that they issue from God,
who has given them as the basis on which to judge acts of will. Strictly speaking, no act of will is virtuous in itself, since it need not occur and its effects
can be performed by God alone. Nevertheless, it can be virtuous through conformity with another act, which itself would refer to another act for its own
virtuousness, until reaching the first act, which emanates from God's will.
Thus the only necessarily virtuous act can be the love of God for his own sake,
from which other acts are judged. But to love God in this way simply means
to act in conformity with his will. This leaves God's will entirely free with
regard to its commands. With no essential order between his will and knowledge, God can without contradiction even command that a creature not love
him, although the creature cannot obey, since obedience would signify love
for its creator. Ockham therefore holds such a command to be logically possible but ethically self-contradictory (Ockham 1990:144–47).

A clarity of the Law fills in for the diminished intelligibility of the world,
while a conventional agreement on the definitions of terms is held sufficient
to establish the internal coherence necessary for a truth now fully removed

to language. These are Ockham's unwarranted assumptions—the faith that grounds his faith—comparable to those he criticizes. Perhaps this is truly more in line with Christian belief, but it is inconsistent with his refusal to accept ontological guarantees and his insistence on the contingency of lived experience. There is little value in debating whether Ockham, who is clearly a believer himself, should be vilified (or perhaps praised?) as a harbinger of skepticism and agnosticism or held responsible for the collapse of the Scholastic synthesis or the rise of "Ockhamism."[30] If he indeed upsets the delicate balance between reason and faith, it is right to ask why it was so fragile in the first place. The point, however, is that his alternatives to the answers he attacks in others do not live up to the rigors of his own thought.

Ascribing a common eudaemonic goal to reason and faith, Augustine sought to demonstrate Christianity's rational superiority over paganism. But his attempt was nonsensical: to attack reason for its inability to secure its own foundations does not make it more rational to accept a leap of faith to an infinite God who would provide this certainty. Aquinas, Scotus, and Ockham similarly posit for both philosophy and theology the demand for a ground that is the highest in being, unity, and goodness, although they are perhaps more respectful than Augustine regarding the independence of the two forms of knowledge. Nevertheless, the concessions necessary for the negotiated settlements between reason and faith they proffer are ultimately unacceptable for both faculties, even if it is impossible for either to dispense with the other. The result is their mutual intertwining and deconstruction. Reason cannot reconcile itself to a foundation remaining outside its grasp; theology cannot coherently synthesize the benevolence and omnipotence of the God who guarantees both knowledge and salvation. In both cases, what fails is the logic of identity and difference. But it is precisely here that an alternative ontology of difference again appears.

Individuation and Difference

Deleuze (1994:35–42) rightly links Scotus's attack on analogy with his analysis of individuation, for the aspiration to unite the various senses of being in the quasi identity of proportion expresses nothing other than the desire to ground difference in unity. Being is therefore said of diverse categories that relate analogically. But a species is predicated of its individuals through simple commonality rather than proportion, so the problem of the primary diversity among individuals cannot be resolved in this way.[31] It is little wonder, then, that the cause of a material substance's singularity—agreed by all to be the ultimate reality of a thing—must be assigned to some nonessential factor: a twofold negation (Henry of Ghent), an act-of-being added to essence, quantity and other accidental traits of the individual (Giles of Rome and Godfrey of Fontaines), or individual matter (Aquinas). Scotus serially dismisses these answers, insisting instead on a principle of individuation[32] both positive and intrinsic to any material thing.

First Scotus must address the charge that individuation is a false problem because universals exist only in the mind. To insist that all real things are singular, he says, is to maintain they are numerically one. If there are real similarities and differences among them, however, there must also be real unities that are not numerically one to serve as measures. These must be real "because what are measured are real and are really measured" (Duns Scotus 1994: n.12). Otherwise, if abstraction is held as the sole cause of universals, it will be left without foundation and will ultimately give rise to paradox, for unless things are *really* similar and different, they cannot be *really* individual: "If every real unity is numerical unity, therefore every real diversity is numerical diversity. The consequent is false. For every numerical diversity, insofar as it is numerical, is equal. And so all things would be equally distinct. In that case, it follows that the intellect could not abstract something common from Socrates and Plato any more than it can from Socrates and a line. Every universal would be a pure figment of the intellect" (n.23). Scotus thus introduces a common nature that does not exist independently of the individuals who share it but that is indifferent to being shared by any particular individual. It is not of itself singular, although it is also not a universal category predicable of many things. Such categories, for Scotus, are indeed produced by the intellect: "Yet in creatures there is something common that is one by a real unity less than numerical unity. This common something is not common in such a way that it is predicable of many, although it is common in such a way that it is not incompatible with it to be in something other than what it is in" (n.39).[33] Because such commonality really exists, Scotus argues, we are right to ask what individuates a thing. Nevertheless, since this common nature cannot exist outside creatures in the manner of a Platonic Form, the distinction within a creature between its common nature and the individuating factor said to "contract" this nature is not a real but only a formal distinction.

Like Scotus, Ockham insists on the reality of relations of similarity and difference, since without them abstractive cognition would not be grounded in intuitive cognition, and nominal signs would not refer back to natural signs, which, although not simply caused by singulars, are the product of interaction between the intellect and real objects (see Ockham 1990:18–27, 47–49). Concerned to avoid the logical error of treating relations between things as things themselves, however, he holds individuals to be similar and different of themselves or on the basis of their individual essences (38; see also Adams 1987: ch. 4) rather than in relation to some third thing. But Scotus does not treat common nature as a concrete thing in the sense Ockham understands; further, he understands a singular to be in excess of mere thinghood. It is not surprising, therefore, that the apparent success of Ockham's attacks comes from the great license he takes in reading his predecessor. He consistently imputes to Scotus the position that all realities outside the mind are singular, even though the passages to which he refers say the very opposite.[34] He blatantly confuses individual contracted nature and common nature to suggest that in Scotus's theory there are as many common natures as individuals. When he does accept the difference, he again claims that Scotus holds all extramental realities to be singular (Ockham 1994: question 6, nn.60–61). At other times he maintains that common nature for Scotus is predicable of individuals prior to any activity of the agent intellect, collapsing its distinction with the universal (q. 6, nn.51–59).

Comparable misrepresentations are made in his criticism of formal difference. Here Ockham holds that since the common nature (whose unity is less than numerical) and the individuating factor (whose unity is numerical) are not really but only formally distinguished, they are really identical, meaning that either the common nature is really individual and thus not common to several things, or the individual difference is common and thus not numerically one. But this misses the fundamental point. Although Scotus accepts that the common nature and individual difference are "really identical," this is true only from the perspective of a notion of real distinction that is inadequate to them. No issue of real identity or difference takes place between a common nature and individual difference because such measures apply only to fully formed individuals. Nevertheless, the real differences and similarities among beings necessitate another form of difference appearing in the synthetic unity of the individual, so that individuals and concepts may correspond. Thus, even though Scotus famously defines formal difference as weaker than the real difference between things but stronger than the conceptual difference between beings of reason (see Scotus, cited in Gilson 1955:765n.63), the formal is not simply a middle position between the real and conceptual but instead a difference of another order. It is necessary to affirm that a thing is at once the same as and different from what it is not and then determine the relation between these two factors within its singular being. Refusing to probe these depths, Ockham places formal and real distinction along a continuum, squeezing Scotus's formal difference into a schema for which it is not suited. He suggests that accepting formal distinc-

tion eliminates the possibility of distinguishing creatures through identity
and contradiction (Ockham 1994: question 6, n.27), an argument that requires reality to conform to the way human cognitions make distinctions and
thus betrays the very insistence Ockham vigorously attacks in others.[35]

Among the various theories of individuation, that of twofold negation—
which holds a thing to be individual if it is not something else and is not
divisible into subjective parts[36]—is insufficient because no negation can make
a thing formally incompatible with what it is not. That a thing is not visible,
for example, does not mean it is of itself or of its nature invisible, just as saying it is not divisible does not make divisibility incompatible with its nature.

> If substance is understood as non-quantified, it is not divisible. That
> is, it cannot be divided by a proximate potency. Yet it is not *incom-
> patible* with it that it be divided, because then it would be incom-
> patible with it to receive a quantity through which it would be for-
> mally able to be divided. . . . Likewise, if not having a seen object
> takes the proximate potency to seeing away [from the sense of sight],
> nevertheless it does not produce an *incompatibility* with seeing. For
> the sense of sight can stay the same positive nature in which there
> was this negation, and yet the opposite of that negation can be in it
> without any incompatibility on the part of the nature. (Duns Sco-
> tus 1994: n.50)

A thing is individual only by being essentially incompatible with other things,
but following Aristotle, Scotus holds that essence must be defined in positive terms, and any negation involved must refer to some higher positivity
(n.52). Further, the theory of negation fails to answer the question, only describing how a thing is singular without explaining why it is "this" singular:
"For just as in Socrates there is a twofold negation, so in Plato there is negation of two kinds. How does it come about therefore that Socrates is a singular by *this* proper and determinate singularity and not by Plato's singularity? There is nothing that can be said unless one finds out how it comes
about that negation is *this* negation. And that cannot be except through something positive" (n.56).

Because individuality is an essential quality, it cannot depend on any act-
of-being added to essence. This is clear, since "this man" is singular regardless of any actual existence (Duns Scotus 1994: nn.64–65). Individuality is
therefore the ultimate actuality of form, not something added to form, and
thus is the lowest order of a categorical hierarchy. But a formal accident such
as quantity or place cannot be posited as the cause of singularity. First, sub-

stance is prior to accidents, and thus an individual substance remains prior to its individual accidents. Further, any combination of accident with substance will produce something only accidental, but the individual is a substantial, not an accidental, unity. Finally, if a nature is said to be individual because it is generated in "this" quantity, it follows that if a form is destroyed and then reimposed on the same quantity, the same individual will be generated twice, which is absurd (nn.66–128). This last criticism obviously applies to the theory of individuation through matter. Matter is also inadequate, however, because both it and form can be taken universally or singularly: the definition of any material thing includes reference to matter as an element of its composite; conversely, an individual thing may be said to have its own particular form (nn.136–41).[37] It must still be asked, therefore, what individuates either matter or form.

Against these theories Scotus insists that the principle of individuation must be a difference that "contracts" a species nature, similar to the way specific differentia contract a genus. Because a species already has a determinate unity, although this is less than numerical unity, it is not *per se* contracted into an individual and so must have something "added" to it. Similar to specific differentia, individual differences are primarily diverse and so not themselves subsumed into a higher identity.[38] But while specific differences constitute a quiddity, individual differences constitute a material reality beyond the quidditative. It is still characteristic of a quiddity that it can be said of several things: quiddity marks a thing as a thing, but not as "this" thing (Duns Scotus 1994: nn.181–82). Individual difference thus cannot constitute the whole of which it is a constituent part in the way that specific difference constitutes the unity of a species: "Therefore, this [individual] entity, which of itself is another entity than the quiddity or the quidditative entity, cannot constitute the whole of which it is a part in its quidditative being, but only in another kind of being" (n.181).

What, then, is this individual difference or entity, this haecceity? Scotus says it is neither form, matter, nor a combination of the two. Form and matter are constitutive of quiddities. Thus, even though it is combined with a nature to make it individual, this is not a real combination of thing and thing. A thing is individual by being at once really similar to and really different from other things, but between similarity and difference within the thing is a relation of a different order in which the identity of indiscernables does not apply. Within a singular being is a difference constituting its unity; the contracted nature and the contracting haecceity are not really but only formally distinct.

Therefore, this individual entity is not matter or form or the composite, inasmuch as each of these is a nature. Rather it is the ultimate reality of the being that is matter or that is form or that is the composite. Thus whatever is common and yet determinable can still be distinguished (no matter how much it is one thing) into several formally distinct realities of which this one is not formally that one. This one is formally the entity of singularity and that one is formally the entity of the nature. These two realities cannot be distinguished as "thing" and "thing," as can the reality the genus is taken from and the reality the difference is taken from. (The specific reality is taken from these.) Rather when in the same thing, whether in a part or in the whole, they are always formally distinct realities of the same thing. (Duns Scotus 1994: n.188)

In this way Scotus proffers a determinate entity—although this entity is not a "thing"—as the cause of individuation. As determinate, it is intelligible, although its nonquidditative nature places it outside the definition of the thing, so that it transcends the sphere of human knowledge: "I grant that the singular is *per se* intelligible as far as it itself goes. But . . . it is not *per se* intelligible to some intellect—say, to ours" (n.192). Human thought, based on abstraction and representation, cannot reach this level of difference and so apprehends haecceity as indistinguishable from genera and species. Scotus blames this deficiency on the Fall, reserving its recognition for the soul lifted to the height of the divine intellect in the afterlife (see Scotus, in Bettoni 1978:40).

It is obvious what Deleuze finds useful in Scotus, for this individual difference is virtual in the Deleuzean sense of being a fully real and positive excess, inhering in the synthetic structure of actual beings but never localizable or definable. But it is also clear that Scotus takes only a first step in the rethinking of difference, since haecceity remains subordinate to the substance in which it inheres. Although only the individual exists in the full sense of the term, it is not made ontologically prior to the common nature, which makes possible the definition of the individual within a higher identity. The move to an ontology of difference is thereby foreclosed. What is required is

a plastic, anarchic and nomadic principle, contemporaneous with the process of individuation, no less capable of dissolving and destroying individuals than of constituting them temporarily; intrinsic modalities of being, passing from one "individual" to another, circulating and communicating underneath matters and forms. The individuating is not the simple individual. In these conditions, it is not enough to say that individuation differs in kind from the determination of species. It is not even enough to say this in the manner of Duns Scotus, who was nevertheless not content to analyse the elements of an individual but went as far as the conception of individuation as the "ultimate actuality of form." We must show not only how individuating difference differs in kind from specific difference, but primarily and above all how individuation properly *precedes* matter and form, species and parts, and every other element of the constituted individual. (Deleuze 1994:38)

Scotus privileges common nature because, he says, although it is a product of the individuals themselves, it is indifferent and therefore prior to any particular individual.[39] But this response—which in no way organizes individual differences according to a common sense but only affirms that fully formed individuals fall within the higher identity of their species—suggests the very Platonism Scotus explicitly rejects; moreover, it is insufficient on its own terms, because the fully actual individual with a haecceity exceeding categorical determinations is likewise indifferent to the existence of others with which it might share features in common.[40] It also conceals a more profound anxiety, reflected in Scotus's deployment of univocity. As a quidditative concept, being never directly but only virtually (in the Scotist sense) relates to specific and individual differences, even while extending to substances that share nothing in common. This is necessary from a Scotist viewpoint because the individuation of God is based on his infinity and simplicity rather than any composition and contraction (see Duns Scotus 1994: nn.190–91).[41] Haecceity therefore applies only to finite beings, while for Scotus the indifference of a transcendental means it applies either to God alone or to God and some or all of his creatures but not to creatures alone. Otherwise every predicate would be transcendental and so univocal between God and creatures, and any basis on which to determine what can and cannot be said affirmatively of God would vanish. The result would be either pantheism or a negative theology that Scotus (1987:15–16) maintains is incoherent. The need to protect divine transcendence is thus what ultimately demands that being not be said univocally of differentia generally and haecceity in particular and necessitates the ontological priority of quiddities.

It is therefore essential to overturn the primacy of substance, of the self-subsistent or identical, and so too any infinite being that transcends and governs the world of finite beings and becoming. It is necessary to situate an originary web of differences from which individual identities both appear and dissolve. This move not only demolishes the Christian God but affirms the differences by which individuals always exceed categorization according to similarity and sameness, enabling the extension of univocity to the primary diversity of individual differences. The consequent collapse of divine heterogeneity and infinity, however, eliminates the possibility of an ultimate intelligible recuperation of difference, in either this life or an afterlife. An individual being, constituted through a formal difference linking a common nature and haecceity that are forever irreducible, now takes on the character of a singular-multiple event, and thus an ontology of difference is born. The univocity of being no longer remains indifferent to the difference between the infinite and finite so as to protect the separation of the two realms. Rather, it embodies a positive but unrepresentable difference that now breaches this sacred divide: what is common to all beings is not their quiddity but instead this very excessiveness. Being qua being thereby expresses the eventness of all beings, the lost movements by which they overflow every pseudocontinuum of space and time on which representative thinking rests. Such thought reveals its clumsiness in dealing with the most delicate differences from which the identities and differences it recognizes arise, appearing as the product of the most profound amnesia. What is forgotten is the originary movement and synthesis of differences, by which they relate not through an underlying identity—established through a teleological logic of totality, an appeal to transcendence, or a movement of negation—but only through difference as their groundless ground. Univocity becomes the sameness of that which differs, the difference that links beings *through their difference.*

In this project Scotus may appear more important than Ockham, who, in his demolition of ontology, privileges the simple and fully constituted individual, excluding the possibility of such excess. But the critique of universals is integral to the liberation of individual difference. The fundamental error in Ockham's nominalism is that it fails to take its own radical logic far enough, maintaining the relation between singular and universal by merely inverting their causal order. Only in this way can Ockham maintain with his opponents a definitive foundation for knowledge. To free individuals from the concepts imperfectly applied to them, as Ockham sought to do, requires articulating a prior disunity and dispersion escaping all identity, from which the simple individual as a ground for abstraction both appears and disintegrates. It is only appropriate, even if ironic, that this conclusion—which dissolves the Christian God as well—should follow from Christian philosophy itself.

6. The Ethics of a Pluralism Made of Stolen Bits

> I like the word [curiosity]. . . . It evokes "care"; it evokes the care
> one takes of what exists and what might exist; a sharpened sense of
> reality, but one that is never immobilized before it; a readiness to
> find what surrounds us strange and odd; a certain determination
> to throw off familiar ways of thought and to look at the same
> things in a different way . . . ; a lack of respect for the traditional
> hierarchies of what is important and fundamental.
> —Michel Foucault, "The Masked Philosopher"

WE HAVE BEEN SEEKING a difference of a very special sort: a groundless difference that differs from identity and difference as such. This search arises from the need for a postmetaphysical philosophy that avoids both an appeal to transcendence and the comforts of continuity and coherence that may be retained even after metaphysical foundations have been denounced. The empiricism and historicism often considered adequate responses to the death of God remain complicit in the erasure and forgetting that characterize metaphysics. What metaphysics, empiricism, and historicism disregard is the full power of the event. Assigning the event an unambiguous meaning or place—regulated by the likes of telos, causality, providence, or mere serialization, which purportedly does not appeal to any such principles—always domesticates its effects. But resisting this maneuver opens thought to another domain. For this reason, rejecting both metaphysical foundations and the customary responses to their loss produces neither a simplistic skepticism that denies truth, knowledge, and certainty while remaining parasitically attached to these categories nor a negative theology that continues to put forward an origin but places it out of reach. The groundless difference that these positions ignore is therefore more than a mere remainder of dialectical or other representational schemata. It carries with it a positive content glimpsed in the mutation it enacts on such schemata.

Dialectics demands a harmonization of differences greater than any promised by previous philosophies. This approach derives the identity of identity and difference from immediate experience as the condition for experience to have meaning and then develops this identity through a series of purportedly internal transitions toward the concrete, with the promise of providing a final meaning and proper place for nature, society, history, and God. Yet the instantiation of the Notion, which is to occur ultimately in the modern state, remains at an abstract level. In its final form the Notion is nothing more than a unity posited above a social reality Hegel acknowledges to be divided and lacking the internal means of reconciliation. Despite his best efforts, Hegel leaves his portrayal of the modern state at the level of what ought to be. This remaining abstraction indicates how opposition—said to be the most extreme and so most inclusive difference—fails to be exhaustive. Dialectical negation gives way to another difference that is not simply "beyond" or "outside" the Absolute and so is subject not to mediation but rather to another form of synthesis.

If the mediation of opposites fails, their traditional hierarchical pairings must certainly suffer a similar fate. Aristotle elevates the limited and determinate over indeterminate infinitude using the concepts of telos and continuity. These twin logics allow becoming to be grasped as an intelligible movement, yet they are ultimately both necessary and incompatible. The final cause, while appearing last in the order of development, is nonetheless logically prior to other causes in terms of potentiality and actuality: the whole is more actual than its parts, and the parts, as parts, gain their being only through reference to the whole that organizes them. This establishes a finite and determinate universe while relegating the unlimited to a principle of division. This divisibility, however, can never be other than potentially infinite, violating the central rule of Aristotelian metaphysics that potency necessarily carries with it the possibility of becoming actual. Here Aristotle stumbles on a potential—or, rather, a fully real virtuality—greater and more dangerous than a plastic material substrate that assumes various forms according to determinate principles. The infinite, even in this thinking, which endeavors to contain it, is revealed as a chaotic excess over all possible settlements, orderings, and determinations.

Augustine recognizes the power of such chaos but treats it as evil, a fault whose existence must not undermine the benevolence and omnipotence of his God. At stake here is the hierarchy of positive and negative and the model of a fully positive being grounding a created harmony but remaining transcendent and unaffected by a negation that is not a mere absence but the corruption of Being. Augustine suggests that the first evil will has no cause, but this makes it a *causa sui* sufficient unto itself; he holds humans responsible for sin, yet the innocence he must ascribe to them precludes their decision from being a genuine operation of free will; and he maintains that sin and suffering are necessary components of a greater good, which undermines God's absolute power. Despite these maneuvers, evil stubbornly remains a difference subverting the metaphysical dualism that is supposed to leave it behind.

Even without the question of evil, medieval Christian thought confronts issues of irreducible difference involving the heterogeneous relation between the created world and the God who transcends it. Drawn from Aristotle's analysis of the categories, the concepts of analogy and univocity are applied to both this theological dilemma and the question of individuation. Being is clearly not a highest genus, for it is predicated of both genera and differentia, of what is common to beings as well as what is different. Aquinas argues that being need not be purely univocal or equivocal but can instead be analogical, and from this he suggests a proportional relation between God and creation, so that the universe resembles God, who does not resemble it, establishing a hierarchy that reason can trace to move closer to knowledge of the divine. This solution, however, not only privileges the goodness of God over his omnipotence; it also presupposes an understanding of him, since an analogy can be constructed only between terms that are both known. Duns Scotus, therefore, turns to a univocal conception in which being is indifferent to the differences among the categories and likewise indifferent to the division between infinite and finite being. Nonetheless, constrained by a Scholastic demand for a natural hierarchy that demonstrates—albeit imperfectly—the existence and perfections of God, he designs an essential order of causes grounded in a highest being, and in order to maintain the transcendence of this being, he limits the concept of univocity to quiddities and excludes differentia. Differentia are held to remain deficient in relation to the substances that provide them with being and that therefore virtually include them. Ockham's attacks on universals demolish the confidence with which reason can posit these Thomistic and Scotist hierarchies in order to unite it with faith. In doing so, however, they clear a path for a univocal conception extended to all differences, including Scotus's individuating haecceities, which exceed all formal determinations. The univocity of being, freed from theological requirements and the dominance of substance, thereby gives rise to an ontology of difference.

Although it is inadequate on its own terms, dialectics can nonetheless be used to take the first steps toward a thought of the event. Hegel demonstrates how there can be no thing-in-itself and how each thing is nothing but its relations to others. In this way, he displaces the notion of an atomic thing in favor of relational forces. If one seeks the meaning of any particular phenomenon, this virtual network of forces is presupposed as its condition of possibility. Hegel characterizes the relations among forces as negative, since a negative relationship invokes moments of both separation and unity. This negativity allows us to conceive a totality of relations, since anything posited outside the whole—the thing-in-itself, a transcendent being, or any other standard metaphysical crutch—would be negatively related to it and thus accounted for within its schema. It is thus a totality that embraces even contradictories. The resulting movement of forces is one from being-in-itself to being-for-another and finally back to a higher state of being-for-self *through* being-for-another.

But Hegel remains committed to a spatialized conception of difference. Contradictories are seen to be separated by an infinite distance—even if this space is not a separate medium—while other differences are similarly thought in spatial terms. Time is likewise understood in terms of space, so that space becomes the visualization of difference as such, even though this distance also vanishes in dialectical mediation. Conceiving difference in this manner means comprehending it in terms of equality and measure. Here lies the source of the continuing abstraction within dialectics: its reduction of differences to a single conceptualization so as to reconcile them.

Disconnecting the relationality that dialectics introduces from the latter's insistence on equality and similitude as its means and goal results in another movement and association. Forces are now related but also irreducibly heterogeneous, brought together through a disjunctive synthesis linking differences *through their difference* and expressing an agonism that cannot be grasped through oppositional logics. On the one hand, this coupling of forces constitutes not a being within a dialectical process but an event that is at once singular and multiple; on the other, it introduces an active will to power that dissolves the opposition between self and other. As Nietzsche makes clear, in unequal relations, despite the strife and resistance immanent to them, one force necessarily dominates the other. Only from the position of the dominated force, of the force unable to express itself and so turned back on itself, do the demands for foundation, identity, and a strict separation of good and evil arise. Exceeding this is a noble morality that affirms itself through an immediate differentiation—not a mediated difference of any dialectical sort but a repetition in which it transcends its limits and overcomes itself. It is a repetition of not identity but rather a virtual difference. The noble or active will to power, in short, produces or actualizes an event.

The virtual event that underlies actual relations and differences is a real infinity: it is neither the spurious infinity attacked by both Hegel and Aristotle—an endless extension that remains an "ought"—nor the purely potential infinity of division that Aristotle posits in violation of his own metaphysics of potency and act. The event is in this sense the Epicurean *clinamen*, occurring in a time and space discontinuous with the minimum thinkable continuity, thereby multiplying both spatial and temporal dimensions. But the Epicurean atom is deficient insofar as it remains a self-identity. It is necessary to add to the insight of the *clinamen* an attack on such a substantive notion. Again Nietzsche is central, not only with his relational forces and will to power, but also with his eternal return. Although the eternal return may appear to invoke an infinite repetition of the identical, this reading overlooks a central aspect of Zarathustra's response to the dwarf: the moment itself recurs, not merely the state of being captured by it (Nietzsche 1966b:3.2.2). The present moment, at once also past and future, is no longer a marker of a temporal continuum but rather an untimely event. There can be no moment in itself, and so any moment must be related to others through an irreducible heterogeneity that puts it beyond any fixed position. The eternal return in this way embodies a disjunctive synthesis of time that moves it "out of joint." Similarly, the Deleuzean "fold" is a spatial discontinuity that follows from a primary disjoining, which displaces the notion of the point as a primary marker of space and distance. The movements of eternal return, heterogeneous folding, and self-overcoming characterize the event as being in excess of any dialectical transition.

Through such movement, multiplication, and linking, the event provides the conditions of real rather than possible meaning without the appeals to identity or totality that underpin representational thought. Whereas the virtual event is constituted through a synthesis of heterogeneous forces, it is actualized through a similar organization that links differences through their difference. The actualization of the virtual, as outlined by Deleuze and Guattari, maintains the discontinuity between the two levels of virtual and actual within their mutual immanence and imbrication. It is thus not a relation of simple cause and effect or original and copy: the virtual cannot be copied, either well or badly, because its actualization is a genuine creation. Similarly, Foucauldian micropowers are not simply the small-scale components of a macroscopic totality, and they establish relations of noncorrespondence in the institutions, subjects, and objects of knowledge that create social meaning, littering them with sites of resistance, reversal, and mutation.

With the turn from dialectics, characterizing a force as nothing but its relations no longer means that it is equal or identical to them. This sameness is no longer an identity or similarity but a *sameness of that which differs*. The univocity of being, when separated from the requirements of Christian theology, is this very sameness. It invokes neither a hierarchy of beings—

if this means a hierarchy grounded in Oneness—nor an equality on a level surface but rather a rhizomatic pluralism. As the Gnostic description of the Pleroma—often confused with a Neoplatonic model—makes clear, the rhizome retains connectedness, but without a fixed center or limit. It introduces a dimension of depth exceeding any determinate or oppositional order, which appears as a shadow of the rhizome when this depth is erased, forgotten, or treated as a fault or sin to be overcome. The ontological rethinking of difference thus comes to have ethical and political import.

Epicurus and Lucretius, in their critique of teleological thought, show how the demands for a universal truth rest on a resentment and denial of the contingencies of life. Lyotard, by differentiating xenophobia from anti-Semitism, shows how typical responses to the Holocaust mimic the very phenomenon they seek to attack by refusing to engage with the unrepresentable "jews." And Nietzsche, in his critique of slave morality, locates a distortion and forgetting of difference in the moral opposition of good and evil. Against these erasures, an affirmation of difference requires a more subtle and strategic approach than any representational thinking allows—strategic precisely in the sense that the rules for engagement with this groundless difference cannot be fixed outside the context of action. Notions of a moral law give way here to an ethical sensibility that does not dispense with "law" but refuses to be restricted to it. As Foucault notes in this regard, it is a matter not of escaping games of truth but rather of playing them differently (see Foucault 1988a:15). Playing them differently means approaching them with a sense of curiosity and care for that which remains opaque and different and a willingness to press thinking beyond its traditional limits. At issue here is the capacity to produce or experience an event, to introduce the impossible newness of the untimely, which complicates the oppositional relations between universal and particular, self and other, and identity and difference. This dissolves the self as a subject or identity, but not to disperse it into nothingness or deny its relationality. The Nietzschean overman, for example, is a being that, in affirming its groundless and contingent difference, overcomes itself and moves "beyond" good and evil. Similarly, the Epicurean sage is one who fights off the fear of death, which produces the moralizing resentment of contingency that seeks to apportion blame. And the individual with gnosis affirms the chaotic, excessive element within the self that compels an ethic of care. Another form of community follows from these modes of living, one of a belonging together of beings with no identity in common.

The responsibilities carried by this sensibility are not denied by the lack of foundations but rather follow from it. They follow precisely because the singular-multiple event, which exceeds the identity of identity and difference, remains inescapable, as evidenced by the consistent failures of metaphysical philosophies to dispense with it fully. This does not mean, however, that the ethical pluralism of the event can ever make an unadulterated, fully actualized appearance—such a utopian ideal in fact expresses yet another forgetting of difference. The event thereby invokes an "ought," but this "ought" is not an abstraction of the sort Hegel criticizes and yet repeats. For the virtual does not mark a gap between a truth presupposed in thought and a reality it is supposed to mirror. It rather arises when both thought and action, refusing to be restricted by the logic of identity, dispense with the abstractions that this logic invokes. Here thinking and action enter an always uncertain terrain—hence, once again, the need for a strategic approach.

Notes

Chapter 1: The Quest for Lost Time and Space

1. Berlin, for example, declares a need to "fall back on the ordinary resources of empirical observation and ordinary human knowledge" (1969:168) in order to establish an "empirical, as against the metaphysical, view of politics" (171n).

2. This becomes clear in criticisms of work by Taylor charging that despite his attempts, he cannot escape the need to presuppose the truth of his theism. See, for example, B. Williams 1990.

3. Hence the later Rawls insists he never intended to provide an ahistorical grounding for liberal politics but only "tries to draw solely upon basic intuitive ideas that are embedded in the political institutions of a constitutional democratic regime and the public traditions of their interpretation" (1985:225). Berlin ties the negative conception of freedom to the historical conditions of late capitalism (1969:xli). Rorty (1989) calls for Western societies to recognize their historical contingency and seeks to secure liberal rights on pragmatic considerations while dismissing communitarian attacks on liberalism as resting on defunct language games that remain premised on metaphysical assumptions of an Archimedean point.

4. "What must be maintained is the possibility of dating within the impossibility of its providing the frame of thinking time. . . . The displacing of chronology does not mean that it has been replaced. All interpretations will bear a date. Dating, however, does not provide the temporality of interpretation; it merely allows it to bear a signature—to be signed—and thus to bring into play the attendant risk that interpretation henceforth will always be able to take place in relation to the signature" (Benjamin 1993:17).

5. The logic of secularization theorems is traced in Blumenberg 1983, pt. 1. For a detailed account of Blumenberg's argument, see Widder 2000a.

6. See Nietzsche 1974: §§83 and 337, where historical sense is understood as the capacity to bear within oneself fundamentally alien and heterogeneous elements. For Nietzsche's attacks on a false historical sense used to secure either a divine truth (à la Hegel) or the purity of a national identity, see §§357 and 337.

7. See Foucault 1986, 1984c.

8. Hegel (1977: §§202–6) maintains that skepticism negates itself by making a truth claim in its denial of truth, whereas Jürgen Habermas (1990:80–82, 98–100) declares Nietzsche and Foucault to be contemporary exponents of "value scepticism" who are similarly caught in performative contradiction. Habermas (1987) also labels Nietzsche, Heidegger, Derrida, and Foucault as modern bearers of nihilism. Plotinus (1956:2.9.15) equates Epicureans and Gnostics in their devaluation of world order and corresponding lack of focus upon virtues. Keffer (1985) and Patrick (1987) link postmodernism to Gnosticism in order to disparage both.

Chapter 2: Force, Synthesis, and Event

1. Hegel's dubious claim is that "a truth cannot lose anything by being written down, any more than it can lose anything through our preserving it" (1977: §95).

2. On Hegel's adoption and remodulation of Kant's concept of force in order to collapse the Kantian separation of noumenal and phenomenal, see Heidegger 1988: ch. 3.

3. Slavoj Žižek employs the dialectic of "force and the understanding" to argue against the idea of Hegel as a totalizing thinker. Absolute knowledge, he contends, is not knowledge of the totality of negative relations but instead the structural failure of this totality. The lesson of the dialectic of forces is that essence is not a thing-in-itself beneath appearances; rather, there is nothing beneath them, and essence is this very fact: "The appearance implies that there is something behind it which appears through it; it conceals a truth and by the same gesture gives a foreboding thereof; it simultaneously hides and reveals the essence behind its curtain. But what is hidden behind the phenomenal appearance? Precisely the fact that there is nothing to hide. What is concealed is that the very act of concealing conceals nothing" (1989:193). This, Žižek continues, reveals the crucial difference between Hegel and Kant in relation to the sublime. Instead of being a transcendent positivity, as it is in Kant, the sublime is for Hegel "an object which occupies the place, replaces, fills out the empty place of the Thing as the void, as the pure Nothing of absolute negativity—the Sublime is an object whose positive body is just an embodiment of Nothing" (206). The sublime object is therefore a suture closing the play of differences—that is, the play of appearances or forces—but it is also a mere projection. It thereby both conceals and reveals a radical Lack, a failure of differences to gather into a whole: "It is not only that the appearance, the fissure between appearance and essence, is a fissure internal to the essence itself; the crucial point is that, inversely, *'essence' itself is nothing but the self-rupture, the self-fissure of appearance*" (214).

Žižek's interpretation is challenging, although his contention that Hegel locates a Lack that both enables and dissolves the closed structure of differences is mitigated by his penchant to translate Hegel—and every other thinker, for that matter—into a Lacanian discourse that does locate this Lack. Further, his reading does not seem to square with many of Hegel's more conservative statements—especially in, but not limited to, the political register—that seem to demand a closed system. On this point, see Connolly 1993:185–97.

Judith Butler similarly registers problems with those who treat Hegel as a thinker of metaphysical closure, because "'inclusion' as a spatial relation is a poor way of describing the relationship of the infinite to the system itself. To be able to think Hegel's absolute, the infinite and the systematic at once, is to think beyond spatial categories, to think the essence of time as Becoming. But if the Absolute is not a principle of spatial stasis, if it is a temporal modality, the internal complexity of temporality itself, then satisfaction no longer carries the meaning of finality, stasis, closure" (1987:13–14). Thus, on her reading, the lesson of the concept of force is "that there is something that does not appear, but that is nevertheless crucial to any given appearance; moreover, it indicates that reality is not coextensive with appearance, but always sustains and is sustained by a hidden dimension" (27). This hidden dimension perhaps corresponds to Žižek's Lack. Nevertheless, Butler's argument seems to be based primarily on a restricted definition of closure. And while it is certainly true that Hegel's totality is not one of objects enclosed in space, this does not justify understanding his system as "open" according, presumably, to the same sort of spatial thinking—but if there is a rethinking of space being presented, why not a rethinking of closure? This point would be minor if it did not govern Butler's reading of other thinkers who aspire to think "beyond" dialectical thought. Because she treats this as a spatial beyond, she suggests, for example, that Deleuze treats desire as a precultural plenitude to be accessed directly through emancipation, while she differentiates Deleuze and Lacan simply on the basis of whether this plenitude can be tapped (186–217). Against such a conflation of Lacan's Lack/Real/*jouissance* and Deleuze's virtual, see Widder 2000b.

4. The organic is the only syllogism in nature. Inorganic nature—from its barest form, space, onward—presents itself as merely given, without mediation. Only the organism, according to Hegel, contains an active principle to negate its surrounding environment, making mediation possible.

5. Hegel 1977: ch. 5, esp. §§293–97. Put succinctly by Heidegger and Adorno respectively: "Hegel does not deny that nature is something real; yet, he does show that it cannot be reality, the Being of beings" (Heidegger 1983:59); "wherever the object itself is mediated by 'spirit,' knowledge becomes fruitful not by excluding the subject but through its utmost exertions, through all its impulses and experiences" (Adorno 1993:7).

Alexandre Kojève (1969: chs. 5–6) shows how this separation of nature and spirit allows Hegel to conceive of historical time as the negation of the natural world into a mediated whole, with human labor power serving as the motor force. Vincent Descombes (1980: ch. 2) effectively argues that the dual ontology is both necessary and fatal to Kojève's reading. Judith Butler (1987:63–79) criticizes Kojève's depiction of Hegelian desire as a disembodied pursuit, a path intimately related to his characterization of Hegel as atheist, proto-Marxist, and individualist.

6. Kojève (1969: ch. 2) erroneously treats these chapters of the *Phenomenology* as historically consecutive, producing a very skewed and selective reading of chapters 4–6. By contrast, Hyppolite (1974:27–74) holds that only in the chapters on spirit and religion is there a movement coinciding with actual historical development, while the developments traced in consciousness, self-consciousness, and reason are abstractions of spirit that are accounted for in greater richness in the later chapters.

7. A similar criticism of Marx's historical dialectic is made by Laclau (1990: ch. 1).

8. See generally Hegel 1977: §§166–77. To review these sections briefly: self-consciousness, as the truth of consciousness that has learned that its object is not alien to it, is seen to have two moments: in the first, consciousness confronts a distinctive world, and in the

second, it negates this difference and returns to itself. The second moment—self-consciousness proper—presents a movement of negation that is labeled desire, so that self-consciousness is defined as "desire in general." The first moment, in which difference resists incorporation into the self and so negates the latter, is defined as life, in contradistinction to self-consciousness. Life, in turn, is itself explained as a movement of self-related negativity in which a living being first establishes its independence from both the universal (genus) and its environment and then returns to the universal through an act of self-negation (procreation). This movement, which preserves its moments within it, is then equated with the movement of consciousness becoming self-consciousness. From all this Hegel concludes that the other of self-consciousness, which it desires to sublate, must be another self-consciousness in order for genuine satisfaction to be attained.

Warminski (1998) shows that this failure to provide a proper transition from the dialectic of life to self-consciousness has devastating consequences for Hegel's attempt to relate life and consciousness.

9. Adorno makes the point clearly: "While Hegel is forced to integrate the historical moment into the logical, and vice versa, his attempt to do so turns into a critique of his own system. The system has to acknowledge the conceptual irreducibility of the concept, which is inherently historical: in terms of logical-systematic criteria the historical, all else notwithstanding, is disturbing; it is a blind spot" (1993:124).

10. Hardt (1993) develops a similar line of argument running from Hegel to Deleuze.

11. "This event is not the 'sensational.' Under the guise of the sensational, it is forgotten" (Lyotard 1990:51).

12. For Hegel, the singular both mediates and is mediated by the universal and particular in such a way that each term, while different, is nonetheless nothing but the other two terms. In Hegel's scheme, the concrete universal is no more than the totality of particulars, which itself is nothing other than the totality of individual singularities. Each term is thus identical to the others, yet distinct as well. See Stace 1924:226–62.

13. This text figures prominently in one of Deleuze's most focused and revealing engagements with Heidegger. Sameness as the belonging together of differences opens the possibility of a univocal conception of being as difference, although Deleuze suggests that Heidegger does not go far enough in this direction, as evidenced by the latter's critique of Nietzsche's eternal return. See Deleuze 1994:64–66.

14. Some hold Deleuze's harsh attacks on Hegel, especially in *Nietzsche and Philosophy*, to create a binary opposition to dialectical thought that is inconsistent with the philosophy of difference he seeks to articulate. It is no small irony that many of these critics, who also seek to appropriate Nietzsche, do not level the same criticism against the latter's clearly more vicious polemic. Hardt (1993:27–28, 52–53) suggests that the development of Deleuze's thought shows a progressively refined relation to Hegel, moving away from crude opposition toward a strategy of more indirect attacks. Malabou, however, finds Deleuze's position, with and without Guattari, to be "univalent and univocal" (1996:115) and argues that in trying to conceive a becoming that banishes all negativity, Deleuze reinvokes the very negative unity he wants to escape. Her reading, however, completely overlooks Deleuze's many characterizations of both Hegel and the dialectic that portray dialectical difference not in simple opposition to multiplicity but rather as a shadow or incomplete version of it. She similarly overlooks how Deleuze and Guattari explicitly align

Hegel's understanding of the Concept with their own but criticize him for overreaching and reducing the divergent realms of science and art to philosophy (see Deleuze and Guattari 1994:12). I owe this last point to Michael Rooney.

15. "Nietzsche's most general project is the introduction of the concepts of sense and value into philosophy" (Deleuze 1983:1). On this valuation's being prior to any notion of subjectivity, see Nietzsche 1974: §374.

Against the Heideggerian criticism that Nietzsche is unable to fully consider the problem of the Being of beings because he poses it in terms of evaluation, Deleuze may appear to simply take the Nietzschean position in the debate. But Philip Goodchild argues that Deleuze "overcomes this false dichotomy. For the question of values brings a radical reversal in philosophy: thought can no longer be subjected to any guiding *or* grounding question but instead must begin by creating its own questions and problems. *The question of values is not a grounding question, but an 'ungrounding' or abyssal question, because scales of evaluation must themselves be evaluated.* . . . According to this perspective, Heidegger had only partially posed the question [of philosophy], for he did not question his ultimate presuppositions about the nature of philosophy and its relation to ontology" (1996:25–26). That said, Goodchild's contention that Deleuze's thought amounts to a rejection of ontology in favor of a "philosophy of life" or "vitalism" seems to draw excessively on one particular line of Deleuzean rhetoric and instates at the level of Deleuzean and Heideggerian discipleship another false dichotomy. It also serves as the basis for a series of reductions performed by Goodchild, in which he attributes the "incompleteness" of Deleuze's thought to a "sterile, privileged, materialist perspective" that "recurs in various guises throughout the tradition of European reason and may even extend back as far as Thales" (156) and that is itself deterritorialized by a turn to "Spirit" (which does not recur throughout the tradition of European reason?).

16. I follow Lyotard's use of "jews" here because it would be absurd to construe Nietzsche's attacks as aimed specifically at historical Jews.

17. For an example of such misconceptions, see Detwiler 1990. For a counterpoint, see McIntyre 1997.

18. Vincent Descombes challenges Deleuze's claim to distinguish noble affirmation of difference from slavish affirmation through opposition. If the master does not oppose but rather differentiates in a nonnegative fashion, then even the oppositional logic of the slave will *appear* to be another difference. If the slave recognizes only oppositions to his identity, then the master's affirmation of difference will *appear* only as another negation. From the perspective of each, then, nonnegative difference and negative opposition seem identical. Descombes then argues that Deleuze is left with two options: if the master simply affirms himself without any relation to the slave, it will not be an affirmation of difference but rather identity in itself; alternatively, if the master affirms himself through comparison with the slave, it will be impossible to distinguish difference and opposition. The choices, then, are between simple positivity and negative difference. See Descombes 1980:156–67.

Descombes, however, not only fails to accurately portray the dynamic of noble affirmation, which is established in relation to other nobles rather than to the slaves, but also refuses to distinguish power relations from the will to power. The movement of forces is one thing; a will's capacity to distinguish between groundless, nonnegative difference and opposition is quite another. It should be apparent that neither Nietzsche nor Deleuze takes the master and slave types to exhaust the possible forms of will: the overman, for example, fits neither category neatly. Acknowledging these factors makes it rather more difficult to dismiss Deleuze's attempt to think a nonnegative difference as a pipe dream.

Ronald Bogue disagrees with aspects of Descombes's reading but nevertheless accepts that the relations between forces must be characterized by "concepts . . . that are essentially oppositional and agonistic. The problem arises because Nietzsche's conception of mastery is much more conflictual than Deleuze allows" (1989:33). But again it is a question of whether agonism, conflict, and opposition are all the same. Nietzsche's distinctions between fights of annihilation and fights that are contests (Nietzsche 1954), his approval of the spiritualization of enmity (Nietzsche 1990:53–54), and Zarathustra's numerous exhortations to hate but not despise one's enemies (Nietzsche 1966b) all suggest they are not.

19. Those who do argue for such reconciliation include Deleuze (1983) and Ansell Pearson (1997).

20. Simmel (1986:170–81), for example, finds the eternal return incoherent as a cosmological doctrine but retains it as an answer to the psychological need for a metaphysical reconciliation of finite and infinite; for that reason, he maintains, it need not conform to the dictates of logic. Similarly, Schacht (1983:253–66) sees the cosmological presentation as a failed thought experiment but argues that this does nothing to damage the other aspects and uses of the idea, and Nehamas (1985:141–50) argues that Nietzsche never seriously entertained the cosmological doctrine and that claiming he did obscures the more important psychological influences. None of these thinkers entertains the possibility of the eternal return as an ontological doctrine that is more than a fiction posed for psychological purposes but also something different from an attempted scientific cosmology.

21. This is "the new world conception" against which earlier thinkers have sought to find contradiction, often through "other ulterior considerations (—mostly theological, in favor of the *creator spiritus*)" (Nietzsche 1967a: §1066).

22. Commentators have charged that Nietzsche fails to demonstrate the necessity of the circular return, either because he fails to consider simple models where such repetition cannot occur even given infinite time (Simmel 1986:172–73n) or because he himself rejects the discrete centers of force on which the argument is based (Schacht 1983:264–65), but such criticisms are of no great concern insofar as his aim is to show that modern science leads to nihilism on its own terms. Put simply, the scientific eternal return is not Nietzsche's.

23. David Wood (1988), however, argues that the "scientific" eternal return, precisely by extending the serial notion of time, begins its subversion.

24. As White (1990:86) points out, Zarathustra rebukes the dwarf for seeking to use the image of the circle so as to step outside temporality and view it as a whole.

25. See Deleuze 1983:47–49, which presents the eternal return as a problem of the passage of the present; see also Stambaugh 1972:29–45.

26. Cauchi (1998) considers the overman to be an impossible romantic ideal that Zarathustra projects to hide his own ressentiment toward the fact that he cannot escape the old morality. This nihilism, she says, is exposed in the final part of the text. Her reading, however, completely ignores the fact that Nietzsche never intended part 4 as the conclusion and that he died before writing the final two parts of the text. Moreover, it requires

ascribing to Nietzsche's overman the characteristic of radical autonomy that Nietzsche himself undermines when, for example, he holds that free spirits could not exist without the Church (1967b:1.9) and when he counsels treating the self as a work of art (1974: §290). In contrast to Cauchi's position, see Conway 1990.

27. Similar but less sophisticated readings are offered by May (1994) and Hallward (1997). May argues that although Deleuze opposes transcendental principles of unity, he is not opposed to an underlying unity or sameness per se and indeed articulates such a unity through the concept of a surface organizing divergent singularities. Indeed, he says, Deleuze becomes incoherent when he posits differences as prior to this unitary surface. Hallward holds that Deleuze's is a philosophy of redemption structurally similar to that of St. Paul, seeking an escape from this world to a Real beyond all representation and finitude and understanding this Real not as multiplicity but rather as the self-differentiation of the One. Both May and Hallward severely distort the theme of univocity, and May in particular forces on Deleuze the spurious alternative between a co-relation of unity and difference and some sort of oxymoronic "pure difference" in which differences are merely indifferent to one another.

28. For a detailed argument against Badiou on this point, see Widder 2001.

29. See, for example, the reference to "the chaotic interference of all the virtualities in the One" (Badiou 2000:71) and the description of the diagram of outside forces, which "causes the disjointed objects . . . to enter into a formal *composition*, which rests characterized by exteriority, but now activated by its 'forceful' seizure" (87).

30. See, for example, the reference to the virtual as "the deployment of the One in its immanent differentiation" whereby it is its own "process of actualization" (Badiou 2000: 49).

31. See, for example, Deleuze 1993: ch. 7, on the way clear and distinct macroperceptions develop from and fall back into vague microperceptions.

32. It is astounding how often the dynamic of Foucauldian power relations is interpreted in terms of an identity formed against resistance, given that one of the great ironies in both *Discipline and Punish* (Foucault 1990b) and *The History of Sexuality*, vol. 1 (Foucault 1990a), is that power never succeeds in creating a disciplined, normalized self. For an example of such misunderstandings, see MacNay 1992, which goes so far as to turn to Habermasian communicative rationality to supplement and correct Foucault's thought.

33. These are a questioner's words, but Foucault agrees with them.

34. Blanchot suggests May 1968 in this regard: "The impossibility of recognizing an enemy, of taking into account a particular form of adversity, all that was vivifying while hastening the resolution, though there was nothing to be resolved, given that the event had taken place. The event? And had it taken place?" (1988:31).

Chapter 3: A Question of Limits and Continuity

1. Aristotle clearly connects wholeness defined by its telos or end with the good: "If, then, there is some end of the things we do, which we desire for its own sake . . . and if we do not choose everything for the sake of something else (for at that rate the process would go on to infinity, so that our desire would be empty and vain), clearly this must be

the good and the chief good" (1980:1094a19–23); "evil belongs to the class of the unlimited, as the Pythagoreans conjectured, and good to that of the limited" (1106b29–31); "the
Final cause of a thing is an *end*, and is such that it does not happen for the sake of something else, but all other things happen for its sake. So if there is to be a last term of this
kind, the series will not be infinite; and if there is no such term, there will be no Final cause.
Those who introduce infinity do not realize that they are abolishing the nature of the
Good" (1933–35:994b9–14).

2. For his critique of the Forms, see Aristotle 1980: bk. 1, ch. 6; Aristotle 1989: bk. 1, ch.
9. For his critique of division, see Aristotle 1975: bk. 2, chs. 5, 13; see also Balme 1975:183–
85. On Aristotle's use of the homonymity of terms in his early critiques of the possibility
of first science, see Owen 1986: ch. 10; Ferejohn 1980.

3. Many interpreters hold Aristotle's method to be in the first instance empirical, but
they fail to appreciate that the empirical argument rests on a prior dialectical demonstration and is not simply introduced by it. See Owen 1986: chs. 8 and 13, the arguments in
which are taken up and modified by Nussbaum (1986: ch. 8) and Wains (1992). Bolton
(1991) opposes such viewpoints but is unable to fully account for the dialectical argument
presented in *Physics,* bk. 1, ch. 3, treating it as a supplement to Aristotle's empiricism even
while admitting that natural philosophy could not avoid skepticism without it.

4. On contrariety as maximal difference in general, see Aristotle 1933–35: bk. 10, ch. 4;
on its relation to knowledge, see ibid.: bk. 3, ch. 2; on its relation to ethics, see Aristotle
1980: bk. 2, ch. 8, and bk. 4, ch. 4.

5. On this dual meaning of origin arising with Aristotle, see Heidegger 1976:227–28;
Schürmann 1987:95–105.

6. See Heidegger 1976, which shows how this primacy given to presencing over presence also points to a residual understanding of Being as presencing.

7. In the same way, the polis is prior to the family and individual, even though it is last
in the order of development. See Aristotle 1988: bk. 1, ch. 2.

8. Heidegger (1976:259–63) rightly rejects any simple analogy between nature and techne
that implies one can replace the other. Nature, he argues, is the self-inception and domination of form, but it is not a self-making even though it is part of a wider category of self-
production. Nonetheless, Aristotle strictly divides moving beings into natural and artifi-
cial, and in both these fields the movement is understood in terms of telos. Moreover, as
Schürmann (1987:99–100) notes, the origin of this reasoning falls on the side of art.

9. On the uncertain consequences for mathematics, see Hintikka 1979.

10. The reason the term *place* cannot mean "dimensional entity" becomes clear only
when Aristotle ties it to his argument against the existence of void as part of his larger
opposition to atomism; see Aristotle 1934–57: bk. 4, ch. 7.

11. Furley nonetheless finds this answer acceptable because "motion is defined as the
actualization of an *incomplete* potentiality; there is no reason why Aristotle should insist
on the existence of a completed motion as a prior condition. The potentiality of the infinite seems to be as legitimate as the potentiality of motion" (1967:154). This is certainly
odd, since Aristotle is clear that motion presupposes a telos.

12. Hintikka (1979) tries to answer this by suggesting that for Aristotle infinite divisibility is sufficiently actualized by being conceived by the mind, in the sense not that

thought can ever grasp the infinite all at once but that it can continue along its path endlessly. But then there is no reason to reject infinite extension of space as well as time, since it can be conceived by the mind in the same way.

13. Aristotle employs other senses of definition that do not invoke the notion of classification. A thing may be defined by its causes (as a solar eclipse is defined by the moon's being interposed between the sun and earth) or by an account of its material components and their arrangement. But these usages are limited. The first is suitable to events rather than substances and so constitutes a pseudo-definition. The second is appropriate only for artifacts, not natural beings. See LeBlond 1979.

14. There is no consensus on the meaning of matter as Aristotle's principle of individuation. See Lukasiewicz, Ascombe, and Popper 1953; Regis 1976; Rorty 1973.

15. "The reality of a thing is the last such predication to hold of these atoms" (Aristotle 1975:96b12–13), but these predicates must belong further than the subject predicated, even though "all <of them together> will not <belong> further" (96a33–34).

16. This issue is addressed in ch. 6.

17. The two errors are, in fact, the same: if a thing can come into being from absolute nonexistence, it might do so under any condition whatsoever; see Long and Sedley 1987:26.

18. Compare this with Aristotle's criticism of the early atomists, where he holds that first principles must be homogeneous with their products (1984b: bk. 3, ch. 7).

19. On the true and false infinite and limit in Epicureanism, see Deleuze 1990:266–79.

20. All translations of Epicurus are from Epicurus 1993. The page numbers provided are the standard ones for those writings preserved in book 10 of Diogenes Laertius's *Lives of the Eminent Philosophers.* The fragments quoted in other ancient texts, and the *Vatican Sayings,* discovered in the nineteenth century, are cited with the fragment or saying number provided in Epicurus 1993.

21. On whether the Epicurean void is extended, empty space or an "impalpable substance" that is neither matter nor mere nothingness, see Bailey 1964:294–96; Rist 1972:56; Inwood 1981; Sedley 1982.

22. See Epicurus 1993:56–60; Lucretius 1992:1.599–34. On the analogical relation between perceptual, physical, and theoretical minima, see Furley 1967:7–43.

23. The key statements of Epicurus are 1993:56, 59. On whether this implies any "mathematical atomism," see Vlastos 1965; Mau 1973.

24. Against those who hold that such directions cannot exist in infinite space, Epicurus (1993:60) defines up and down relative to any fixed point.

25. On the reason the theory of atomic swerve does not appear in Epicurus's surviving writings, see Rist 1972:48n.1; Englert 1987:9–11. On the underlying reason for introducing the swerve, see Long and Sedley 1987:52; O'Keefe 1996.

26. For the young Marx (1975:49), the declination of the atom sustains its individuality, albeit in a still abstract form.

27. For the many interpreters who hold Epicurus to a theory of absolute minimal parts, this swerve of the least possible distance is the minimum of conceivable extension, or the size of a part of an atom. This leads to the geometrical dilemma already noted. However, Richard Sorabji, using the logic of analogy, suggests that for Epicurus, "the smallest visible speck is probably too small for us to *perceive* any edge to it, and hence any shape. By

analogy, we should be unable to *conceive* an edge or shape in the smallest *conceivable* part. There has been much discussion of the shape to be ascribed to the minimal parts in Epicurus' atom. My suggestion is that they have no shape at all. If they have no shape, Epicurus will be able to escape certain geometrical objections, for example, the objection that the diagonal of a square minimum part would have to exceed the side by less than a minimal length" (1983:371–72). In short, the way out of the impasse is to go beyond the minimum—or to see the minimum itself as a beyond—and treat the swerve as a movement in which normal notions of space (and, using the same reasoning, one can add time, although Sorabji [375–77] does not do so) no longer apply. That is, the space and time of the *clinamen* would be only analogous with perceived space and time, as the atom itself is only analogous to a perceived body divided into parts. Deleuze maintains that this is exactly what Lucretius intends: "The meanings of the terms which qualify it [the *clinamen*] have in fact this origin: '*incertus*' does not mean indeterminate, but rather unassignable; '*paulum*,' '*incerto tempore*,' '*intervello minimo*' mean 'in a time smaller than the minimum of continuous, thinkable time'" (1990:269–70).

28. Furley (1967:161) holds that the terminology of free will is not part of the original Epicurean doctrine.

29. On the mechanisms by which the swerve is meant to ensure free will, see Bailey 1964:433–37; Furley 1967: study 2, 161–237; Englert 1987. Connolly (1999) argues that the *clinamen* effects a rethinking of free will, opening it to practices applied to the self that never entirely escape cultural, environmental, and other forces but that in turn are not reducible to them.

30. Lucretius thereby refuses a paradigm of objectivity resting on a militarist approach that seeks domination, a move with consequences for both his science and his politics. See Cabisius 1984–85; Fowler 1989; Serres 1982: ch. 9.

31. "Philosophy as the art of discovering truth: according to Aristotle. Contradicted by the Epicureans, who made use of Aristotle's sensualistic theory of knowledge: they rejected the search for truth with irony; 'Philosophy as an art of *living*'" (Nietzsche 1967a: §449).

32. But Aristotle does state that "temples should also be scattered throughout the country, dedicated some to gods and some to heroes" (1988:1331b17–18), and that the divination of heavenly bodies and the anthropomorphization of the gods are "an inspired saying" that serve "to influence the vulgar and as a constitutional and utilitarian expedient" (1933–35:1074b10, 1074b5). On Aristotle's early Platonism see Jaeger 1948. Against Jaeger, see Owen 1986: ch. 11.

33. On the distinction between "katastematic" and "kinetic" pleasures, see Merlan 1960: ch. 1; Rist 1972: ch. 6.

34. Foucault maintains that care of the self for its own sake begins with Epicureanism. See Foucault 1984b, 1986.

35. It is therefore insufficient to subsume the Epicurean withdrawal from politics as part of the general apathy that followed the fall of the Greek polis. See Farrington 1967:1. However, against the typical understanding of a total Epicurean rejection of activism, see Fowler 1989.

36. This is clear in the tactics by which Lucretius seeks to downplay the more unappealing implications of Epicurean thought. See Nichols 1976:50–52 and chs. 3–4 generally.

Chapter 4: The One and the Many

1. There is no need to consider here whether the good is supposed to operate on a co-originary force of disorder and evil or the latter is seen merely as a derivation of the former. By the time of Plotinus, the issue is clearly resolved in the second way. For a brief review of the key historical positions, see Armstrong 1992. In all cases, the good is identified with order, form, and reason, and what is at issue here, regardless of whether a principle of disorder and irrationality is said to coexist, is the attempt to maintain the separation and purity of the good from its "dark other."

2. Deleuze levels a related critique against Plato; see 1990:253–66.

3. For the influences of Greek, and specifically Platonic, philosophy on early Christian theology, see Stead 1994.

4. On the distinction Augustine enacts between time (*chronos*) and eternity (*aion*), see Augustine 1961: bk. 11; Augustine 1984:11.11; see also Rist 1994:73–85; Dewart 1987; Quinn 1992.

5. On the extent to which the problem of evil remained largely unthematized prior to Augustine, see Rist 1994:262–66.

6. The Manichean heresy is "the notion that the Devil has evil as the essential principle of his being, that his nature derives from some hostile First Principle" (Augustine 1984:11.13).

7. Augustine further insists that the universe was created solely due to God's goodness and not to restrain a prior evil (1984:11.23).

8. See Evans 1982: ch. 1; as well as Augustine 1961:2.8, where Augustine, reflecting on an incident when he stole pears from a neighbor simply for the thrill of sin, cannot find any "thing" in it that could have provided him with happiness.

9. Whether Augustine has this firmly in mind when celebrating the burning of heretics at the stake is uncertain.

10. Not surprisingly, Augustine insists elsewhere that God had the power to prevent evil from arising (1984:14.27). Gilson misses this point, holding that for Augustine the possibility of evil use is a necessary condition for the goodness of will (see 1960:143–48).

11. Augustine tries to avoid this conclusion by treating evil will not as an efficient cause but as a deficiency (1984:12.7). On the accusations of hidden Manicheanism Augustine faced in his lifetime, see Bonner 1986: chs. 8–9.

12. This logic underlies Augustine's argument regarding Christ as the true mediator; see 1984:9.16–17.

13. Since "future citizens" of the city of God remain hidden in the worldly city (Augustine 1984:1.35), the Church must assemble them "where they can hear how they ought to live a good life on earth for a space, so that they may deserve hereafter to live a life of bliss for ever" (2.28).

14. The structure of the *Nag Hammadi Library* supports this view (Filoramo 1990:18). There is also evidence in the meaning of gnosis, which "emphasizes the act of knowing rather than knowledge itself" (39).

15. The connections between antifoundationalism and Gnosticism are widely recognized, with Hans Jonas famously linking Gnosticism to Heidegger's twentieth-century

rethinking of ontology (see 1970: ch. 13 and epilogue). The works of Patricia Cox Miller and Joel Fineman, cited later, locate Gnosticism's affinities with the work of Derrida and Lacan. Nonetheless, such likenesses are often used to disparage Gnostic thought as nihilistic. See, for example, Keffer 1985; Patrick 1987.

16. Gnosticism is certainly not a monolithic doctrine, and consequently the use of such an overarching term—and even the names given to various sects—has been strongly criticized. On challenges to the internal unity of Sethianism, see Wisse 1981; Schenke 1981. Against the Church Fathers' depiction of Gnosticism as a heresy internal to Christianity, see Jonas 1970; Pearson 1990; Perkins 1993: pt. 1; Mansfeld 1981. Jonas's syncretic reading has been challenged from a postcolonialist studies perspective by King (1994).

Despite their sophistication, it is rare within these debates to challenge the logic of naming itself or the assumption that a properly descriptive term is to be sought. M. Williams (1996), for example, holds the term *Gnosticism* to be incoherent and unproductive, but the force of his argument rests largely on explicit comparison with other terms of identity—e.g., *Christian* or *Jew*—simply asserted to be better defined and less burdened with caricatures and problematic metaphors. Hence the alternative he suggests is to maintain the names of various sects, such as Valentinianism, which purportedly have sufficient internal coherence, and replace the overarching category with less inclusive but still wide typological groupings such as the sterile "biblical demiurgical tradition" used throughout the text.

The Nag Hammadi texts may generally be described as Christian Gnostic writings, although several tractates clearly derive from non-Christian sources, and others have added to them a "superficial Christianizing 'veneer'" (Hendrick and Hodgson 1986:4). The tractates themselves are categorized as largely Valentinian and Sethian, the sects with the most sophisticated ontologies and against whom Plotinus most likely directed his anti-Gnostic polemic. Without either dismissing the scholarly divisions or ignoring the challenges to them, this chapter will draw out a set of ontological and ethical themes from these diverse tractates. The purpose is not to suggest that they are all saying the same thing but rather to articulate through them an ontology and ethic of difference directly related to this chapter's examination of the Neoplatonist Christian attempt to secure unity through transcendence. Toward this end, themes gathered from the entire range of tractates can be seen to complement one another.

17. References to Nag Hammadi texts take the form of the name of the tractate in the *Nag Hammadi Library* (*NHL*); the numbers indicate the codex, tractate, page, and line. Tractate names are abbreviated after first use. All translations are from Robinson 1988, which uses a variety of scholarly apparatus: square brackets indicate lacunae in the original texts and contain either the translator's attempted reconstruction or an ellipsis if reconstruction is impossible; parentheses indicate material the editor or translator provided as material useful to the reader; and angle brackets indicate a correction of a scribal omission or error.

18. Focusing on the Nag Hammadi tractate *The Gospel of Truth*, Fineman (1980) argues that the Valentinian practice of naming follows a logic of metaphoric slippage that establishes the Godhead as a Lacanian-style Lack.

19. Emanationism as a productive process is specifically linked to Valentinian Gnosticism, but Sethian tractates are similarly read to present a Neoplatonic hierarchy of being

organized around a Godhead and fading progressively into nonbeing. The important point here is that an equation of distance with loss is commonly ascribed to both sects. On the relations between Gnosticism and Neoplatonism, see Wallis 1992.

20. Marcionite and Manichean eschatologies are significantly different; see Jonas 1970: chs. 6, 9.

21. On the difference between emanation and immanence, see Deleuze 1992:169–74.

22. On the similarity between the language of Plotinus and the Gnostics, see Bazán 1992; Dillon 1992; Hancock 1992.

23. Miller (1992) argues that Gnostic criticisms of the concept of creation are based precisely on its failure to capture the erotic dimension of making. Begetting, she argues, does not separate creator from created but rather institutes an ambiguous bond of Eros between them.

24. Plotinus clearly misunderstands the distinction between creation and begetting when attacking Gnosticism. Challenging the idea that the material world could result from a fallen soul, he asserts "its creative act to be a proof not of decline but rather of its steadfast hold. Its decline could consist only in its forgetting the Divine: but if it forgot, how could it create? Whence does it create but from the things it knew in the Divine?" (1956:2.9.4). But such ignorance is precisely what marks the difference between creation and begetting. Hence, "he who creates cannot beget. He who begets also has power to create" (*Gos. Phil., NHL* 2.3.81.23–24).

25. In some Gnostic myths, the Fall is presented in highly positive terms. In *The Tripartite Tractate*, for example, the cause of sin is "an abundant love" of the Father and a desire to glorify him (*NHL* 1.5.76.19–20).

26. See Filoramo 1990: ch. 4. The distinction between the two sects is not entirely consistent (Jonas 1970:182n.11). Other sects, notably Manicheanism, tie the Fall to an external force of darkness (ch. 9).

27. On Gnostic depictions of the physical creation in terms of a two-dimensional painting of a three-dimensional living face, see Pépin 1992:316–18.

28. Compare the following with the analysis of *The Tripartite Tractate* by Miller (1989), who argues that the universe created by the fallen Logos is constructed on a literalist and representationalist logic reflecting the demiurge's misrecognition of the play of polyvalence and dissemination that characterizes the Pleroma.

29. As Jonas remarks with regard to Heidegger and Gnosticism, "Only where there is a whole is there a law" (1970:334). The whole must be broken to escape the demiurge.

30. For the Gnostic interpretation of Genesis and the original sin, see especially *Ap. John, NHL* 2.1; *The Hypostasis of the Archons, NHL* 2.4; *The Testimony of Truth, NHL* 9.3.

31. The embodiment of light escaping, tricking, and mocking the demiurge is a common feature among diverse mythemes of the *Nag Hammadi Library,* whether the figure of illumination is Jesus (*The Second Treatise of the Great Seth, NHL* 7.2; *The Apocalypse of Peter, NHL* 7.3), Eve (*On the Origin of the World, NHL* 2.5), or Sophia (*Ap. John, NHL* 2.1; *Hyp. Arch., NHL* 2.4).

32. Bloom (1980) finds in Valentinian gnosis a negative form of knowledge exceeding any Christian negative theology or Hegelian dialectical negation.

33. Of the Carpocrates and Caïnites, for example, Irenaeus writes: "According to their own writings their souls must try out every possible way of living so that when they de-

part they have nothing left to do" (*Against Heresies* 1.25.4, in Grant 1997:93; see also ibid.:1.31.2, in Grant 1997:105; Jonas 1970:270–74). Oddly, Irenaeus admits doubt as to the truthfulness of the charges against these sects (Grant 1981:166–67). On the inconsistencies and hesitations in Irenaeus's account, see M. Williams 1996:167–69. On the question of the actual existence of a Cainite sect, see Pearson 1990: ch. 6.

Chapter 5: Reason and Faith

1. On the difference between univocal and homonymous terms see Aristotle 1984: bk. 1. On "being" having a common sense see Aristotle 1933–35: bk. 4, ch. 2.

2. This reasoning requires that God's power of cause and effect be analogous to that known through sense experience, so that the analogy of being depends on accepting a prior analogy. For Gilson, however, there is no such problem. The analogous relation of cause and effect follows from the analysis of being: a cause can give to its effect only what it *is;* being is thus the ultimate root of causality, and God is most purely and simply being (see Gilson 1991: ch. 5).

3. Against the standard interpretation of Aquinas as adopting a metaphysical analogy of being, see McInerny 1961.

4. God's existence may seem to be not a demonstrable fact but the first article of faith. Aquinas holds instead that it follows from undemonstrable first principles of reason that are not held by faith but rather self-evident in themselves, if not necessarily self-evident to the human mind; see Aquinas 1993:196–99.

5. Gilson (1991: chs. 3–4) attributes this and other differences to the Christian privileging of God as being over truth and goodness, a position drawn from Exodus 3:14 ("I am that I am") and alien to Greek thought.

6. Here Aquinas distinguishes between "change" as an activity occurring in time and involving a common temporality and a subject that undergoes alteration, and "creation," in which "the only thing in common is imaginary" (1993:258).

7. On the differences between Aquinas's hierarchy of being and a Platonist model of participation, see Henle 1956.

8. The essence of a man, for example, can be signified fully by the term *man* or only in part by terms such as *humanity.* The latter names only the formal aspect of the being's essence without reference to its material embodiment. One can therefore say, "Socrates is a man" but not, "Socrates is humanity" (see Aquinas 1968: ch. 2). An immaterial substance can be signified only in full "because nothing is there beside the form as its recipient. That is why the essence of a simple substance, no matter how we conceive it, can be attributed to the substance" (ch. 4., sect. 4). Hence, just as Aristotle maintains, "soul and essence of soul are the same, but man and essence of man are not" (Aristotle 1933–35:1043b3–4).

9. On the use of the distinction between essence and existence or act-of-being against Platonist essentialist ontologies, see Gilson 1994: pt. 1, chs. 1–3 and 6; Henle 1956: pt. 2, chs. 5–6.

10. On the differences with the being that Aquinas similarly makes the first object of the intellect, see Gilson 1991: chs. 12–13; Bettoni 1978: pt. 2, ch. 1.

11. Scotus here draws on Aristotle 1933–35:1030a17–21; see Harris 1927: vol. 2, pp. 55–57.

12. On the way Scotus negotiates between the Augustinian rejection of sense experience and Aristotelian empiricism, see Gilson 1955:10.2; Bettoni 1978:41–46; Wolter 1946:71–77. On his attacks on the theory of illumination, see Brown 1978.

13. Heidegger (1978) shows how this conversion gives rise to excess. Oneness opens a domain of mathematics; truth, one of logic and meaning. These realms are not reducible to the field of actuality and require categories other than the ten traditionally given for being. Heidegger argues that the theory of categories breaks down here, for it must address problems of judgment and the subject that are significantly greater than that of maintaining the primary diversity of the categories while avoiding complete equivocity.

14. This does not mean that this agent can violate the law of contradiction. If two effects cannot exist simultaneously, however, it is because of the nature of the effects, not a weakness on the part of the agent (Duns Scotus 1987:64).

15. The idea in dispute here is the claim that a power capable of creating being from nothing must be infinite by virtue of bridging the infinite distance between these extremes. But Scotus argues that this is not a truly infinite distance and that being and nothing are not extremes connected by any space, infinite or otherwise, since the slightest deviation from one immediately and fully invokes the other (Duns Scotus 1987:67).

16. These divisions are famously introduced in Duns Scotus 1966: ch. 1. However, Scotus notes early on (1.5) that he is not using "essential order" in the strict sense, in which the posterior is ordered and the prior transcends that order. This allows him to treat as essential orders series of cause and effect that are not ontologically ordered (2.34–51). On the various subdivisions of essential order, see Prentice 1970: ch. 4.

17. An order can be essential where it is necessary for A to come before B if B is to exist, but this does not imply an ontological ordering of A and B.

18. The link between the orders of eminence and dependence lies in the final cause, for anything with a final cause implies a being of greater eminence (Harris 1927: vol. 2, pp. 71–72; Prentice 1970:123).

19. On Scotus's attempt to reconcile an Aristotelian-inspired proof of a first mover with Anselm's ontological argument, see Bettoni 1978:143–45. On his rejection of physicalist proofs, see Gilson 1955:457–59; Prentice 1970:124–32; Effler 1965. Harris (1927: vol. 2, ch. 5) and R. Wood (1987) hold that Scotus does provide an a posteriori proof based on experience.

20. An accidental effect is not ordered to its cause, but following Aristotle, Scotus holds that accident presupposes purposeful action (see Duns Scotus 1966:2.9–10; Duns Scotus 1987:47–48).

21. Their common necessity must arise from what they share in common. The question is simply whether their differences are also part of what makes them necessary.

22. Here is where the problem of the origin of evil arises for Scotus, and he employs the same responses as Augustine, with as little success; see Harris 1927: vol. 2, pp. 336–44.

23. The authenticity of the *Theoremata* is unimportant here, since even the accepted works, such as Duns Scotus 1966:4.67–72, admit that the Catholic understanding of infinite power cannot be demonstrated.

24. Since Ockham does not completely sever the connection between thought and reality, some hold the nominalist label to be inappropriate. See Boehner 1958: esp. 156–74 ("The Realistic Conceptualism of William Ockham").

25. See Ockham 1990:18–25; Adams 1987: ch. 13; Coleman 1992: ch. 22; Leff 1975: chs. 1–2.

26. On Ockham's acceptance of Boethius's distinction between *quod est* (what a thing is) and *quo est* (by which a thing is) but not that of essence and existence, see Boehner 1958:373–99 ("The Metaphysics of William Ockham").

27. Since the same general effect can often be produced by several causes—fire, for example, can substitute for the heat of the sun—it is not necessary to posit any partial cause as permanent (Ockham 1994:117–18). The only constituent that can be said to be absolutely necessary to the production of a human is another human, and so it cannot be proven that one human is not the total cause of another.

28. This passage is part of an objection to the question at issue, but Ockham agrees with it on this point.

29. Hence, Ockham maintains, the word for "man" may differ in various languages, but they all refer to the same mental concept. As Gilson (1938:71–74) notes, Ockham provides no basis for asserting this commonality of perception.

30. Gilson (1938: ch. 3) follows Hochstetter in accusing Ockham of opening the door to skepticism by admitting that God can cause intuitive cognition of nonexistents. Against Gilson see Boehner 1958:268–300, 300–319; Leff 1975: ch. 1. Adams (1987: ch. 14) admits Ockham's position has skeptical implications but claims he is no more vulnerable than his predecessors.

31. "It is henceforth inevitable that analogy falls into an unresolvable difficulty: it must essentially relate being to particular existents, but at the same time it cannot say what constitutes their individuality. For it retains in the particular only that which conforms to the general (matter and form), and seeks the principle of individuation in this or that element of the fully constituted individuals" (Deleuze 1994:38).

32. On the idea of a principle of individuation being mistakenly ascribed to Scotus, see Gracia 1996.

33. On real and cognitive formalities, see Bettoni 1978:2.4; Coleman 1992: ch. 21. On the background to Scotus's conceptions of common nature and individuation, see Tweedle 1993; R. Wood 1996.

34. Most often, Ockham quotes Duns Scotus 1994: n.34.

35. In support of Ockham see Adams 1987: vol. 1, ch. 2; Boehner 1958. Ockham does accept formal distinction for the three divine persons.

36. Subjective parts can be predicated of the whole they divide, just as individuals can be predicated of their species and species of their genus.

37. Here Scotus holds, against Aquinas, that matter cannot be reduced to pure potentiality. It is created and must have some degree of act-of-existence, and so it cannot be an individuating principle but rather requires one.

38. This does not mean, though, that the individuals constituted by these differences are absolutely diverse and so not of any common species. See Duns Scotus 1994: nn.185–86.

39. "Every quidditative entity (whether partial or total) in some genus is of itself indifferent as a quidditative entity to this individual entity and that one, in such a way that as a quidditative entity it is naturally prior to this individual entity insofar as it is a 'this'" (Duns Scotus 1994: n.187).

40. Heidegger (1978:69–82) levels a similar criticism against Scotus's treatment of individuals in relation to quantitative and analogically derived standards that measure them.

41. Ockham rightly notes that formal difference is compatible with divine simplicity—which Scotus himself maintains in holding that the various perfections in God can be formally distinguished—but incorrectly suggests that this invokes a real rather than a simply conceptual univocity between God and creatures. Ockham (1994: question 6, nn.87–90) argues that there is no basis for excluding the merely formally distinct factors of nature and contracting difference from the pseudocomposition of the divine essence. But nature and difference are derived from the existence of real relations among real finite beings, and since God does not participate in such relations, there is sufficient reason to exclude these factors from his essence. Against this, see Adams 1987:931–41.

Bibliography

Adams, Marilyn McCord. 1987. *Ockham*. 2 vols. Notre Dame, Ind.: University of Notre Dame Press.

Adorno, Theodor. 1993. *Hegel: Three Studies*. Trans. Sherry Weber Nicholson. Cambridge, Mass.: MIT Press.

———. 1995. *Negative Dialectics*. Trans. E. B. Ashton. New York: Continuum.

Ansell Pearson, Keith. 1997. *Viroid Life: Perspectives on Nietzsche and the Transhuman Condition*. London: Routledge.

Aquinas, St. Thomas. 1968. *On Being and Essence*. Trans. Armand Maurer, CSB. Toronto: Pontifical Institute of Medieval Studies.

———. 1988. *St. Thomas Aquinas on Politics and Ethics*. Trans. Paul E. Sigmund. New York: Norton.

———. 1989. *Summa Theologiae: A Concise Translation*. Ed. Timothy McDermott. Westminster, Md.: Christian Classics.

———. 1993. *Selected Philosophical Writings*. Trans. Timothy McDermott. Oxford: Oxford University Press.

Aristotle. 1933–35. *Metaphysics*. 2 vols. Trans. Hugh Tredennick. Cambridge, Mass.: Loeb Classics.

———. 1934–57. *Physics*. 2 vols. Trans. P. H. Whicksteed and F. M. Cornford. Cambridge, Mass.: Loeb Classics.

———. 1975. *Posterior Analytics*. Trans. Jonathan Barnes. Oxford: Clarendon.

———. 1980. *Nichomachean Ethics*. Trans. David Ross. Oxford: Oxford University Press.

———. 1984a. *Categories*. In *The Complete Works of Aristotle: The Revised Oxford Translation*, 2 vols., ed. Jonathan Barnes, trans. J. L. Ackrill, 1:3–26. Princeton, N.J.: Princeton University Press.

———. 1984b. *On the Heavens*. In *The Complete Works of Aristotle: The Revised Oxford Translation*, 2 vols., ed. Jonathan Barnes, trans. J. L. Ackrill, 1:447–511. Princeton, N.J.: Princeton University Press.

———. 1988. *Politics*. Trans. Benjamin Jowett. Cambridge: Cambridge University Press.

Armstrong, A. H. 1992. "Dualism: Platonic, Gnostic and Christian." In *NeoPlatonism and Gnosticism*, ed. Wallis, 33–54.

Augustine, St. 1961. *Confessions.* Trans. R. S. Pine-Coffin. London: Penguin Books.

———. 1984. *City of God.* Trans. Henry Bettenson. London: Penguin Books.

———. 1993. *On Free Choice of the Will.* Trans. Thomas Williams. Indianapolis, Ind.: Hackett.

Badiou, Alain. 2000. *Deleuze: The Clamor of Being.* Trans. Louise Burchill. Minneapolis: University of Minnesota Press.

Bailey, Cyril. 1964. *The Greek Atomists and Epicurus: A Study.* New York: Russell and Russell.

Balme, D. M. 1975. "Aristotle's Use of Differentiae in Zoology." In *Articles on Aristotle I,* ed. Jonathan Barnes, Malcolm Schofield, and Richard Sorabji, 183–93. London: Duckworth.

Barnes, Jonathan, Malcolm Schofield, and Richard Sorabji, eds. 1979. *Articles on Aristotle III: Metaphysics.* London: Duckworth.

Baugh, Bruce. 1992. "Transcendental Empiricism: Deleuze's Response to Hegel." *Man and World* 25, no. 2:133–48.

Bazán, Francisco Garcia. 1992. "The 'Second God' in Gnosticism and Plotinus's Anti-Gnostic Polemic." In *NeoPlatonism and Gnosticism*, ed. Wallis, 55–83.

Benjamin, Andrew. 1993. *The Plural Event: Descartes, Hegel, Heidegger.* London: Routledge.

Bergson, Henri. 1955. *An Introduction to Metaphysics.* Trans. T. E. Hulme. New York: Macmillan.

Berlin, Isaiah. 1969. *Four Essays on Liberty.* Oxford: Oxford University Press.

Bettoni, Efrem, OFM. 1978. *Duns Scotus: The Basic Principles of His Philosophy.* Trans. Bernadine Bonansea, OFM. Westport, Conn.: Greenwood.

Blanchot, Maurice. 1988. *The Unavowable Community.* Trans. Pierre Joris. Barrytown, N.Y.: Station Hill.

Bloom, Harold. 1980. "Lying against Time." In *The Rediscovery of Gnosticism,* ed. Layton, 1:57–72.

Blumenberg, Hans. 1983. *The Legitimacy of the Modern Age.* 2d rev. ed. Trans. Robert M. Wallace. Cambridge, Mass.: MIT Press.

Boehner, Philotheus, OFM. 1958. *Collected Articles on Ockham.* Ed. Eligius M. Buytaert, OFM. New York: Franciscan Institute.

Bogue, Ronald. 1989. *Deleuze and Guattari.* London: Routledge.

Bolton, Robert. 1991. "Aristotle's Method in Natural Science: *Physics* I." In *Aristotle's Physics: A Collection of Essays,* ed. Lindsay Judson, 1–29. Oxford: Clarendon.

Bonner, Gerald. 1986. *St. Augustine of Hippo: Life and Controversies.* 2d ed. Norwich, U.K.: Canterbury.

Boundas, Constantin. 1994. "Deleuze: Serialization and Subject Formation." In *Gilles Deleuze and the Theater of Philosophy,* ed. Constantin V. Boundas and Dorothea Olkowski, 99–116. London: Routledge.

———. 1996. "Deleuze-Bergson: An Ontology of the Virtual." In *Deleuze: A Critical Reader,* ed. Patton, 81–106.

Brown, Jerome V. 1978. "John Duns Scotus on Henry of Ghent's Theory of Knowledge." *The Modern Schoolman* 65, no. 1 (Nov.): 1–29.

Butler, Judith. 1987. *Subjects of Desire: Hegelian Reflections in Twentieth Century France.* New York: Columbia University Press.

Casibius, Gail. 1984–85. "Social Metaphor and the Atomic Cycle in Lucretius." *The Classical Journal* 80, no. 2:109–20.

Cauchi, Francesca. 1998. *Zarathustra contra Zarathustra: The Tragic Buffoon.* Aldershot, U.K.: Ashgate.

Cicero. 1991. *On Duties.* Ed. M. T. Griffin and E. M. Atkins. Cambridge: Cambridge University Press.

Coleman, Janet. 1992. *Ancient and Medieval Memories: Studies in the Reconstruction of the Past.* Cambridge: Cambridge University Press.

Connolly, William. 1993. *Political Theory and Modernity.* 2d ed. Ithaca, N.Y.: Cornell University Press.

———. 1995. *The Ethos of Pluralization.* Minneapolis: University of Minnesota Press.

———. 1999. "Brain Waves, Transcendental Fields and Techniques of Thought." *Radical Philosophy* 94 (Mar.–Apr.): 19–28.

Conway, Daniel W. 1990. "Nietzsche contra Nietzsche: The Deconstruction of Zarathustra." In *Nietzsche as Postmodernist,* ed. Clayton Koelb, 91–110. Albany: State University of New York Press.

Deleuze, Gilles. 1983. *Nietzsche and Philosophy* Trans. Hugh Tomlinson. London: Athlone.

———. 1988. *Foucault.* Trans. Seán Hand. London: Athlone.

———. 1990. *The Logic of Sense.* Trans. Mark Lester with Charles Stivale. New York: Columbia University Press.

———. 1991. *Bergsonism.* Trans. Hugh Tomlinson and Barbara Habberjam. New York: Zone Books.

———. 1992. *Expressionism in Philosophy: Spinoza.* Trans. Martin Joughin. New York: Zone Books.

———. 1993. *The Fold: Leibniz and the Baroque.* Trans. Tom Conley. Minneapolis: University of Minnesota Press.

———. 1994. *Difference and Repetition.* Trans. Paul Patton. London: Athlone.

Deleuze, Gilles, and Félix Guattari. 1983. *Anti-Oedipus: Capitalism and Schizophrenia.* Trans. Robert Hurley, Mark Seem, and Helen R. Lane. Minneapolis: University of Minnesota Press.

———. 1987. *A Thousand Plateaus: Capitalism and Schizophrenia.* Trans. Brian Massumi. Minneapolis: University of Minnesota Press.

———. 1994. *What is Philosophy?* Trans. Hugh Tomlinson and Graham Burchell. New York: Columbia University Press.

Descombes, Vincent. 1980. *Modern French Philosophy.* Trans. L. Scott-Fox and J. M. Harding. Cambridge: Cambridge University Press.

Detwiler, Bruce. 1990. *Nietzsche and the Politics of Aristocratic Radicalism.* Chicago: University of Chicago Press.

Dewart, Joanne McWilliam. 1987. "Augustine's Struggle with Time and History." *Congresso Internationale Su S. Augustino Nel XVI Centenaris Della Conversione* [International Congress on St. Augustine in the sixteenth centenary of his conversion], acts 1–3, vol. 2:467–82.

Dillon, John. 1992. "*Pleroma* and Noetic Cosmos: A Comparative Study." In *NeoPlatonism and Gnosticism,* ed. Wallis, 99–110.

Diogenes Laertius. 1965. *Lives of Eminent Philosophers.* 2 vols. Trans. R. D. Hicks. Cambridge, Mass.: Loeb Classics.

Duns Scotus, John. 1966. *A Treatise on God as First Principle*. Trans. Allan Wolter, OFM. Chicago: Franciscan Herald.

———. 1987. *Philosophical Writings*. 2d ed. Trans. Allan Wolter, OFM. Indianapolis: Hackett.

———. 1994. "Six Questions on Individuation from His *Ordinatio*, II. d. 3, part 1, qq. 1–6." In *Five Texts on the Medieval Problem of Universals*, ed. and trans. Vincent Spade, 57–113. Indianapolis: Hackett.

Effler, Roy. 1965. "Duns Scotus and the Physical Approach to God." In *Studies in Philosophy and the History of Philosophy, Volume III: Duns Scotus*, ed. John Ryan and Bernadine Bonasea, 171–90. Washington, D.C.: Catholic University of America Press.

Englert, Walter G. 1987. *Epicurus on the Swerve and Voluntary Action*. American Classical Studies, no. 16. Atlanta: Scholars.

Epicurus. 1993. *The Essential Epicurus: Letters, Principal Doctrines, Vatican Sayings, and Fragments*. Trans. Eugene O'Connor. Buffalo, N.Y.: Prometheus Books.

Evans, Gillian R. 1982. *Augustine on Evil*. Cambridge: Cambridge University Press.

Farrington, Benjamin. 1967. *The Faith of Epicurus*. London: Weidenfeld and Nicolson.

Ferejohn, Michael T. 1980. "Aristotle on Focal Meaning and the Unity of Science." *Phronesis* 25, no. 2:117–28.

Festugière, A. J. 1956. *Epicurus and His Gods*. Trans. C. W. Chilton. Cambridge, Mass.: Harvard University Press.

Filoramo, Giovanni. 1990. *A History of Gnosticism*. Trans. Anthony Alcock. Oxford: Blackwell.

Fineman, Joel. 1980. "The Gospel of Truth." In *The Rediscovery of Gnosticism*, ed. Layton, 1:289–318.

Foucault, Michel. 1977. "Revolutionary Action: 'Until Now.'" In *Language, Counter-Memory, Practice*. Trans. Donald F. Bouchard and Sherry Simon, 218–33. Ithaca, N.Y.: Cornell University Press.

———. 1984a. "The Order of Discourse." In *Language and Politics*, ed. Michael Shapiro, 108–38. Oxford: Blackwell.

———. 1984b. "On the Genealogy of Ethics: An Overview of Work in Progress." In *The Foucault Reader*, ed. Paul Rabinow, 340–72. New York: Pantheon Books.

———. 1984c. "Politics and Ethics: An Interview." In *The Foucault Reader*, ed. Paul Rabinow, 373–80. New York: Pantheon Books.

———. 1986. *The History of Sexuality, Volume 3: The Care of the Self*. Trans. Robert Hurley. London: Penguin Books.

———. 1988a. "The Ethic of Care for the Self as a Practice of Freedom." In *The Final Foucault*, ed. James Bernauer and David Rasmusson, 1–20. Cambridge, Mass.: MIT Press.

———. 1988b. "The Masked Philosopher." In *Politics Philosophy Culture*, trans. Alan Sheridan et al., ed. Lawrence D. Kritzman, 323–30. London: Routledge.

———. 1989. *The Archaeology of Knowledge*. Trans. A. M. Sheridan Smith. London: Routledge.

———. 1990a. *The History of Sexuality, Volume I: An Introduction*. Trans. Robert Hurley. New York: Vintage Books.

———. 1990b. *Discipline and Punish: The Birth of the Prison*. Trans. Alan Sheridan. New York: Vintage Books.

————. 1991. *Remarks on Marx: Conversations with Duccio Trombadori.* Trans. R. James Goldstein and James Cascaito. New York: Semiotext(e).

Fowler, D. P. 1989. "Lucretius and Politics." In *Philosophia Togata: Essays in Philosophy and Roman Society,* ed. Miriam Griffin and Jonathan Barnes, 120–50. Oxford: Clarendon.

Furley, David. 1967. *Two Studies in Greek Atomists.* Princeton, N.J.: Princeton University Press.

Gilson, Étienne. 1938. *The Unity of Philosophical Experience.* London: Sheed and Ward.

————. 1955. *History of Christian Philosophy in the Middle Ages.* London: Sheed and Ward.

————. 1960. *The Christian Philosophy of St. Augustine.* Trans. L. E. M. Lynch. New York: Random House.

————. 1991. *The Spirit of Medieval Philosophy.* Trans. A. H. C. Downes. Notre Dame, Ind.: University of Notre Dame Press.

————. 1994. *The Christian Philosophy of St. Thomas Aquinas.* Trans. L. K. Shook, CSB. Notre Dame, Ind.: University of Notre Dame Press.

Golding, Sue. 1995. "The Politics of Foucault's Poetics, or, better yet: The Ethical Demand of Ecstatic Fetish." *Michel Foucault: J'Accuse (New Formations)* 25 (June): 40–47.

————. 1997. "Curiosity." In *The Eight Technologies of Otherness,* author/editor Sue Golding, 10–27. London: Routledge.

Goodchild, Philip. 1996. *Gilles Deleuze and the Question of Philosophy.* London, Ont.: Associated University Presses.

Gracia, Jorge J. E. 1996. "Individuality and the Individuating Entity in Scotus's *Ordinatio:* An Ontological Characterization." In *John Duns Scotus: Metaphysics and Ethics,* ed. Ludgar Honnefelder, Rega Wood, and Mechthild Dreyer, 229–49. Leiden: E. J. Brill.

Grant, Robert M. 1981. "Charges of Immorality against Various Religious Groups in Antiquity." In *Studies in Gnosticism and Hellenistic Religions: Presented to Gilles Quispel on the Occasion of His 65th Birthday,* ed. R. Van Den Broek and M. J. Vermaseren, 161–70. Leiden: E. J. Brill.

————. 1997. *Irenaeus of Lyons.* London: Routledge.

Habermas, Jürgen. 1987. *The Philosophical Discourse of Modernity.* Trans. Frederick Lawrence. Cambridge: Polity.

————. 1990. *Moral Consciousness and Communicative Action.* Trans. Christian Lenhardt and Shierry Weber Nicholsen. Cambridge, Mass.: MIT Press.

Hallward, Peter. 1997. "Gilles Deleuze and the Redemption from Interest." *Radical Philosophy* 81 (Jan.–Feb.): 6–21.

Hancock, Curtis L. 1992. "Negative Theology in Gnosticism and Neoplatonism." In *Neo-Platonism and Gnosticism,* ed. Wallis, 167–86.

Hardt, Michael. 1993. *Gilles Deleuze: An Apprenticeship in Philosophy.* London: University College London.

Hare, J. E. 1979. "Aristotle and the Definition of Natural Things." *Phronesis* 24, no. 2:168–79.

Harris, C. R. S. 1927. *Duns Scotus.* 2 vols. Oxford: Clarendon.

Hegel, G. W. F. 1967. *Philosophy of Right.* Trans. T. M. Knox. Oxford: Oxford University Press.

————. 1969. *Science of Logic.* Trans. A. V. Miller. Atlantic Highlands, N.J.: Humanities.

————. 1975. *Lectures in the Philosophy of World History, Introduction: Reason in History.* Trans. H. B. Nisbet. Cambridge: Cambridge University Press.

————. 1977. *Phenomenology of Spirit.* Trans. A. V. Miller. Oxford: Oxford University Press.

Heidegger, Martin. 1969. *Identity and Difference.* Trans. Joan Stambaugh. New York: Harper and Row.

———. 1971. *On the Way to Language*. Trans. Peter D. Hertz. New York: HarperCollins.

———. 1976. "On the Being and Conception of *Phusis* in Aristotle's *Physics*, B, 1." Trans. Thomas J. Sheehan. *Man and World* 9, no. 3:219–70.

———. 1983. *Hegel's Concept of Existence*. Trans. Kenley Royce Dove. New York: Octagon Books.

———. 1985. *Duns Scotus's Theory of the Categories and of Meaning*. Trans. and with an intro by Harold Robbins. Ann Arbor, Mich.: University Microfilms International.

———. 1988. *Hegel's Phenomenology of Spirit*. Trans. Parvis Emad and Kenneth Maly. Bloomington: Indiana University Press.

Hendrick, Charles W., and Robert Hodgson Jr., ed. 1986. *Nag Hammadi, Gnosticism and Early Christianity*. Peabody, Mass.: Hendrickson.

Henle, Rev. R. J. 1956. *St. Thomas and Platonism: A Study of the Plato and Platonici Texts in the Writings of St. Thomas*. The Hague: Martinus Nijhoff.

Hintikka, Jaakko. 1979. "Aristotelian Infinity." In *Articles on Aristotle III*, ed. Barnes, Schofield, and Sorabji, 125–39.

Hyppolite, Jean. 1974. *Genesis and Structure of Hegel's Phenomenology of Spirit*. Trans. Samuel Cherniak and John Heckman. Evanston, Ill.: Northwestern University Press.

Inwood, Brad. 1981. "The Origin of Epicurus' Concept of Void." *Classical Philology* 76, no. 4 (Oct.): 273–85.

Jaeger, Werner. 1948. *Aristotle: Fundamentals of the History of His Development*. Trans. Richard Robinson. Oxford: Clarendon.

Jonas, Hans. 1970. *The Gnostic Religion: The Message of the Alien God and the Beginnings of Christianity*. 2d ed. London: Routledge.

Keffer, Michael. 1985. "Deconstruction and the Gnostics." *University of Toronto Quarterly* 55, no. 1 (Fall): 74–91.

King, Karen L. 1994. "Translating History: Reframing Gnosticism in Postmodernity." In *Tradition und Translation: Zum Problem der interkulturellen Übersetzbarkeit religiöser Phänomene* [Tradition and translation: on the problem of the intercultural translatability of religious phenomena], ed. Christoph Elsas, 264–77. Berlin: Walter de Gruyter.

Klossowski, Pierre. 1997. *Nietzsche and the Vicious Circle*. Trans. Daniel W. Smith. London: Athlone.

Kojève, Alexandre. 1969. *An Introduction to the Reading of Hegel*. Trans. James H. Nichols Jr. New York: Basic Books.

Krauss, Lawrence M. 1997. *The Physics of Star Trek*. Foreword by Stephen Hawking. London: Flamingo.

Kuhn, Thomas. 1970 [1962]. *The Structure of Scientific Revolutions*. 2d ed., enl. Chicago: University of Chicago Press.

Laclau, Ernesto. 1990. *New Reflections on the Revolution of Our Time*. London: Verso.

Layton, Bentley, ed. 1980–81. *The Rediscovery of Gnosticism: Proceedings of the International Conference on Gnosticism at Yale, New Haven Connecticut, March 28–31, 1978*. 2 vols. Leiden: E. J. Brill.

LeBlond, J. M. 1979. "Aristotle on Definition." In *Articles on Aristotle III*, ed. Barnes, Schofield, and Sorabji, 63–79.

Leff, Gordon. 1975. *William of Ockham: The Metamorphosis of Scholastic Discourse*. Manchester, U.K.: University of Manchester Press; Totowa, N.J.: Rowman and Littlefield.

Long, A. A., and David Sedley. 1987. *The Hellenistic Philosophers, Volume I: Translations of the Principal Sources with Philosophic Commentary.* Cambridge: Cambridge University Press.

Lucretius. 1992. *On the Nature of Things.* Trans. W. H. D. Rouse. Revised by M. F. Smith. Cambridge, Mass.: Loeb Classics.

Lukasiewicz, Jan, G. E. M. Anscombe, and Karl R. Popper. 1953. "Symposium: The Principle of Individuation." *Proceedings of the Aristotelian Society,* suppl. vol. 27:69–120.

Lyotard, Jean-François. 1984. *The Postmodern Condition: A Report on Knowledge.* Trans. Geoff Bennington and Brian Massumi. Manchester, U.K.: Manchester University Press.

———. 1990. *Heidegger and "the jews."* Trans. Andreas Michel and Mark S. Roberts. Minneapolis: University of Minnesota Press.

———. 1994. "Discussions, or Phrasing 'after Auschwitz.'" In *Auschwitz and After: Race, Culture and "The Jewish Question" in France,* ed. Lawrence D. Kritzman, 149–79. New York: Routledge.

McInerny, Ralph. 1961. *The Logic of Analogy: An Interpretation of St. Thomas.* The Hague: Martinus Nijhoff.

McIntyre, Alex. 1997. *The Sovereignty of Joy: Nietzsche's Vision of Grand Politics.* Toronto: University of Toronto Press.

MacNay, Lois. 1992. *Foucault and Feminism: Power, Gender and the Self.* Oxford: Polity.

Malabou, Catherine. 1996. "Who's Afraid of Hegelian Wolves?" In *Deleuze: A Critical Reader,* ed. Patton, 114–38.

Mansfeld, Jaap. 1981. "Bad World and Demiurge: A 'Gnostic' Motif from Parmenides and Empedocles to Lucretius and Philo." In *Studies in Gnosticism and Hellenistic Religions: Presented to Gilles Quispel on the Occasion of His 65th Birthday,* eds. R. Van Den Broek and M. J. Vermaseren, 261–314. Leiden: E. J. Brill.

Mau, Jürgen. 1973. "Was There a Special Epicurean Mathematics?" In *Exegesis and Argument: Studies in Greek Philosophy Presented to Gregory Vlastos,* ed. E. N. Lee, A. P. D. Mourelatos, and R. M. Rorty, 421–30. New York: Humanities.

Marx, Karl. 1964. *Economic and Philosophic Manuscripts of 1844.* Trans. Martin Milligan. New York: International.

———. 1970. *Critique of Hegel's "Philosophy of Right."* Trans. Annette Jolin and Joseph O'Malley, ed. Joseph O'Malley. Cambridge: Cambridge University Press.

———. 1975. "Difference between the Democritean and Epicurean Philosophy of Nature." In Karl Marx and Fredrick Engels, *Collected Works,* 47 vols., 1:25–107. New York: International.

May, Todd. "Difference and Unity in Gilles Deleuze." In *Gilles Deleuze and the Theater of Philosophy,* ed. Constantin Boundas and Dorothea Olkowski, 33–50. London: Routledge.

Merlan, Philip. 1960. *Studies in Epicurus and Aristotle.* Wiesbaden: Otto Harrassowitz.

Miller, Patricia Cox. 1989. "'Words with an Alien Voice': Gnostics, Scripture, and Cannon." *Journal of the American Academy of Religion* 57, no. 3:459–83.

———. 1992. "'Plenty Sleeps There': The Myth of Eros and Psyche in Plotinus and Gnosticism." In *NeoPlatonism and Gnosticism,* ed. Wallis, 223–38.

Nancy, Jean-Luc. 1996. "The Deleuzean Fold of Thought." In *Deleuze: A Critical Reader,* ed. Patton, 81–106.

Nehemas, Alexander. 1985. *Nietzsche: Life as Literature.* Cambridge, Mass.: Harvard University Press.

Nichols, James H., Jr. 1976. *Epicurean Political Philosophy: The De rerum natura of Lucretius.* Ithaca, N.Y.: Cornell University Press.

Nietzsche, Friedrich. 1954. "Homer's Contest." In *The Portable Nietzsche,* trans. and ed. Walter Kaufmann, 32–39. New York: Viking.

———. 1966a. *Beyond Good and Evil: Prelude to a Philosophy of the Future.* Trans. Walter Kaufmann. New York: Vintage Books.

———. 1966b. *Thus Spoke Zarathustra.* Trans. Walter Kaufmann. New York: Viking.

———. 1967a. *The Will to Power.* Trans. Walter Kaufmann and R. J. Hollingdale. New York: Vintage Books.

———. 1967b. *On the Genealogy of Morals.* Trans. Walter Kaufmann and R. J. Hollingdale. New York: Vintage Books.

———. 1974. *The Gay Science.* Trans. Walter Kaufmann. New York: Vintage Books.

———. 1982. *Daybreak.* Trans. R. J. Hollingdale. Cambridge: Cambridge University Press.

———. 1983. *Untimely Meditations.* Trans. R. J. Hollingdale. Cambridge: Cambridge University Press.

———. 1986. *Human, All Too Human: A Book for Free Spirits.* Trans. R. J. Hollingdale. Cambridge: Cambridge University Press.

———. 1990. *Twilight of the Idols/The Anti-Christ.* Trans. R. J. Hollingdale. Harmondsworth: Penguin Books.

Nussbaum, Martha. 1986. *The Fragility of Goodness: Luck and Ethics in Greek Tragedy and Philosophy.* Cambridge: Cambridge University Press.

Ockham, William of. 1990. *Philosophical Writings.* Ed. and trans. Philotheus Boehner, OFM; rev. Stephen F. Brown. Indianapolis, Ind.: Hackett.

———. 1994. "Five Questions on Universals from his *Ordinatio,* d.2, qq. 4–8." In *Five Texts on the Medieval Problem of Universals,* ed. and trans. Vincent Spade, 114–231. Indianapolis, Ind.: Hackett.

O'Keefe, Tim. 1996. "Does Epicurus Need the Swerve as an Archê of Collisions?" *Phronesis* 41, no. 3:305–17.

Owen, G. E. L. 1986. *Logic, Science and Dialectic: Collected Papers on Greek Philosophy.* Ed. Martha Nussbaum. London: Duckworth.

Pagels, Elaine. 1979. *The Gnostic Gospels.* New York: Vintage Books.

———. 1988. *Adam, Eve and the Serpent.* New York: Random House.

Patrick, James. 1987. "Modernity and Gnosis." *Modern Age* 31 (Summer–Fall): 222–33.

Patton, Paul. 1996. *Deleuze: A Critical Reader.* Oxford: Blackwell.

Pearson, Birger A. 1990. *Gnosticism, Judaism and Early Christianity.* Minneapolis: Fortress.

Pépin, Jean. 1992. "Theories of Procession in Plotinus and the Gnostics." In *NeoPlatonism and Gnosticism,* ed. Wallis, 297–336.

Perkins, Pheme. 1986. "Ordering the Cosmos: Irenaeus and the Gnostics." In *Nag Hammadi, Gnosticism and Early Christianity,* ed. Hendrick and Hodgson, 221–238.

———. 1992. "Beauty, Number, and Loss of Order in the Gnostic Cosmos." In *NeoPlatonism and Gnosticism,* ed. Wallis, 277–96.

———. 1993. *Gnosticism and the New Testament.* Minneapolis: Fortress.

Phelan, Rev. Gerald B. 1948. *The Aquinas Lecture, 1941: St. Thomas on Analogy.* Milwaukee, Wis.: Marquette University Press.

Plato. 1974. *Republic.* Trans. G. M. A. Grube. Indianapolis, Ind.: Hackett.

Plotinus. 1956. *Enneads.* Trans. Stephen MacKenna. London: Faber and Faber.

Prentice, Robert P. 1970. *The Basic Quidditative Metaphysics of Duns Scotus as Seen in His De Primo Principio.* Rome: Antonianum.

Quinn, John M. 1992. "Four Faces of Time in St. Augustine." *Recherches Augustiniennes* 26:181–231.

Ramirez, J. Rolland. 1982. "The Priority of Reason over Faith in Augustine." *Augustinian Studies* 13:123–31.

Rawls, John. 1971. *A Theory of Justice.* Cambridge, Mass.: Harvard University Press.

———. 1985. "Justice as Fairness: Political not Metaphysical." *Philosophy and Public Affairs* 14, no. 3:223–51.

Readings, Bill. 1991. *Introducing Lyotard: Art and Politics.* London: Routledge.

Regis, Edward, Jr. 1976. "Aristotle's Principle of Individuation." *Phronesis* 21, no. 2:157–66.

Rist, John. 1972. *Epicurus: An Introduction.* Cambridge: Cambridge University Press.

———. 1994. *Augustine: Ancient Thought Baptised.* Cambridge: Cambridge University Press.

Robinson, James, ed. 1988 [1978]. *The Nag Hammadi Library in English.* Rev. ed. San Francisco: HarperCollins.

Rorty, Richard. 1967. "Relations, Internal and External." In *Encyclopedia of Philosophy,* 8 vols., ed. Paul Edwards, 7:125–33. London: Collier Macmillan.

———. 1973. "Genus as Matter: A Reading of *Metaphysics* Z-H." In *Exegesis and Argument: Studies in Greek Philosophy Presented to Gregory Vlastos,* ed. E. N. Lee, A. P. D. Mourelatos, and R. M. Rorty, 393–420. New York: Humanities.

———. 1989. *Contingency, Irony, and Solidarity.* Cambridge: Cambridge University Press.

Schacht, Richard. 1983. *Nietzsche.* London: Routledge and Kegan Paul.

Schenke, Hans-Martin. 1981. "The Phenomenon and Significance of Gnostic Sethianism." In *Rediscovery of Gnosticism,* ed. Layton, 2:588–616.

Schürmann, Reiner. 1987. *Heidegger on Being and Acting: From Principles to Anarchy.* Trans. Christine-Marie Gros. Bloomington: Indiana University Press.

Sedley, David. 1982. "Two Conceptions of Vacuum." *Phronesis* 27, no. 2:175–93.

Serres, Michael. 1982. *Hermes: Literature, Science, Philosophy.* Ed. Josué V. Harari and David F. Bell. Baltimore, Md.: Johns Hopkins University Press.

Simmel, Georg. 1986. *Schopenhauer and Nietzsche.* Trans. Helmut Loiskandl, Deena Weinstein, and Michael Weinstein. Amherst: University of Massachusetts Press.

Simpson, Dean. 1985. "Epicureanism in the *Confessions* of St. Augustine." *Augustinian Studies* 16:39–48.

Sorabji, Richard. 1983. *Time, Creation and Continuum: Theories in Antiquity and the Early Middle Ages.* Ithaca, N.Y.: Cornell University Press.

Stace, W. T. 1924. *The Philosophy of Hegel: A Systematic Exposition.* London: Macmillan.

Stambaugh, Joan. 1972. *Nietzsche's Thought of Eternal Return.* Baltimore, Md.: Johns Hopkins University Press.

Stead, Christopher. 1994. *Philosophy in Christian Antiquity.* Cambridge: Cambridge University Press.

Summers, Kirk. 1995. "Lucretius and the Epicurean Tradition of Piety." *Classical Philology* 90, no. 1:32–57.

Taylor, Charles. 1975. *Hegel.* Cambridge: Cambridge University Press.

———. 1989. *Sources of the Self: The Making of Modern Identity.* Cambridge: Cambridge University Press.

Tweedle, Martin M. 1993. "Duns Scotus's Doctrine on Universals and the Aphrodisian Tradition." *American Catholic Philosophical Quarterly* 67, no. 1:77–93.

Vlastos, Gregory. 1965. "Minimal Parts in Epicurean Atomism." *Isis* 56, no. 2:121–47.

Wains, William. 1992. "Saving Aristotle from Nussbaum's Phainomena." In *Essays in Ancient Greek Philosophy V: Aristotle's Ontology,* ed. Anthony Preuss and John P. Anton, 133–49. Albany: State University of New York Press.

Wallis, R. T, ed. 1992. *NeoPlatonism and Gnosticism.* Albany: State University of New York Press.

Warminski, Andrzej. 1998. "Hegel/Marx: Consciousness and Life." In *Hegel after Derrida,* ed. Stuart Barnett, 171–93. London: Routledge.

White, Alan. 1990. *Within Nietzsche's Labyrinth.* London: Routledge.

Whitlock, Greg. 1996. "Roger Boschovich, Benedict de Spinoza and Friedrich Nietzsche: The Untold Story." *Nietzsche-Studien* 25 (1996): 200–220.

Widder, Nathan. 2000a. "On Abuses in the Uses of History: Blumenberg on Nietzsche; Nietzsche on Genealogy." *History of Political Thought* 21, no. 2 (Summer): 308–26.

———. 2000b. "What's Lacking in the Lack: A Comment on the Virtual." *Angelaki* 5, no. 3 (December): 117–38.

———. 2001. "The Rights of Simulacra: Deleuze and the Univocity of Being." *Continental Philosophy Review* 35, no. 4 (December).

Williams, Bernard. 1990. "Republican and Galilean." *New York Review of Books,* November 8, pp. 45–49.

Williams, Michael Allen. 1996. *Rethinking "Gnosticism": An Argument for Dismantling a Dubious Category.* Princeton, N.J.: Princeton University Press.

Wisse, Frederick. 1981. "Stalking Those Elusive Sethians." In *The Rediscovery of Gnosticism,* ed. Layton, 2:563–76.

Wolter, Allan, OFM. 1946. *The Transcendentals and Their Function in the Metaphysics of Duns Scotus.* New York: Franciscan Institute.

Wood, David. 1988. "Nietzsche's Transvaluation of Time." In *Exceedingly Nietzsche,* ed. David Farrell Krell and David Wood, 31–62. London: Routledge.

Wood, Rega. 1987. "Scotus's Argument for the Existence of God." *Franciscan Studies* 47:257–77.

———. 1996. "Individual Forms: Richard Rufus and John Duns Scotus." In *John Duns Scotus: Metaphysics and Ethics,* ed. Ludgar Honnefelder, Rega Wood, and Mechthild Dreyer, 251–72. Leiden: E. J. Brill.

Žižek, Slavoj. 1989. *The Sublime Object of Ideology.* London: Verso.

Index

Adorno, Theodor: on Hegel, 159n.5, 160n.9; on identity, 4–5

analogy (of being): Aquinas on, 17–18, 116, 118–20, 125, 151, 170nn.2–3; and the categories, 116; Deleuze on, 141, 172n.31; Duns Scotus on, 125, 141; and the relation between God's and creatures' attributes, 116, 118–21, 128–29; restricted to the realm of judgment, 125; retains hierarchy and transcendence, 107, 128; unable to address the diversity of individuals, 116, 141–42, 172n.31; between univocity and equivocity, 119

Ansell Pearson, Keith, 47, 48, 162n.19

antifoundationalism: and Gnosticism, 167–68n.15; mistakenly conflated with ontological minimalism, 2, 12; and the postmetaphysical, 2, 12; and the retention of metaphysical components, 2–3, 12

Aquinas, St. Thomas, 14, 115–24, 151, 170nn.1–10; on analogy, 17–18, 116, 118–20, 125, 151, 170nn.2–3; on Aristotle, 17, 116, 118, 121, 123, 125; on essence vs. act-of-being, 122, 125, 170n.9; Gilson on, 119, 124; on individuation, 142, 172n.37; and the ladder of being, 18, 117, 121–22; on telos, 117, 123; on time, 121

—on God: and Aristotle's prime mover, 121; and creation ex nihilo, 121, 170n.6; his essence is his existence, 122; his essence remains unknowable, 120, 125; his goodness is elevated over his omnipotence, 18,

116, 124; and his providence, 122–23; and proofs for his existence, 120, 124, 170n.4; relates to creatures through analogy, 119–21, 125–26, 170n.2; words must positively apply to God, 118, 139

Aristotle, 13, 60–75, 150, 163–65nn.1–15, 18; on analogy and univocity, 17–18, 116, 151, 170n.1; Aquinas on, 17–18, 116, 118, 121, 123, 125; on archê, 66–67, 164n.5; on atomism, 71, 165n.18; on becoming, 63–67; and the Christian West, 17–18, 62, 115, 116–17, 151, 171n.19; on the closed universe, 60, 69; on continuity, 14, 16, 70–71; on contraries and contradictories, 64–65, 71, 164n.4; Deleuze on, 61–62, 65; on demonstrative proof, 125; on difference, 61–62; Duns Scotus on, 18, 116, 127, 132, 144, 170n.11, 171nn.19–20; on essence and definition, 61, 73–75, 144, 165nn.13, 15, 170n.8; fails to appreciate existential suffering, 82, 83; on the good, 60, 163–64n.1; Heidegger on, 16, 164nn.5–6, 8; his encounter with virtual excess, 70, 75, 150; on the homogeneity of first causes and their effects, 165n.18; on the necessity of the limit for knowledge, 61, 67–68, 93; Ockham on, 18, 117, 134; on place, 69, 164n.10; and Plato, 16, 61–62, 83, 166n.32; on the polis, 60, 164n.7; on potency and act, 16, 60, 66, 69–71, 164n.11; on the prime mover, 121; on relation, 68–69; on the subordination of the material cause, 62, 65–67, 75; and superfluous mul-

historical, 29–30, 31, 32–34; on identity, 14–15, 151–52; moving from abstract to concrete, 21, 22–23, 24, 28–31, 150; and quantity and quality, 41; remaining abstract, 22, 31–34, 35, 50–51, 150, 152; resting on external final cause, 32, 34; and time/temporality, 15; and totalization, 23, 24, 35, 149–50. *See also* Hegel, G. W. F.

difference: Aristotle on, 16, 62, 73–74; different from identity and opposition, 4, 40, 149; equality as abstraction of, 40–41; and the event, 5, 35; misunderstood as division, 109; multiple affirmation of, 56–59; multiplying spatial and temporal dimensions, 4–5, 153; and naming, 4–5, 149; and political discourse, 35; and spacing, 35–36; treated as evil by Christian Neoplatonism, 17, 89, 100; virtual, 51–52, 152

disjunctive synthesis: against dialectics, 15–16, 41, 55–56; and eternal return, 44, 46–47; and the event, 5–6, 35, 51, 148, 152; exceeding linear space, 41, 55; following from dialectics, 21, 35, 50, 150, 152; and individuation, 148; in relation to opposition, 6; and the rethinking of quantity, 41; structuring meaning, 5–6, 16, 35, 41–42, 52–53; and the virtual, 51–52, 53–54

Duns Scotus, John, 14, 125–34, 141–48, 151, 170–71nn.11–23, 172–73nn.32–41; against Aquinas, 18, 125–26, 172n.37; on Aristotle, 18, 116, 127, 132, 144, 170n.11, 171nn.19–20; on common nature, 134, 142, 143, 145, 146–47, 172n.39; Deleuze on, 141, 146–47; on essential order, 18, 116–17, 129–31, 132, 171nn.16, 18; on essential order of causes, 129–30, 131, 136, 171nn.17–18; on formal and real difference, 134, 143, 145–46; on haecceity, 18, 117, 134, 135, 145–46, 147; Heidegger on, 126, 171n.13, 172n.40; on individuation, 8, 117, 134, 141–48, 172n.38; on transcendentals, 127–28; on virtual primacy of quidditative being, 126–27, 147, 172n.39

—on God: absolute knowledge of effects, 129; absolute omnipotence is presupposed, 117, 133–34; absolute omnipotence is undemonstrable, 129, 133, 171n.23; impossibility of two gods, 132, 138; and univocity, 116, 125–27, 130, 173n.41

—on univocity: as a condition of knowledge of God, 116, 125–27; indifferent to finite/infinite division, 18, 127; limited to

quiddities, 126–27, 146–47; not a hierarchical concept, 128; of transcendentals beyond being, 127–28

Epicurean atoms: and clinamen, 11–12, 16, 61, 78–79, 81, 153, 165nn.24–26; as first beginnings, 76, 78–79, 102; and free will, 78–79, 166n.29; and gnosis, 102; infinity of, 77; movement of, 78, 79–80; and perception, 76, 79–80; shape and parts analogous to sensible objects, 77–78, 165nn.22–23, 165–66n.27; as thinkable minimum, 77–78; and void, 77, 165nn.21, 24

Epicurus/Epicureanism, 76–87, 165–66nn.17–36; against Aristotle, 16, 60–61, 72, 75, 76, 80, 82, 83, 87; Augustine on, 89, 90; against Augustinianism, 10; Blumenberg on, 10–11, 86–87; Cicero on, 82; on continuity, 16, 77, 79; on death, 11, 16, 82–83, 83–84; does not escape metaphysics, 61, 76, 85–87; on ethics, 16–17, 72, 82–85, 166n.34; and Gnosticism, 18, 102, 158n.8; on the gods and religion, 84, 86–87; on the infinite and limit, 16, 60–61, 76–77, 165n.19; and Lucretius, 11, 14, 16, 60, 72, 75, 76–87, 154; and Nietzsche, 10–12, 82, 85–86, 166n.31; on pain and pleasure, 84–85, 166n.33; and pluralism, 16, 80–82, 83; raised to the postmodern condition, 14; on repetition, 81; on resentment, 11, 16, 82–83, 85, 154; still relies on teleology, 10–11, 86–87, 154; on time, 79; against teleology, 80–81, 82–83. *See also* Epicurean atoms

eternal return, 6, 15, 35, 44–48, 153, 162nn.22–25

event, the: as the being of becoming, 6; and chaos, 18; and continuity, 5, 36, 153; and the "death of God," 47; and difference, 5, 35; and disjunctive synthesis, 5–6, 35, 51, 148, 152; escaping the One and the Many, 5; and eternal return, 44, 46, 47; and ethical "ought," 155; Foucault on, 9; and genealogy, 12; Holocaust as, 37–38; and "lost time," 36–37, 46; Lyotard on, 36–38; and meaning, 5–6, 35, 50–51, 153; and multiple-singularity, 5, 36, 51, 152, 154; not a being-in-itself, 51; novelty of 5, 38, 160n.11; ontological priority over particular and universal, 75; politics and, 37–38; and repetition, 6; and univocity, 148; unlocalizable, 5, 6, 36–37; as virtual, 35, 51, 152, 155

NATHAN WIDDER is a lecturer in political theory at the University of Exeter (U.K.). His research interests focus on issues of power, meaning, truth, and subjectivity, approached through both contemporary philosophy and a rereading and rethinking of the Western tradition. His work has appeared in such journals as *Theory & Event, History of Political Thought, Parallax, Angelaki,* and *Continental Philosophy Review.*

The University of Illinois Press
is a founding member of the
Association of American University Presses.

Composed in 10.5/13 Adobe Minion
by Barbara Evans
at the University of Illinois Press
Manufactured by Thomson-Shore, Inc.

University of Illinois Press
1325 South Oak Street
Champaign, IL 61820-6903
www.press.uillinois.edu